THE PRECENSORSHIP OF BOOKS

A History and a Commentary

THE CATHOLIC UNIVERSITY OF AMERICA
CANON LAW STUDIES
No. 329

THE PRECENSORSHIP OF BOOKS

(Canons 1384-1386, 1392-1394, 2318,§2)

A History and a Commentary

A DISSERTATION

SUBMITTED TO THE FACULTY OF THE SCHOOL OF CANON LAW OF THE CATHOLIC UNIVERSITY OF AMERICA IN PARTIAL FULFILLMENT OF THE REQUIREMENTS FOR THE DEGREE OF DOCTOR OF CANON LAW

BY THE
REV. DONALD H. WIEST, O.F.M.CAP., S.T.B., J.C.L.
OF THE PROVINCE OF ST. JOSEPH

THE CATHOLIC UNIVERSITY OF AMERICA PRESS
WASHINGTON 17, D. C.
1953

NIHIL OBSTAT:
Brendan Morrissey, O.F.M.Cap.
Ignatius McCormick, O.F.M.Cap.
Censores Ordinis

IMPRIMI POTEST:
Cyprian Abler, O.F.M.Cap.
Minister Provincialis
Detroit, die 10 Junii, 1952

NIHIL OBSTAT:
Clement V. Bastnagel, J.U.D.
Censor Deputatus

IMPRIMATUR:
Patrick A. O'Boyle, D.D.
✠ Archiepiscopus Washingtoniensis
Washingtonii, die 1 Octobris, 1952

MANUFACTURED BY
UNIVERSAL LITHOGRAPHERS, INC.
BALTIMORE, MD., U. S. A.

To
MY FATHER AND MOTHER

TABLE OF CONTENTS

CHAPTER VII

FOREWORD

In exercising her teaching office, the Catholic Church utilizes every legitimate means of communication at her disposal. Not the least of these is the medium of books. The value of the written word needs no demonstration. Owing to its peculiar character, it possesses distinct advantages over the spoken word. Books are permanent; they are available at all times; they can reach persons separated from the writer by time and place; they can be read at leisure by persons who have little or no opportunity of attending the spoken word. In view of present conditions, books are not merely a useful, but also a necessary, means to the effective preservation, defense, and propagation of the Christian faith and good morals.

From the very beginning the Church accepted books at their true worth. Evidence abounds showing her wise use of good books. And evidence is also at hand to show how she dealt with pernicious books. The incident involving Paul at Ephesus is but the first in a long chain: "And many who had practiced magical arts collected their books and burnt them publicly; and they reckoned the prices of them, and found the sum to be 50,000 pieces of silver."[1] One cannot discern from the text whether the destruction of the books was voluntary or prescribed, but in later years, especially at the Councils, heretical books were proscribed and burnt. At a much later date Luther gained prominence and notoriety by making a bonfire of Catholic books.

In the early days, when scrolls, books, etc., were produced by hand, their multiplication was a slow and tedious process. The Church found that she could effectively curb the spread of pernicious books by prohibiting, confiscating and destroying them. In the later middle ages, however, when printing set in, the Church faced a new problem. She took immediate cognizance of the immense power for good in the "divine art of printing," as it was described by Berthold, the Archbishop of Mainz, in 1486. But she also learned that, when pernicious books were circulated, their spread was so rapid as to render nugatory any attempt at control by prohibition, confiscation and destruction.

The Church countered with an adequate remedy. She made obligatory what had been a voluntary custom among ecclesiastics for centuries, namely, the submission of books for ecclesiastical censorship before printing. At first this procedure was enforced locally, at the points where grievances

[1] Acts, XIX, 19–20.

were acute. It was aimed particularly at the presses of the German University towns of Erfurt, Cologne, etc. Within a few decades, however, the popes extended this legislation to the entire Church. The Council of Trent re-enacted and improved the initial universal legislation. Pope Leo XIII modernized it, and the law as we know it today was promulgated in the Code of Canon Law in 1917, and became effective in 1918.

It is the purpose of the present dissertation to investigate briefly the history and development of the Church's legislation on the censorship of books. This study will limit itself to precensorship, i.e. censorship of books before they are printed. The correlative problem of subsequent censorship has been ably treated, at least in its repressive angle, by Joseph Pernicone in his dissertation *The Ecclesiastical Prohibition of Books*, Canon Law Studies, n.72, published by the Catholic University of America in 1932.

In treating of precensorship this work will further limit itself to a consideration of the general norms, i.e., to canons 1384-1386 and 1392-1394. Canons 1387-1391 have already been treated in a companion volume by Nathaniel Sonntag, O.F.M.Cap., in his dissertation *The Censorship of Special Classes of Books*, published as n.262 of the Canon Law Studies of the Catholic University of America in 1947. To the consideration of the general norms will be added a study of the penal sanction enacted in canon 2318, §2.

The writer wishes to express his sincere gratitude to his Superiors in the Capuchin Order for the opportunity of completing his graduate studies in canon law; to the members of the Faculty of the School of Canon Law of the Catholic University of America for their kind assistance and helpful direction; to friends, relatives, confrères, and especially to Rev. Nathaniel Sonntag, O.F.M.Cap., J.C.D., whose interest, encouragement, prayers and valuable help have made the completion of this dissertation possible.

For kind permission to quote several definitions from their works in Chapter V of this dissertation, acknowledgement is gratefully made to the following publishers: G. & C. Merriam Co., Springfield, Mass. (*Webster's New Collegiate Dictionary*, copyright 1949, 1951); Funk and Wagnalls Co., New York, N. Y. (*The New College Standard Dictionary*, copyright 1947); The American Library Association, Chicago, Ill. (*A. L. A. Glossary of Library Terms*, prepared by Elizabeth H. Thompson, copyright 1943). The writer also expresses his appreciation to the following for permission to use copyright material: Rev. T. Lincoln Bouscaren, S.J., and the Bruce Publishing Co., Milwaukee, Wis. (*Canon Law Digest*, vol. II, copyright 1943); the Bruce Publishing Co. (*Canon Law*, by Revs. T. Lincoln Bouscaren, S.J., and Adam C. Ellis, S.J., copyright 1946); the Pontifical Institute of Mediaeval Studies, Toronto, Canada (*Mediaeval Studies*, vol. IV).

PART ONE

THE HISTORY OF PRECENSORSHIP

History shows us that precensorship existed in the Church from the early days of antiquity. For centuries precensorship was associated, though not identified, with the prohibition of evil literature. The precensorship found in the early Church was rather primitive in form; still, the principle of precensorship which was employed then was fully capable of development into the type of precensorship that is exercised today.

Long before precensorship was imposed on the faithful, it was exercised on a voluntary basis, particularly by the Fathers of the Church. Precensorship may have been a widespread custom as early as the fifth century. Obligatory precensorship appeared in the Church in certain sectors, e.g., in religious orders, in universities, in dioceses, after the twelfth century. Precensorship was not imposed upon the entire Church until after the appearance of printing in the fifteenth century. During the sixteenth century the law on precensorship received much attention. Little was done after that time until the time of Pope Leo XIII, who, in 1897, completely reorganized the law concerning the publication of books. Much of the law of the Code was taken from the legislation of Leo XIII.

The entire history of precensorship in the Church may be covered under three convenient headings: the evolution of the concept of precensorship, the appearance of voluntary precensorship, and obligatory precensorship.[1]

CHAPTER I

THE EVOLUTION OF THE CONCEPT OF PRECENSORSHIP

Precensorship means the official examination and judgment on a work before it is published. Precensorship is part of a much broader concept, censorship, which means the review of any work, whether published or

[1] See also Gagnon, *La Censure des Livres*, Les Thèses Canoniques de Laval, n. 3 (Québec: Université Laval, 1945), pp. 21–57 (hereafter cited as *La Censure*).

not, whether official or not. Censorship had its origins in Roman law, whence it passed into ecclesiastical usage. Hence, it will be advantageous to divide the first chapter on the evolution of the concept of precensorship into three articles: the useage of censorship in Roman law; the appearanc of censorship in ecclesiastical discipline; the initial form of precensorship in the Church. A fourth article will summarize the first chapter.

Article I. The Usage of Censorship in Roman Law

The Romans used the word censorship (*censura*) in several different meanings. In its original acceptation it meant the office and activity of the ancient Roman Censor, one of two magistrates charged with the duty of registering the names of Roman citizens and fixing their rank according to their property holdings.[2] Hence, in its first meaning, censorship meant an examination and judgment, with particular reference to civil status.

At a later date, when the Roman Censors became custodians of public conduct and morals, the term took on an added meaning of an examination and judgment of moral status.[3]

In the course of time, the term *censura* was also used for a third thing, namely, for the *nota censoria*, i.e., the penalty invoked upon a guilty person in consequence of a condemnatory judgment.[4]

Article II. The Usage of Censorship in Ecclesiastical Discipline

Censura as a penalty was taken over directly into ecclesiastical discipline in earliest times. It was used to designate all punishments inflicted by the Church, e.g., those which were known then or later came to be known as

---

[2] Cram has published a scholarly paper entitled "The Roman Censors," *Harvard Studies in Classical Philology* (Cambridge, 1890—), LI (1940), 71–110, in which he gives ample treatment to this question.

[3] A sample edict of the Roman Censors, dating from 662 B.C., is as follows· "Renuntiatum est nobis esse homines, qui nouum genus disciplinae instituerunt, ad quos iuuentus in ludum conueniat; eos sibi nomen imposuisse Latinos rhetoras; ibi homines adulescentulos dies totos desidere. Maiores nostri, quae liberos suos discere et quos in ludos itare uellent, instituerunt. Haec noua, quae praeter consuetudinem ac morem maiorum fiunt, neque placent neque recta uidentur. Quapropter et iis, qui eos ludos habent, et iis, qui eo uenire consuerunt, uidetur faciundum, ut ostenderemus nostram sententiam, nobis non placere."—*Fontes Iuris Romani Antejustiniani, Pars Prima—Leges* (ed. S. Riccobono, Florentiae: Apud S.A.G.Barbèra, 1941), pp. 305–306.

[4] C (4.7) 3; C (9.9) 23. Examples in the Theodosian Code are: 1, *de off. rect. prov.*, I, 7; 5 *ne s. bapt. iter.*, XVI, 6.

excommunication, suspension, public penances, deposition, degradation, etc.[5] The Code of Canon Law retains the term *censura* in the meaning of a penalty, e.g., in canons 2216, 1°; 2241, §1; 2242, §1. The English equivalent for the term in this sense is "censure," and, according to present usage, has a very precise and technical meaning.

Censura as a judgment of moral status is met in the early usage of the Church, particularly in connection with the condemnation of a doctrinal lapse by one of its members. The judgment of moral status was indirect rather than direct. The fact that a doctrine was censured rendered the position of those who held that doctrine objectively reprehensible. Primarily, the *censura* attached to the doctrine, not to the person.[6] The Church still uses the term *censura* in this condemnatory sense in her discipline.[7] The English equivalent is the noun "censure" or the verb "to censure," both of which are always understood in a condemnatory sense.

The use of the term *censura* as an examination of books and writings is not found in early ecclesiastical discipline as far as could be ascertained. It appears much later. However, the concept of censorship was in evidence. It will be the purpose of this dissertation to investigate the evolution of this particular phase of censorship.

Article III. The Initial Form of Precensorship in the Church

The initial example of "censorship" in the Church is the incident of St. Paul at Ephesus. When the Ephesians were converted, it was necessary for

---

[5] C. 38, C. XII, q. 2. The idea, though not the word, is contained in cc. 23, 24, 29, C. VII, q. 1. Kober cites Tertullian and Cyprian as using the term *censura* in this meaning, but fails to identify the passages. Cf. "Censuren, kirchliche"—Wetzer-Welte, *Kirchenlexikon oder Encyclopedie der katholischen Theologie und ihrer Huelfswissenschaften* (2. ed., 12 vols. & Index, Freiburg im Breisgau, 1883–1903), II, 2107 (hereafter cited as *Kirchenlexikon*). A fairly complete history of the term in this sense, and its gradual evolution, may be found in Moriarty, *The Extraordinary Absolution from Censures*, The Catholic University of America Canon Law Studies, n. 113 (Washington, D. C.: The Catholic University of America Press, 1938), p. 4.

[6] C. 13, X, *de iudiciis*, II, 1. The distinction is brought out clearly in this citation, which dates from 1204.

[7] A detailed explanation of censures applicable to doctrines may be found in Quilliet, "Censures doctrinales," *Dictionnaire de Théologie Catholique*, 15 vols. in 30, (Paris: Letouzey et Ané, 1903–1950), II, 2101–2113 (hereafter cited as *DTC*). These terms are also explained in dogmatic textbooks, e.g., Perrone, *Praelectiones Theologiae de Virtute Fidei, Spei et Caritatis* (Ratisbonae, 1865), pp. 178–179 (hereafter cited as *Praelectiones*); Pesch, *Praelectiones Dogmaticae* (9 vols., Friburgi Brisgoviae, 1895–1899), I, 336–337 (hereafter cited as *Praelectiones*); Van Noort, *Tractatus de Fontibus Revelationis nec non de Fide Divina* (Bussum, 1920), pp. 184–190 (hereafter cited as *Tractatus*).

those who had exercised magical arts to renounce their former practices. They did so, and brought their books and burned them publicly. "And they reckoned up the prices of them, and found the sum to be fifty thousand pieces of silver."[8] It seems that this was a voluntary externalization of an act necessarily involved in their conversion.

It should not surprise us that few documents exist from the period of the persecutions. Diocletian (284-305), as well as other emperors, purposely destroyed all records of Christianity. In spite of that we do possess an isolated instance of presumptive approval for certain writings as early as the second century. Later there is evidence of antecedent disapproval of anonymous works; and also antecedent disapproval of apocryphal works.

(1) *The Presumptive Approval for Certain Writings*

Although we do not possess records of precensorship as we know it today, there is evidence that the principle of precensorship was invoked in the early Church. Certain works were presumed good, and others harmful. This principle is found in the *Muratorian Fragment*, is developed in the *Constitutiones Apostolorum*, in the *Decretum Gelasianum*, and in the writings of St. Jerome.

(a) The *Muratorian Fragment* (Second Century)

The *Muratorian Fragment* is of paramount importance to biblical scholars for its biblical canon. It also contains a veiled reference to precensorship in the form of a presumptive approval given to the works of certain authors. The text reads:

> Fertur etiam [epistula] ad Laodicenses, alia ad Alexandrinos Pauli nomine finctae ad haeresem Marcionis et alia plura, quae in catholicam Ecclesiam recipi non potest; fel enim cum melle misceri non congruit. Epistula sane Iudae et superscripti Iohannis duae in catholica habentur et Sapientia ab amicis Salomonis in honorem ipsius scripta. Apocalypses etiam Iohannis et Petri tantum recipimus, quam quidam ex nostris legi in Ecclesia nolunt. Pastorem vero nuperrime temporibus nostris in urbe Roma Hermas conscripsit sedente cathedra urbis Romae ecclesiae Pio Episcopo fratre eius; et ideo legi eum quidem oportet, se publicare vero in Ecclesia populo neque inter prophetas completo numero, neque inter Apostolos in fine temporum potest.[9]

---

[8] Acts, XIX, 19.

[9] Cf. *Enchiridion Biblicum: Documenta ecclesiastica sacram Scripturam spectantia auctoritate Pontificiae Commissionis de re Biblica edita* (Romae, 1927), pp. 1–3, lines 63–80.

The author of this document states that the Scriptures have been accepted by the Church. In fact, they have received a special approval, sanctioning their use in the Church. He also mentions that some non-scriptural writings, e.g., *The Shepherd* by Hermas, have also received favorable judgment, and stand recommended for reading by the faithful, but that they do not belong in the same category as the books of the prophets and apostles. He finally refers to the writings of the heretics, e.g., those favoring the Marcionite heresy, and notes that they cannot be received by the Church.

Admittedly, the author is concerned with subsequent censorship. However, in view of the triple division made and the reasons alleged, it is logical for us to infer that over and above the subsequent approval given to the writings of the prophets and apostles, the works of Hermas, the Pope's brother, received an automatic antecedent approval, while the works of heretics received an automatic antecedent disapproval. The former produced honey; the latter only gall.

(b) The *Constitutiones Apostolorum* (Fourth or Fifth Century)

Were the testimony of the *Muratorian Fragment* to stand alone, it would afford little proof for the existence of precensorship in the early Church. However, when viewed in conjunction with later testimony, it takes on greater importance. The identical concept is brought out more explicitly in the *Constitutiones Apostolorum*.[10] In this work, two successive chapters deal with books. Chapter V refers to approved books under the title "*Qui libri scripturae legendi*"[11] while Chapter VI refers to the books which are automatically excluded under the title "*Quod oporteat abstinere a lectione omnium librorum Gentilium.*"[12] In the title prefixed to Chapter VI there is a noticeable broadening of the concept of presumptive precensorship. The *Muratorian*

---

[10] It is generally admitted that the *Constitutiones Apostolorum* date from the end of the fourth or beginning of the fifth century. Cf. Lijdsman, *Introductio in Jus Canonicum cum uberiori fontium studio* (2 vols., Hilversum, 1924–1929), I, 96–97; Van Hove, *Prolegomena ad Codicem Iuris Canonici*, Commentarium Lovaniense in Codicem Iuris Canonici editum a Magistris et Doctoribus Universitatis Lovaniensis, Vol. I, tom. 1 (2 .ed., Mechliniae-Romae: H. Dessain, 1945), pp. 128–219 (cited hereafter as *Prolegomena*); Kurtscheid-Wilches, *Historia Iuris Canonici, Historia Fontium et Scientiae Iuris Canonici* (Romae: Officium Libri Catholici, 1943), p. 56.

[11] Lib. I, Cap. V—Mansi, *Sacrorum Conciliorum Nova et Amplissima Collectio* (53 vols. in 60, Parisiis, Arnhem, Lipsiae, 1901–1927), I, 278 (hereafter cited as Mansi).

[12] Mansi, I, 279.

Fragment had disapproved of the works of heretics. The *Constitutiones Apostolorum* disapproved of the works of Gentiles as well.

(c) The *Decretum Gelasianum* (Fifth Century)

Still later the *Decretum Gelasianum,* also known by its title *De libris recipiendis et non recipiendis*, gave a general antecedent approval to the writings of the Fathers whose orthodoxy was known:

> Item opuscula atque tractatus omnium Patrum orthdoxorum, qui in nullo a sanctae Romanae ecclesiae consortio deuiauerunt, nec ab eius fideli predicatione seiuncti sunt, sed communionis ipsius gratia Dei usque ad ultimum diem uitae suae participes fuerunt, legenda decernimus.[13]

Similarly, it pronounces a general disapproval on works of heretics:

> Ceterum que ab hereticis siue scismaticis conscripta uel praedicata sunt, nullatenus recipit catholica et apostolica Romana ecclesia . . . [14]

(d) St. Jerome (+420)

Although the Fathers were not legislators for the universal Church, and some were not bishops, they do afford an insight into the attitude of the

[13] §15—Mansi, VIII, 145; C. 3, D. XV. It is beyond the scope of this dissertation to attempt a solution of the authenticity and date of this document. Experts cannot come to full agreement. The majority hold that the scriptural section dates back to Pope Damasus I (366–384), who made use of the services of St. Jerome (+420), and that the remainder is the addition of Pope Gelasius (492–496). Some attribute the whole to Pope Hormisdas (514–523), though it seems that the documents bearing his name indicate a re-issuance of the decree of Gelasius. In 1921 Dobschuetz printed the text which is accepted as the most critical in his "Das Decretum Gelasianum de libris recipiendis et non recipiendis in kritischem Text herausgegeben und untersucht"—*Texte und Untersuchungen.* Dritte Reihe, Band 8, Heft 4, Leipzig, 1912. He devotes a sizeable portion of the 365 pages to an attempt to establish the opinion that the work is not of pontifical origin, but must have been the work of a private individual during the first quarter of the sixth century. His conclusions have not met with general acceptance. For a survey of all opinions and an evaluation of each, cf. Bardy, "Gélase (Décret de)," *Dictionnaire de la Bible* (ed. F. Vigoroux, 3. ed., 5 vols. in 10, Paris, 1926–1928), *Supplément* (ed. L. Pirot, 3 vols., 1928–1938), III, 581 (hereafter cited as *DB* and *DBS* respectively). Cf. also Jaffé, *Regesta Pontificum Romanorum ab condita Ecclesia ad annum post Christum natum MCXCVIII* (2. ed., by F. Kaltenbrunner [ad annum 590], P. Ewald [590–882], and S. Loewenfeld [882–1198], and so referred to as: JK, JE, and JL, Lipsiae, 1885–1888), JK, n. 699.

[14] §27—Mansi, VIII, 145; c. 3, D. XV; JK, n. 700.

Church. St. Jerome had taken a precise stand regarding books. His antecedent approval of the Fathers reads:

> Post Sacras Scripturas, doctorum hominum tractatus lege eorum dumtaxat, quorum fides nota est.[15]

And, conversely, his disapproval of the works of heretics reads:

> Nemo enim in perforatam intrat cymbam, ut discat vitare naufragium, et ad haeresibus plenum volumen animam diriges immunem doli, ut ibi discas catholicam veritatem.[16]

(2) *The Antecedent Disapproval of Anonymous Works*

The principle of precensorship also gave rise to the antecedent disapproval of anonymous works. The reason was simple. The orthodoxy of the writer could not be known or proven. The *Decretum Gelasianum* contains the following text:

> Sed ideo secundum antiquam consuetudinem singulari cautela in sancta Romana ecclesia non leguntur, quia et eorum, qui conscripsere, nomina penitus ignorantur, et ab infidelibus aut idiotis superflua, aut minus apta, quam rei ordo fuerit, scripta esse putantur . . . propter quod, ut dictum est, ne uel leuis subsannandi oriretur occasio, in sancta Romana ecclesia non leguntur.[17]

The same document makes an exception:

> Item actus B. Siluestri, apostolicae sedis praesulis, licet eius, qui conscripsit, nomen ignoremus, a multis tamen in urbe Roma catho-

---

[15] *Ep. LIV* (ad Furiam), n. 11—Migne, *Patrologiae Cursus Completus*, Series Latina (221 vols., Parisiis, 1844–1864; new ed. 1865–1896), XXII, 555 (289). Citations will be from the new edition, and, wherever possible, the pagination of the first edition will be added in parentheses. If the first edition alone is used, special mention of that fact will be made (hereafter cited as *MPL*).

[16] Arndt attributes this statement to St. Jerome, citing his letter to Laeta, in *De Libris Probibitis Commentarii* (Ratisbonae, Neo Eboraci & Cincinnati, 1895), p. 44 (hereafter cited as *Commentarii*). The passage cannot be found in the letter cited (*MPL*, XXII, 867), though the letter does give advice about books.)

[17] §17—Mansi, VIII, 145; c. 3, D. XV; JK, n. 699.

licis legi cognouimus, et pro antiquo usu multae hoc imitantur ecclesiae.[18]

(3) *The Antecedent Disapproval of Apocryphal Works*

Still another application of the same principle of precensorship appears in the antecedent disapproval of apocryphal writings. Certain authors had attributed their works to men whose orthodoxy was known, hoping thereby to obtain a ready acceptance for their work. Such a procedure was condemned, as is observed in the *Constitutiones Apostolorum:*

> Haec enim scripsimus vobis, ut scire possitis, qualis sit nostra scientia, et ne libros quos impii nostri inscriptione munierunt, approbetis, neque enim nomine apostolorum attendere debetis, sed naturam rerum et scientiam nunquam a recto deflexam . . .. Fugite ergo horum doctrinam, ne supplicii eorum, qui ista ad fallendum fideles et probos Domini Jesu discipulos scripserunt, participes efficiamini.[19]

Article IV. Summary

After investigating the history of the early Church, we find that the evidence for precensorship is rather meager. However, the principle underlying precensorship, as we know it today, is clearly discernible. Early documents show that the writings of persons whose orthodoxy was generally known enjoyed a certain presumptive approval. This is deduced from the wording of the *Muratorian Fragment*; it becomes more evident in the *Constitutiones Apostolorum*, and is contained explicitly in the *Decretum Gelasianum*. The same principle led the early Christians to disapprove of anonymous and apocryphal writings. This disapproval intervened not merely subsequent to their appearance, but even antecedent to it. If the merits of an individual anonymous work warranted reception for that work, an exception to the general rule was made.

---

[18] *Loc. cit.*

[19] Lib. VI, Cap. 16—Mansi, I, 462. Tertullian, at the beginning of the third century, mentions a case wherein a man was convicted of such an imposition on the faithful.—*MPL*, I, 1328–1329 (1219–1220). Arndt (*Commentarii*, p. 44) quotes a passage, admittedly from St. Augustine, which describes how the Manichaeans were misled by apocryphal writings. Unfortunately the reference is inaccurate, for the *Ennar. in Ps. LXI* (*MPL*, XXXVI, 729–740) does not contain this passage.

From these early documents it seems permissible to conclude that the theory of precensorship existed, in primitive form, in the Church from the very beginning. The development and application of this principle took place when the Church gained civil freedom, and when the Fathers were enabled to spread the Church far and wide by means of books.

CHAPTER II

VOLUNTARY PRECENSORSHIP

Specific examples of the exercise of the principle of precensorship begin to appear with the divulgation of the writings of the Fathers. Some of the earliest Fathers submitted their writings to others for review and criticism and correction before spreading them among the people. This procedure was a purely personal precaution taken by each writer; though, in the course of time, it seems to have become a prevalent usage. There are two incidents which might indicate that precensorship was obligatory as early as the ninth century; however, as will be shown, evidence points against such a conclusion.

Chapter two will be divided into four articles, the first dealing with individual precensorship; the second with customary precensorship; the third with the two incidents that seem to indicate obligatory precensorship; and the fourth with a summary of the entire chapter.

Article I. Individual Precensorship

St. Ambrose (+397) sent one of his writings to his friend, Bishop Sabinus, requesting him to examine and correct the work. St. Ambrose stated explicitly that he is doing this before he will allow the work to be divulged.[1]

St. Augustine (+430) dedicated his *Libri Quattuor contra duas epistolas Pelagianorum* to Pope Boniface I (418-422) and declared that it was his intention to send the work to him for correction and approval:

> . . . Haec ergo quae istis, ut dixi, duabus epistulis illorum, ista disputatione respondeo, ad tuam potissimum dirigere Sanctitatem, non tam discenda, quam examinanda, et ubi forsitan aliquid displicuerit, emendenda constitui.[2]

Gennadius, a priest of Marseilles (+between 492 and 505) sent his *De Scriptoribus Ecclesiasticis* to Pope Gelasius, Bishop of Rome (492-496), for censorship.[3] Possessor, an African Bishop, commissioned his deacon Justinus

[1] Epistola XLVIII, ad Sabinum, n. 1: "Priusquam foras prodeat, unde iam revocandi nulla facultas sit."—*MPL*, XVI, 1201 (990).

[2] Cap. I, n. 3—*MPL*, XLIV, 551.

[3] Cap. C—*MPL*, LVIII (1. ed.), 1120. The editors of the Migne edition of this letter note that Chapter "C" is absent in several manuscripts. It is in this chapter that Gennadius refers to two other instances of pontifical censorship, one in favor of Caesar of Arles (+542) and the other in favor of Honoratus, Bishop of Marseilles (+after 492). Cf. *MPL*, LVIII (1. ed.), 1111.

to carry a letter to Pope Hormisdas I (514-523), requesting the latter to examine a book written by Faustus, another bishop, with a view to pronouncing authoritative judgment upon it. The same letter indicates that Possessor had previously sent his own work (an exposition of the Epistles of St. Paul) for censorship; but, since he had not had a reply, he renews his petition.[4] It is also known that Eulogius (+607), Patriarch of Alexandria, sent his writings against the Agnoitae to Pope St. Gregory the Great (590-606) for examination and correction, and that the latter actually passed judgment:

> Rescribo . . . quia de doctrina vestra contra haereticos qui dicuntur Agnoitae, fuit valde quo admiraremur; quod autem displicerit, non fuit.[5]

Pope Stephen III (768-772) performed a similar task for Ambrose Autpert (+778), a Benedictine monk.[6] Anastasius (+c.880), librarian of the Holy Roman Church, obtained the approval of Pope Nicholas I (858-867) before putting his work in codex-form. He deemed it improper to spread a book among the people without leave of the Vicar of God.[7]

These few examples of individual precensorship prove beyond a doubt that the principle of precensorship was known and exercised in the early Church. Some of the texts, it is true, do not specify whether the censorship was antecedent or subsequent to divulgation; but others do. The purpose of all seems to have been the same, namely, to guarantee the orthodoxy of the work before spreading it among the people.

The examples cited are scattered over five centuries and over several Mediterranean countries. They indicate that precensorship was requested by a layman, a religious, a priest, by bishops, and even by a patriarch. Yet, the evidence is too meager to prove anything more than the existence of the concept of precensorship. It would be well nigh impossible to collect all the possible instances, nor is it necessary for the purpose of this dissertation.

Article II. Customary Precensorship

There seems to be no way of determining with any accuracy just when the practice of precensorship became a general custom in the Church. Baronius (1538-1607) made the assertion, when treating of the year 490, that the

[4] *Relatio Possessoris Episcopi Afri per Justinum Diaconum ejus*—*MPL*, LXIII, 490.

[5] *Register Epistolarum*, lib. X, *Ep. XXXIX* (ad Eulogium Patriarcham Alexandrinam)—*MPL*, LXXVII, 1096 (1069).

[6] According to Baillet (*Les Jugements des Savants* [9 vols., Paris, 1685], I, 26) cited by Putnam (*The Censorship of the Church of Rome* [2 vols., New York, 1906–1907], I, 63) Ambrose Autpert stated that he was the first [sic] author to seek the approval of the head of the Church for a work. In view of the evidence cited above, his statement may be disregarded.

[7] *Vita Sancti Joannis Eleemosynarii*, auctore Leontio, Neapoleos Cyprorum Episcopo, Praefatio Anastasii Interpretis ad Dominum Nicolaum Papam—*MPL*, LXXIII, 339 (178).

practice of precensorship was customary from the first centuries, and when treating of the year 600 stated that for certain works the custom seemed to have obtained universal application:

> . . . Hoc temporum decursu praxis invaluisse videtur, ut nullus de fide tractatus libere in fidelium manus tradi posset, qui Romani Pontificis non obtinuisset adprobationem.[8]

Similarly, the late twelfth century shows a decided preoccupation among writers to have their works precensored. As far as is known, precensorship was still performed on a voluntary basis, and there is no evidence to believe that a regular machinery existed in the Church at this time for such a task. The case of Ralph Niger, in particular, whose efforts to have his works precensored extended over a period of thirty years, offers a picture of unparalleled detail. All in all, precensorship proved to be an important factor in the life of the Church, a measure designed to guarantee the orthodoxy of the author and to protect the faithful.[9]

Of all the examples of precensorship available, only two suggest that the custom might have been obligatory rather than voluntary. The first is a letter of Pope Nicholas I to King Charles the Bald of France in 867; and the second is the citation of Abelard before the Council of Soissons in 1121.

(1) The Letter of Pope Nicholas I (867)

The tenor of the letter of Pope Nicholas I to King Charles of France seems to be based on the assumption that precensorship was obligatory at that time:

> Relatum est apostolatui nostro quod opus beati Dionysii Areopagitae, quod de divinis nominibus, vel coelestibus ordinibus, Graeco descripsit eloquio, quidam vir Joannes, genere Scotus, nuper in Latinum transtulerit. *Quod iuxta morem nobis mitti et nostro debuit judicio approbari;* praesertim cum idem Joannes, licet multae scientiae esse praedicetur, olim non sane sapere in quibusdam frequenti rumore diceretur. *Itaque quod hactenus omissum est, vestra industria suppleat, et nobis praefatum opus sine ulla cunctatione mittat;* quatenus dum a nostri apostolatus judicio fuerit approbatum, ab omnibus incunctanter nostra auctoritate acceptius habeatur.[10]

The wording of the letter seems to indicate that precensorship was required, though the obligation seems to be mitigated by the phrase "*juxta morem.*" However, it could easily be imagined that precensorship was required in

[8] *Annales Ecclesiastici* (37 vols., Bar-le-duc, Parisiis, 1864–1883), ad an. 490, nn. 21–47; Lib. VII, pp. 486–496.

[9] For the full data on precensorship in the twelfth century consult Flahiff's detailed and scholarly studies "The Ecclesiastical Censorship of Books in the Twelfth Century," *Mediaeval Studies* (Toronto, 1939—), IV (1942), 1–22; and "Ralph Niger, an introduction to his Life and Works," *Mediaeval Studies*, II (1940), 104–126.

[10] *Epistola CXV* (ad Carolum [Calvum] Regem)—*MPL*, CXIX, 1119. Emphasis added.

view of the fact that the translator, though a man of great knowledge, was widely rumored to have been of questionable orthodoxy on certain points. Hence, the need of precensorship. There is no record of a law imposing precensorship at this time, nor any record that the faithful felt obliged to observe such a procedure.[11]

(2) The Citation of Abelard before the Council of Soissons (1121)

Abelard (1079-1142) was summoned before the Council of Soissons (1121) to give an account of his work *De Unitate et Trinitate Divina*. At the conclusion of the hearings he was obliged to throw his book into the fire and recant the heresies contained therein. The only record of this event, unfortunately, is that given us by Abelard himself, in his *Historia Calamitatum:*

> Dicebant enim, ad dampnationem libelli satis hoc esse debere, quod nec romani pontificis nec ecclesiae auctoritate eum [libellum] commendatum legere publice praesumpseram atque ad transcribendum iam pluribus eum ipse praestitissem . . . Dicebant et hoc perutile futurum fidei Christianae, si exemplo mei multorum similis praesumptio praeveniretur.[12]

Since Abelard's is the sole allegation of the existence of obligatory precensorship in the twelfth century, one hesitates to accept his testimony, particularly because it is not free from self-interest. Flahiff offers a conjectural, and likely, explanation of Abelard's statements:

> Abelard, piqued at the condemnation which appeared to him so unjustifiable, may have put these words into the mouth of his adversaries, as the ground on which they condemned him, in order to represent an admission on their part that no doctrinal error could be found; *or* his adversaries may have spoken the actual words and advanced this reason as sufficient for condemnation in the particular case, because of his extreme temerity, without it being necessarily evidence of a general usage of the kind. The latter hypothesis is strengthened by the fact that the accusers make no appeal to custom; on the contrary, they urge a condemnation in order that it may be a lesson to others for the future.[13]

This view receives strong confirmation in the letters of other authors who sought precensorship shortly after the incident of Abelard. Some went to

[11] It is interesting to note that just at this time obligatory precensorship obtained among the Nestorians. This is evident from their synodal legislation, promulgated by the Patriarch in 806. Cf. Arndt, *Commentarii*, p. 48, for the complete text of this extraordinary document.

[12] The text itself is subject to dispute. *MPL*, CLXXVIII, 149–150, presents the one usually known, but the critical text cited above is that given by Denifle, *Die Entstehung der Universitaeten des Mittelalters* (Berlin, 1885), p. 765, n. 31. Cf. Flahiff, "Ecclesiastical Censorship," *Mediaeval Studies*, IV (1942), 4, n. 16.

[13] *Mediaeval Studies*, IV (1942), 4.

amusing lengths in order to preclude their own condemnation.[14] Hence, it seems in place to support the opinion that precensorship was voluntary and not obligatory during the twelfth century.

Article III. Summary

Actual cases of precensorship date from the time of St. Ambrose in the fourth century, and multiply during the succeeding centuries. Baronius held that precensorship was customary as early as the fifth century, and also asserted that for certain works the custom was universal at the beginning of the seventh century. Precensorship was excercised on a voluntary basis, however. The two incidents which bespeak obligatory precensorship fail to produce convincing evidence in their behalf. There is a complete absence of any record of legislation imposing precensorship; and history fails to mention that the faithful considered themselves bound to follow the procedure of precensorship. Still, precensorship did become very widespread, especially in the later middle ages.[15]

---

[14] *Ibid.*, 4–14.

[15] In view of these facts it is misleading, if not also erroneous, to state that there was no precensorship in the early Church, or that precensorship did not exist before the invention of the art of printing in the fifteenth century. Regatillo, for example, states: "Ante inventam typographiam, nulla fuit lex nec consuetudo censurae."—*Institutiones Iuris Canonici* (2 vols., Santander, Madrid: Sal Terrae, Vol. I, 2. ed., 1946; Vol. II, 1942), II, 110 (hereafter cited as *Institutiones*). Similar statements may be found in Pruemmer, *Manuale Iuris Canonici in usum clericorum* (3. ed., Friburgi Brisgoviae, 1922), p. 484 (hereafter cited as *Manuale*); De Meester, *Juris Canonici et Juris Canonico-Civilis Compendium* (nova ed., 3 vols. in 4, Brugis, 1921–1928, III, pars 1, 249, n. 1 (hereafter cited as *Compendium*); Jombart, "Censure des Livres," *Dictionnaire de Droit Canonique* (Paris: Letouzey et Ané, 1924—), III, 158 (hereafter cited as *DDC*); Beste, *Introductio in Codicem Iuris Canonici* (3. ed., Collegeville: St. John's Abbey Press, 1946), p. 694 (hereafter cited as *Introductio*). It is quite evident that they are writing about law, or, perhaps, about legalized custom which has the force of law.

Some make allowance for the existence of a voluntary custom of precensorship, or at least of isolated instances of voluntary precensorship, e.g., Wernz-Vidal, *Ius Canonicum ad normam Codicis exactum* (7 vols. in 8, Romae: Apud Aedes Universitatis Gregorianae, 1927–1938), IV, pars 2, 128–131) hereafter cited as *Ius Canonicum*); Blat, *Commentarium Textus Codicis Iuris Canonici* (5 vols. in 6, Romae, 1919–1927), III, partes 2–6 (ed. 1923), 328 (hereafter cited as *Commentarium*); Cocchi, *Commentarium in Codicem Iuris Canonici* (8 vols. in 5, Taurinorum Augustae, 1920–1930), VI (i.e. Lib. III, partes 4–6) (2. ed., 1927), 148 (hereafter cited as *Commentarium*); Berutti, *Institutiones Iuris Canonici* (6 vols., [Vol. II, pars 2, et Vol. V adhuc sub praelo], Taurini-Romae: Marietti, 1936–1943), IV, 416 (hereafter cited as *Institutiones*); Claeys Bouuaert-Simenon, *Manuale Iuris Canonici ad usum seminariorum* (3 vols. [Vols. I, III, 4. ed.; Vol. II, 2. ed.], Gandae et Leodii, 1934–1935), III, 132 (hereafter cited as *Manuale*).

CHAPTER III

OBLIGATORY PRECENSORSHIP

Precensorship was not imposed on the universal Church until the fifteenth century. However, long before that time precensorship is found in particular legislation for specific groups of the faithful. Hence, this chapter will deal with both particular and general legislation respecting precensorship.

Article I. Particular Legislation

Three different ecclesiastical units had precensorship before the fifteenth century. The first group is the Franciscan Order, the second group includes many of the medieval universities, and the third group includes certain dioceses, particularly the ones located in the area where printing had its origin.

(1) Precensorship in the Franciscan Order (Thirteenth Century)

The Franciscan Order, it seems, was the first group in the Church to have legislation respecting precensorship. The statute is contained in the famous *Constitutiones Narbonnenses*, which were framed in 1260 by the Chapter held at Narbonne under the presidency of St. Bonaventure (+1274). The pertinent decree reads:

> Item inhibemus ne de cetero aliquod scriptum novum extra Ordinem publicetur, nisi prius examinatum fuerit per generalem Ministrum, vel provincialem et Definitores in Capitulo Provinciali. Et quicumque contra fecerit, tribus diebus tantum in pane et aqua ieiunet et careat illo scripto.[1]

This piece of legislation has remained in the Franciscan Order to the present day, though the penalty is no longer extant. Canon 1385, §3, contains the same idea and applies it to all religious.

(2) Precensorship at the Universities (Thirteenth and Fourteenth Centuries)

The medieval universities instituted precensorship in the thirteenth century. For example, the University of Paris discovered that booksellers (*Librarii* seu *stationarii*) had circulated spurious and adulterated copies of the lectures given at the university. To preclude the repetition of this fraud,

[1] Rubrica VI de occupatione fratrum—*Doctoris Seraphici S. Bonaventurae Opera Omnia* (10 vols. & Index, Ad Claras Aquas [prope Florentiam], 1883–1902), VIII, 456.

the University ruled, in 1275, that books had to conform to the manuscripts, and that they had to be precensored.[2] Within a short time the University required that a teacher obtain the approval of the dean and the faculty for his work before submitting it to a bookseller for multiplication and sale:

> Item quod nullus magister aut bacalaurius, qui sententias legerit, suam lecturam sententiarum committet tractando stationariis directe vel indirecte, quousque sua lectura fuerit per cancellarium et magistros predicte [Theologiae] facultatis examinata.[3]

Hilgers (1858-1918) has established the fact that practically all the universities introduced precensorship of this type during the fourteenth century.[4] However, it should be remembered that this precensorship applied only to lectures given at the university and reproduced by their own booksellers.

Not long after the invention of printing, the University of Cologne broadened its policy of precensorship. The occasion was the printing of an anonymous and libellous pamphlet attacking the immunities of the clergy. The University seemingly failed in its attempt to suppress the work and appealed to Pope Sixtus IV (1471-1484). The latter praised the zeal of the officials of the University and empowered the Rector to take the appropriate steps to coerce the printer, even to the extent of inflicting censures, if necessary.[5] The University then established precensorship for all works printed at Cologne, directing the printers to submit their publications to the rector for examination, and obliging them to note the result of the precensorship in the printed copy of the work. Some books printed at Cologne between 1479-1486 contain such annotations.[6]

The University of Cologne failed in enforcing precensorship. During the years 1479-1486 only six of the fourteen printers cooperated, and five of these persevered for little better than a year. There is no record of a printer

[2] "Donec fuerint approbata per universitatem, correcta et taxata"—Denifle-Chatelain, *Chartularium Universitatis Parisiensis* (4 vols., Parisiis, 1889–1897), I, 531–533 (hereafter cited as *Chartularium*). Citations from this work are taken from Hilgers, *Der Index der verbotenen Buecher* (Freiburg im Breisgau, 1904), pp. 404ff. (hereafter cited as *Der Index*).

[3] Art. 9 of the Papal Statutes drawn up at Avignon, June 5, 1366, for the Faculty of Theology at the University of Paris. Cf. Denifle-Chatelain, *Chartularium*, II (Appendix), 698.

[4] *Der Index*, p. 404.

[5] Evidence for this affair is scanty. The document of Sixtus IV, dated March 17, 1479, is no longer extant, and the oldest source seems to be Ortwin Gratius, *Lamentationes obscurorum virorum* (Coloniae, 1518). Cf. Hilgers, *Der Index*, p. 479; Hansen, "Der Malleus maleficarum," *Westdeutsche Zeitschrift fuer Geschichte und Kunst* (Trier, 1882–1913), XVII (1898), 138 (hereafter cited as *WZGK*).

[6] For example" Admissum et approbatum ab alma universitate studii Coloniensis de consensu et voluntate spectabilis viri pro tempore rectoris."—Hansen, "Der Malleus," *WZGK*, XVII (1898), 138–139. Cf. also Voulliéme, *Der Buchdruck Koelns bis 1500* (Bonn, 1903), p. LXXXVI (hereafter cited as *Buchdruck*); Hartzheim, *Bibliotheca Coloniensis* (Coloniae, 1747), p. 312 (hereafter cited as *Bibliotheca*). Both the latter authors cite several formulae.

being punished for non-compliance. Only twenty-five works show the approval of the University, sixteen of them first editions, and the remainder, reprints. This represents but a small portion of the total output.[7]

Though the efforts of the University of Cologne failed, a book which received such an approval seems to have enjoyed a special prestige, in view of the particular fact that the precensorship was constituted by papal authority.[8]

(3) Episcopal Legislation Respecting Precensorship (Fifteenth Century)

The earliest known episcopal legislation respecting precensorship appears to be a decree of Rudolf II von Scheerenberg, Prince-Bishop of Wuerzburg, during the month of April, 1482. The decree was occasioned by the circulation of a pamphlet by Andrea Zamometic, O.P., which attempted to reconvene the General Council at Basle to pronounce a condemnation on Pope Sixtus IV for alleged heresy, simony, immorality, nepotism, etc. Bishop Rudolf prohibited the libellous pamphlet, and, in order to prevent similar abuses in the future, forbade any work to be printed without the approval of the suffragan [sic] of the bishop.[9]

A second example of episcopal precensorship is found in a letter of Archbishop Berthold of Henneberg for the Archdiocese of Mainz in 1485. The decree concerns only the translation of works into the German language.[10] In January, 1486, Archbishop Berthold issued another decree in which he

---

[7] Voulliéme, *Buchdruck*, pp. LXXXVI–LXXXVII; Hansen, "Der Malleus," *WZGK*, XVII (1898), 138; Kapp, *Geschichte des deutschen Buchhandels bis in das siebzehnte Jahrhundert* (4 vols. & Index, Leipzig, 1886–1923), I, 526 (hereafter cited as *Geschichte*).

[8] Hansen, "Der Malleus," *WZGK*, XVII (1898), 139–140.

[9] The text of the decree is lost. Its existence is known only from a letter of Cardinal Francesco Piccolomini to an unnamed Cardinal in Rome, which letter is published by Schlecht, *Andrea Zamometic und der Basler Konzilsversuch vom Jahre 1482* (Paderborn, 1903), pp. 42*–43*. Kapp (*Geschichte*, I, 525–526) claims that episcopal legislation must have existed already in 1480, or even as early as 1475. He infers this from the presence of an *Imprimatur* in books bearing those dates. Until conclusive evidence is had, it is preferable to consider these as examples of voluntary precensorship, particularly since one of the works cited as proof bears the *Imprimatur* of four different bishops. Kapp himself admits that he has found no signs of precensorship in any of the episcopal laws or statutes of this decade.

[10] The solitary record of this decree is the letter to Conrad Hensel, dated March 22, 1485. In spite of the fact that the letter is addressed to an individual, it is licit for us to conclude to the existence of a decree for the entire archdiocese, since the letter contains the commission whereby Conrad Hensel is appointed precensor for the archdiocese. The complete text may be found in Pallmann, "Des Erzbischofs Berthold von Mainz aeltestes Censuredict," *Archiv fuer Geschichte des deutschen Buchhandels* (Leipzig, 1874—), IX (1884), 238–240 (hereafter cited as *AGDB*).

imposed the observance of the earlier decree on the entire ecclesiastical province.[11] In the following year the first pontifical legislation occurred.

Article II. General Legislation for the Entire Church (1487—)

(1) Legislation of Innocent VIII (1482-1492)

The first record of pontifical legislation enacting precensorship for the entire Church is the Bull "*Inter Multiplices*" of Innocent VIII (1482-1492), issued Nov. 17, 1487, whose text reads:

> Nos . . . auctoritate apostolica praesentium tenore districte praecipiendo inhibemus, ne de caetero, libros, tractatus aut scripturas qualescumque imprimere aut imprimi facere praesumant, nisi consultis prius super hoc in dicta curia magistro sacri palatii seu in ejus absentia ipsius vices gerente, et extra eam locorum ordinariis et eorum speciali et expressa impetrata licentia gratis concedenda, quorum conscientia oneramus, ut antequam huiusmodi licentiam concedant, imprimenda diligenter examinent, sive a peritis et catholicis examinari faciant et procurent ac diligenter advertant, ne quid imprimatur, quod orthodoxae fidei contrarium, impium et scandalosum existat. Et quia parum esset adversus futuras impressiones providere nisi . . . sub simili excommunicationis latae sententiae et eorum arbitrio exigenda pecuniaria poena incurrenda . . . [12]

Some have tried to argue that the Bull was not intended for the universal Church because it was promulgated in Cologne. Hilgers, for example, held that it was sent only to the Archbishop of Cologne.[13] However, the text of the Bull makes it evident that it was meant for the universal Church, for it explicitly mentions that it binds printers residing in Rome, Italy, Germany, France, Spain, England, Scotland, and elsewhere.[14] It is a matter of record that the printers of Cologne resisted attempts to enforce this law. The appearance of the *Imprimatur* in some few books in Spain, and in some in Venice, is the only evidence to show that the Bull was observed.[15]

---

[11] Pallmann (*AGDB*, IX (1884), 238) states that the text of this second decree is practically identical with that of the previous decree. The document itself may be found in Gudenus, *Codex diplomaticus anecdotorum res Moguntinas illustrantium* (5 vols., Francofurti et Lipsiae, 1747–1758), IV, 467–471. Cf. also Reusch, *Der Index der verbotenen Buecher* (2 vols., Bonn, 1883–1885), I, 57 (hereafter cited as *Der Index*); Kapp, *Geschichte*, I, 527–528.

[12] This text, lost for centuries, was finally recovered by Voulliéme and reproduced in *Buchdruck*, pp. LXXXVIII–XC.

[13] "Buecherverbot und Buechercensur des 16 Jahrhunderts in Italien," *Zentralblatt fuer Bibliothekswesen* (Leipzig, 1884—), XXVIII (1911), 113 (hereafter cited as *ZB*).

[14] Cf. Voulliéme, *Buchdruck*, p. LXXXIX; Rest, "Die erste allgemeine paepstliche Zensurordnung," *ZB*, XXXI (1914), 69.

[15] Hilgers, *ZB*, XXVIII (1911), 113.

(2) Legislation of Alexander VI (1492-1503)

Alexander VI (1492-1503) reissued the "*Inter Multiplices*" of Innocent VIII on June 1, 1501. The text and title of this is practically identical with that of Innocent VIII, save for certain changes incidental to the purpose the pope had in mind. This time it was sent to the ecclesiastical provinces of Cologne, Mainz, Trier and Magdeburg. History furnishes us with the reason, namely, that the Bull of Innocent VIII was not being observed, and that many heretical books were being published in these provinces.[16] It is known that the printers of Cologne appealed to Rome against the enforcement of this decree by diocesan authorities.[17] The appeal failed, as is evidenced by the fact that the identical legislation was reaffirmed a few years later by the V General Council of the Lateran.

(3) Legislation of the Fifth General Council of the Lateran (1512-1517)

The V General Council of the Lateran (1512-1517) repeated the earlier legislation and laid more stringent sanctions on its non-observance. The pertinent sections read:

> §2. Statuimus et ordinamus, quod de cetero perpetuis futuris temporibus, nullus librum aliquem, seu aliam quamcumque scripturam, tam in Urbe nostra, quam aliis quibusvis civitatibus, et dioecesibus, imprimere seu imprimi facere praesumat, nisi prius in Urbe per vicarium nostrum, et sacri palatii magistrum, in aliis vero civitatibus et dioecesibus per episcopum, vel alium habentem peritiam scientiae, libri seu scripturae huiusmodi imprimendae, ab eodem episcopo ad id deputandum, ac inquisitorem haereticae pravitatis civitatis sive dioecesis, in quibus librorum impressio huiusmodi fieret, diligenter examinentur, et per eorum manu propria subscriptionem, sub excommunicationis sententia, gratis et sine dilatione imponendam, approbentur.
>
> §3. Qui autem secus praesumpserit, ultra librorum impressorum amissionem, et illorum publicam combustionem, ac centum ducatorum fabricae principis Apostolorum de Urbe, sine spe remissionis, solutionem, ac anni continui exercitii impressionis suspensionem, excommunicationis sententia innodatus existat; ac demum ingravescente contumacia, taliter per episcopum suum, vel vicarium nos-

[16] Kapp, *Geschichte*, I, 530; Pernicone, *The Ecclesiastical Prohibition of Books*, The Catholic University of America Canon Law Studies, n. 72 (Washington, D. C.: The Catholic University of America, 1932), p. 42 (hereafter cited as *Prohibition*). The text of the reissue may be found in *Analecta Ecclesiastica* (Romae, 1893–1911), IV (1896), 422–424 (hereafter cited as *Anal. Eccl.*).

[17] Kapp (*Geschichte*, I, 531) lists the names of the parties involved in the dispute and also names the procurators chosen to represent the principals in Rome. Cf. also Voulliéme, *Buchdruck*, p. XCII.

> trum respective per omnia iuris remedia castigetur, quod alii eius exemplo similia minime attentare praesumat . . . [18]

This is the first pontifical law on precensorship which received adequate publicity and attention. It was adopted by many provincial and diocesan synods, as is evident from the particular law of that period.[19]

(4) Legislation of the Council of Trent (1545-1563)

The Council of Trent, in its fourth session, dealt with the question of the precensorship of books, with particular reference to sacred books. The title and decree are as follows: *Decretum de editione et usu sacrorum librorum:*

> . . . decernit et statuit, ut posthac sacra scriptura, potissimum vero haec ipsa vetus et vulgata editio quam emendatissime imprimatur, nullique liceat imprimere vel imprimi facere quosvis libros de rebus sacris sine nomine auctoris, neque illos in futurum vendere aut etiam apud se retinere, nisi primum examinati probatique fuerint ab ordinario, sub poena anathematis et pecuniae in canone concilii novissimi Lateranensis apposita. Et si regulares fuerint, ultra examinationem et probationem huiusmodi licentiam quoque a suis superioribus impetrare teneantur, recognitis per eos libris iuxta formam suarum ordinationum. Qui autem scripto eos communicant vel evulgant, nisi antea examinati probatique fuerint, eisdem poenis subiaceant, quibus impressores. Et qui eos habuerint vel legerint, nisi prodiderint auctorem, pro auctoribus habeantur. Ipsa vero huiusmodi librorum probatio in scriptis detur atque ideo in fronte libri vel scripti vel impressi authentice appareat. Idque totum, hoc est, et probatio et examen, gratis fiat, ut probanda probentur, et reprobentur improbanda.[20]

In this session the Council dealt primarily with the Sacred Scriptures, but still the decree prescribes precensorship for all books on sacred matters (*de rebus sacris*). The context and purpose of the decree, as well as the rubric placed at its head, seem to indicate that the Council intended to legislate only about editions of the Sacred Scriptures and works on Sacred Scripture. In practice, however, the decree was understood to prescribe precensorship

---

[18] Leo X (in Conc. Lateranen. V) const. "*Inter Sollicitudines,*" 4 maii 1515, §§2–3—*Codicis Iuris Canonici Fontes,* cura Emi Petri Gasparri editi (9 vols., Romae [postea Civitate Vaticana]: Typis Polyglottis Vaticanis, 1923–1939; Vols. XII–IX, ed. cura et studio Emi Iustiniani Card. Serédi), n. 68 (hereafter cited as *Fontes*).

[19] Cf. Hilgers, *Der Index*, p. 408; Reusch, *Der Index*, I, 57; Hefele, *Conciliengeschichte* (9 vols., Freiburg im Breisgau, 1869–1890; Vols. VII–IX, ed. J. Card. Hergenroether), VIII, 750; Hartzheim, *Bibliotheca*, p. 312; Dilgskron, "De revisione et approbatione librorum," *Anal. Eccl.*, IV (1896), 425.

[20] Conc. Trident., sess. IV, *de editione et usu sacrorum librorum—Canones et Decreta Concilii Tridentini ex editione romana a. MDCCCXXXIV repetiti . . . ed. Richter* (Lipsiae, 1853).

for all books on religious matters.[21] Still, this was not as broad as the legislation of the Fifth Lateran Council which had prescribed precensorship for all books without exception.

(5) Legislation of Pius IV (1559-1565)

Shortly after the close of the Council of Trent, Pope Pius IV (1559-1565) published a new revision of the *Index of Forbidden Books*, which contained ten general rules concerning prohibited books. These rules were drawn up by a commission of Fathers appointed by the Council of Trent, and hence the rules are often referred to as the *General Rules of the Council of Trent*, though they were approved by Pope Pius in 1564 after the close of the Council, in the constitution "*Dominici gregis*." Rule Ten, which concerns precensorship, is as follows:

> In librorum aliarumve scripturarum impressione servetur quod in concilio Lateranensi sub Leone X, sess. X, statutum est. Quare, si in alma Urbe Roma liber aliquis sit imprimendus, per vicarium summi pontificis et sacri palatii magistrum, vel personas a sanctissimo Domino nostro deputandas prius examinetur. In aliis vero locis ad episcopum vel alium habentem scientiam libri vel scripturae imprimendae, ab eodem episcopo deputandum, ac inquisitorem haereticae pravitatis eius civitatis vel dioecesis, in qua impressio fiet, eius approbatio et examen pertineat, et per eorum manum propria subscriptione gratis et sine dilatione imponendam sub poenis et censuris in eodem decreto contentis approbetur, hac lege et conditione addita, ut exemplum libri imprimendi authenticum et manu auctoris subscriptum apud examinatorem remaneat; eos vero, qui libellos manuscriptos vulgant, nisi ante examinati probatique fuerint, iisdem poenis subiici debere iudicarunt patres deputati, quibus impressores; et qui eos habuerint et legerint, nisi auctores prodiderint, pro auctores habeantur. Ipsa vero huiusmodi librorum probatio in scriptis detur, et in fronte libri vel scripti vel impressi authentice appareat, probatioque et examen ac caetera gratis fiant. Praeterea in singulis civitatibus ac dioecesibus domus vel loci, ubi ars impressoria exercetur, et bibliothecae librorum venalium saepius visitentur a personis ad id deputandis ab episcopo sive eius vicario, atque etiam ab inquisitore haereticae pravitatis, ut nihil eorum, quae prohibentur, aut imprimatur, aut vendatur aut habeatur . . . [22]

---

[21] Bassaeus, *Flores Totius Theologiae Practicae, tum Sacramentalis tum Moralis* (2. ed., 2 vols., Venetiis, 1690), I, sub verbo "excommunicatio," VIII, n. 1; Bouix, *Tractatus De Curia Romana seu de Cardinalibus, Romanis Congregationibus, Legatis, Nuntiis, Vicariis et Protonotariis Apostolicis* (Reimpressio, Parisiis, 1880), p. 558. (hereafter cited as *De Curia Romana*).

[22] De libris prohibitis regulae decem, Regula X—*Fontes*, n. 426; also in *Bullarum, Diplomatum et Privilegiorum Romanorum Pontificum Taurinensis Editio* (24 vols., & Appendix, Augustae Taurinorum, 1857–1872), VII, 281–282 (hereafter cited as *BRT*).

(6) Legislation of Pius V (1566-1572), Gregory XIII (1572-1585) and Sixtus V (1585-1590)

Pope Pius V (1566-1572) established the Sacred Congregation of the Index on March 5, 1571, with a view to relieving the Sacred Congregation of the Inquisition (Holy Office) of some of its manifold duties. Hence, he entrusted the supervision of harmful books to this new Congregation.[23-24]

Pope Gregory XIII (1572-1585) reorganized this Congregation and gave it full authority to interpret and settle difficulties arising from the *Index* and from the *Ten General Rules*.[25] Hence, this Congregation also had charge of the precensorship of books.

Pope Sixtus V (1585-1590) again reorganized the Roman Curia and granted additional faculties to the Sacred Congregation of the Index.[26] Sixtus V also intended to replace the ten general rules with twenty-one new rules. Despite the fact that the work was printed, it did not pass into law, since Sixtus had died before promulgating it.[27]

(7) Legislation of Clement VIII (1592-1605)

Clement VIII (1592-1605) issued a new edition of the Index in 1593, but, it seems, never promulgated it.[28] In 1595, however, Clement promulgated a new edition of the Index, which was actually printed in Rome in 1596.[29] This edition is of particular interest to the history of the law on precensorship, for, over and above the Index and the Ten Rules, it contained an instruction on the prohibition, expurgation and printing of books, etc. The third section, i.e., the one entitled *De Impressione Librorum*, comprises seven paragraphs. These constitute more detailed regulations concerning the matter originally enacted by Leo X and the Council of Trent, and regarding the Tenth General Rule of Pius IV. Hence, these seven paragraphs are given in full:

> §I. Nullus liber in posterum excudatur, qui non in fronte nomen, cognomen, et patriam praeferat auctoris.
>
> Quod si de auctore non constet aut iustam aliquam ob causam, tacito eius nomine, Episcopo, et Inquisitori liber edi posse videatur, nomen illius omnino describatur, qui librum examinaverit atque approbaverit.

[23-24] Bouix (*De Curia Romana*, p. 449) insists that this Congregation was established Pius V, and not by Sixtus V, as some have held.

[25] Const. "*Ut pestiferarum*," 13 sept. 1572—Cf. Hilgers, *Der Index*, p. 514. This document is not found in the *Fontes* nor in *BRT*.

[26] Const. "*Immensa Aeterni Dei*," 22 ian. 1588—*BRT*, VIII, 988.

[27] Only a few copies of this rare Index of 1590 are still extant. Cf. Hilgers, *Der Index*, pp. 13–14, 524.

[28] Hilgers discovered the two extant copies of this edition. Cf. *Der Index*, pp. 13, 529, 530.

[29] Instr., 17 oct. 1595—*Fontes*, n. 426.

In his vero generibus librorum, qui ex variorum scriptorum dictis, aut exemplis, aut vocibus compilari solent, is qui laborem colligendi, et compilandi susceperit, pro auctore habeatur.

§II. Regulares, praeter Episcopi, et Inquisitoris licentiam (de qua Regula decima dictum est), meminerint teneri se, sacri Concilii Tridentini decreto, operis in lucem edendi facultatem a Praelato, cui subiacent, obtinere.

Utramque autem concessionem, quae appareat, ad principium operis imprimi faciant.

§III. Curent Episcopi et Inquisitores, poenis etiam propositis, ne impressoriam artem exercentes, obscoenas imagines, turpesve, etiam in grandiusculis litteris imprimi consuetas, in librorum deinceps impressione apponant.

Ad libros vero, qui de rebus ecclesiasticis, aut spiritualibus conscripti sunt, ne characteribus grandioribus utantur, in quibus expresse appareat alicuius rei profanae nedum turpis, obscoenaeve species.

Qui etiam invigilabunt summopere, ut in singulorum impressione librorum nomen impressoris, locus impressionis, et annus quo liber impressus est, in principio atque in eius fine adnotetur.

§IV. Qui operis alicuius editionis parat, integrum eius exemplar exhibeat Episcopo, vel Inquisitori: id ubi recognoverint, probaverintque, penes se retineant. Quod Romae quidem in archivo Magistri sacri palatii; extra Urbem vero, in loco idoneo, quem Episcopus, aut Inquisitor elegerit, reservetur.

Postquam autem liber impressus erit, non liceat cuiquam venalem in vulgus proponere, aut quoquomodo publicare, antequam is ad quem haec cura pertinet, illum cum manuscripto apud se retento diligenter contulerit, licentiamque, ut vendi publicarique possit, concesserit.

Idque tum demum faciendum, cum exploratum habebitur, typographum fideliter se in suo munere gessisse, neque ab exemplari manuscripto vel minimum discessisse.

§V. Curent Episcopi et Inquisitores, quorum muneris erit facultatem libros imprimendi concedere, ut eis examinandis spectatae pietatis et doctrinae viros adhibeant, de quorum fide et integritate sibi polliceri queant, nihil eos gratiae daturos, nihil odio, sed omni humano affectu posthabito, Dei dumtaxat gloriam spectaturos, et fidelis populi utilitatem.

Talium autem virorum approbatio, una cum licentia Episcopi et Inquisitoris, ante initium operis imprimatur.

§VI. Typographi et bibliopolae coram Episcopo, aut Inquisitore, et Romae coram Magistro sacri Palatii, iureiurando spondeant, se munus suum catholice, sincere ac fideliter exequuturos, huiusque Indicis decretis ac regulis, Episcoporumque et Inquisitorum edictis, quatenus eorum artes attingunt, obtemperaturos; neque ad suae artis ministerium quemquam scienter admissuros, qui haeretica labe sit inquinatus.

> Quod si inter illos, insignes ac eruditi nonnulli reperiantur, fidem etiam catholicam, iuxta formam a Pio IV fel. rec. praescriptam, eorumdem superiorum arbitrio, profiteri teneantur.
>
> §VII. Liber auctoris damnati, qui ad praescriptum Regularum expurgari permittitur, postquam accurate recognitus, et purgatus, legitimeque permissus fuerit, si denuo sit imprimendus, praeferat titulo inscriptum nomen auctoris, cum nota damnationis, ut quamvis quoad aliqua liber recipi, auctor tamen repudiari intelligatur.
>
> In eiusdem quoque libri principio, tum veteris prohibitionis, tum recentis emendationis, ac permissionis mentio fiat, exempli gratia: *Bibliotheca a Conrado Gesnero Tigurino, damnato auctore, olim edita, ac prohibita, nunc iussu superiorum expurgata et permissa.*[30]

(8) Legislation of Urban VIII (1623-1644)

In 1623, the Sacred Congregation of the Index declared that the text of musical compositions was also subject to precensorship.[31] In 1625, the Sacred Congregation of the Inquisition issued a decree concerning authors who resided in the Papal States, as follows:

> Sanctissimus Dominus noster, pro debito sui pastoralis officii corrigere volens abusus nonnullorum, in statu Sedi Apostolicae mediate vel immediate subiecto existentium, qui libros a se compositos extra praefatum statum, absque ulla Ordinariorum et inquisitorum loci ubi degunt approbatione, imprimendos transmittunt; statuit et decrevit, ut in posterum nemo in statu praedicto degens, cuiusvis conditionis, gradus, ordinis et dignitatis existat, libros de quavis materia tractantes, et ubicumque compositos, audeat alio deferre vel mittere imprimendos, sine expressa in scriptis adprobatione Illustrissimi et Reverendissimi Domini Cardinalis, Sanctissimi Domini Nostri Vicarii, et Magistri Sacri Palatii, si in Urbe; si vero extra Urbem existant, sine Ordinarii et inquisitoris loci illius, sive ab iis deputatorum, facultate et licentia, operi praefigenda. Libros autem, quos contra praesentis decreti tenorem imprimi contigerit, praeter alias poenas arbitrio suae Sanctitatis infligendas, absque alia declaratione ex nunc prohibet et pro expresse prohibitis haberi vult et mandat . . .[32]

(9) Legislation of Alexander VII (1655-1667)

Alexander's new edition of the Index in 1664 is noteworthy, not merely because it initiated the listing of forbidden books in alphabetical order, but also because of the addition of two observations on the tenth Tridentine Rule. These observations are:

---

[30] *Fontes*, n. 426.

[31] Reusch (*Der Index*, I, 340) claims that this declaration was contained in the collection of decrees of the *Index* of Alexander VII, n. 28. It is not listed in later editions of the *Index*, e.g., of 1889.

[32] S.C.S.Off., decr., 18 sept. 1625—quoted by Bouix, *De Curia Romana*, p. 451. The date is given as Oct. 3, 1625, in Pennacchi, *Commentaria in Constitutionem APOSTOLICAE SEDIS qua censurae latae sententiae limitantur* (2 vols., Romae, 1883), I, 141 (hereafter cited as *Commentaria*).

I. Observandum est circa Regulam decimam, quod degentes in statu Sedi Apostolicae mediate, vel immediate subiecto, non possunt transmittere libros a se compositos, alibi imprimendos sine expressa approbatione, et in scriptis eminentissimi, ac reverendissimi d. cardinalis Sanctissimi Domini Nostri Vicarii et Magistri sacri Palatii, si in Urbe; si vero extra Urbem existant, sine Ordinarii loci illius, sive ab his deputatorum facultate, et licentia operi infigenda.

II. Qui vero super impressionem librorum, ordinariam, aut delegatam auctoritatem exercent, dent operam, ne ad examen librorum huiusmodi, personas affectui auctorum quomodolibet addictas, praesertim vero propinquitate illos, aut alia, quantumvis a longe petita ea sit (veri et sinceri iudicii corruptrice) necessitudine contingentes admittant: super omnia autem ab oblatis sibi in hanc operam per eosdem auctores censoribus caveant; sed iis demum utantur, quos doctrina, morumque integritate probatos, ab omni suspicione gratiae intactos, ac, si fieri potest, auctoribus ipsis ignotos, et unius boni publici, Deique gloriae studiosis cognoverint. Quo vero ad auctores regulares, cuiuscumque ordinis et instituti sint, illud praeterea observandum, ut ne eorum scripta, vel opera aliis eiusdem instituti regularibus examinanda committantur, sed alterius ordinis, et instituti viri pii, doctique, et a partium studio, atque ab amoris, et odii stimulis prorsus remoti eligantur: per hoc autem non tollitur, quin intra eorumdem regularium ordinem, per religiosos eiusdem ordinis, superiorum suorum iussu, praefati libri examinari debeant.[33]

(10) Legislation of Benedict XIV (1740-1758)

Benedict XIV (1740-1758) issued a constitution in 1753 which laid down detailed rules to be followed by the Sacred Congregation of the Inquisition and the Sacred Congregation of the Index in their examination and prohibition of books.[34] Since these norms refer exclusively to the Sacred Congregations as such, and since they contain nothing special on precensorship, there is no need to transcribe them here. It is proper to note, however, that the directives given for the appointment and duties of these Roman censors were applicable, in most instances, to all censors. They will be utilized in the commentary on canon 1393.

(11) Legislation of Clement XIII (1758-1769), Leo XII (1822-1829), and Gregory XVI (1831-1846)

During the subsequent century and a quarter, nothing new appeared in regard to the law on precensorship. However, various Popes issued decrees insisting on the observance of previous legislation. Thus, Pope Clement

[33] Brev., 5 mart. 1664—*Index Librorum Prohibitorum Sanctissimi Domini Nostri Leonis XIII Pont. Max. iussu editus* (ed. novissima, Taurini, 1889), p. xxii. As far as is known, the word "censor" is used for the first time in a pontifical document in this second observation.

[34] Const. "*Sollicita ac provida,*" 9 iul. 1753—*Fontes*, n. 426.

XIII (1758-1769) in his encyclical "*Christianae reipublicae,*" dated Nov. 25, 1766, urged the bishops to enforce the laws of the Church.[35] Leo XII (1822-1829) urged regular superiors to enforce the Tridentine Rules.[36] Gregory XVI (1831-1846) issued two encyclicals in which he recalled certain points.[37]

(12) Legislation of Pius IX (1846-1878)

Pius IX (1846-1878) inaugurated a new trend in regard to precensorship by considerably mitigating the law for the Papal States. It had become an impossibility to observe the law enacted by the V General Council of the Lateran in 1515. Hence, acting as civil ruler of the Papal States, Pius IX abolished governmental and political precensorship.[38] And in his encyclical letter to the Papal States, dated June 2, 1848, he mitigated the law of ecclesiastical precensorship as follows:

> Itaque motu proprio et Apostolica Nostra Auctoritate decretum concilii Lateranensis, et caeteras supradictas sanctiones moderando et declarando decernimus, atque permittimus, ut posthac, censores ecclesiastici in locis temporali Nostrae Ditioni subditis de iis tantum solliciti sint, quae Divinas Scripturas, Sacram Theologiam, Historiam Ecclesiasticam, Ius Canonicum, Theologiam Naturalem, Ethicen, aliasque huiusmodi religiosas aut morales disciplinas respiciunt, ac generatim de omnibus, in quibus Religionis vel morum honestatis speciatim intersit. Iuxta haec igitur statuimus atque permittimus ut in omni Ephemeridum et Librorum genere illi dumtaxat sine praevia Ecclesiastica censura edi nequeant, qui moralis aut religiosi, uti diximus, argumenti sint; in caeteris vero ii tantum articuli, qui simile argumentum habeant, vel causam ipsam Religionis aut morum honestatis proxime attingant . . . [39]

Pius IX advanced a step further in the mitigation of the law when he issued his constitution "*Apostolicae Sedis,*" Oct. 12, 1869, the pertinent section of which reads:

> Praeter hos hactenus recensitos, eos quoque quos Sacrosanctum Concilium Tridentinum, sive reservata Summo Pontifici aut Ordinariis absolutione, sive absque ulla reservatione excommunicavit, Nos pariter ita excommunicatos esse declaramus; excepta anathematis poena in decreto Sess. IV, *De editione et usu Sacrorum Librorum constituta*, cui illos tantum subiacere volumus, qui libros de rebus sacris tractantes sine Ordinarii approbatione imprimunt, aut imprimi faciunt.[40]

---

[35] *Fontes*, n. 461.

[36] S. C. Indicis, mandatum, 26 mart. 1825—*Index Librorum Prohibitorum—1889*, p. XLV.

[37] "*Mirari vos,*" 15 aug. 1832—*Fontes*, n. 485; and "*Inter praecipuas,*" 5 maii 1844, ad IV—*Fontes*, n. 502.

[38] Pius IX, motu proprio, 14 mart. 1848—*Pii IX Pontificis Maximi Acta* (9 vols., Romae, 1854–1878), Pars II, vol. I, 222–238.

[39] *Pii IX Pontificis Maximi Acta*, Pars I, I, 99–101.

[40] *Fontes*, n. 552.

This legislation gave rise to considerable discussion about the meaning of the phrase "*de rebus sacris.*" Some limited its meaning to books of Sacred Scripture and to annotations and commentaries of the Scriptures; others held a more extensive view, which was more in accord with the accepted interpretation of the previous law. The Holy Office was asked to render a decision. It reads:

> Censuram nemini reservatam inflictam iis qui libros de rebus sacris tractantes sine Ordinarii approbatione imprimunt aut imprimi faciunt, restringendam esse ad libros Sacrarum Scripturarum, nec non ad eorumdem adnotationes et commentarios, minime vero extendendam ad libros quoscumque de rebus sacris in genere, id est ad religionem pertinentibus tractantes.[41]

(13) Legislation of Leo XIII (1878-1903)

Leo XIII (1878-1903) thoroughly reorganized the entire field of law respecting the precensorship of books. In so doing, he brought to a successful termination the desires expressed at the Vatican Council, which had contemplated and urged this work.[42] Leo's new legislation was promulgated in the celebrated constitution "*Officiorum ac Munerum,*" dated January 25, 1897.[43] Since the decrees of "*Officiorum ac Munerum*" are quite extensive (49 in number) and since they are readily accessible, and since many of them have been embodied in the Code of Canon Law, there is no special reason for transcribing them here. However, it may serve a useful purpose to point out the headings of the various chapters, as follows:

Titulus II. De Censura Librorum
Caput I. De praelatis librorum censura praepositis.
Caput II. De censorum officio in praevio librorum examine.
Caput III. De libris praeviae censurae subiiciendis.
Caput IV. De typographis et editoribus liborum.
Caput V. De poenis in decretorum generalium transgressores statutis.

(14) Legislation of Pius X (1903-1914)

To check the spread of modernism and to warn the clergy and the faithful against its errors, Pius X (1903-1914) issued the encyclical "*Pascendi dominici*

[41] S.C.S.Off., *Ratisbonen.*, 22 dec. 1880, ad II—*Fontes*, n. 1068.

[42] For a history of the proceedings before and during the Vatican Council concerning this matter, see Pennacchi, "In Constitutionem Apostolicam *OFFICIORUM AC MUNERUM* Brevis Commentatio," *Acta Sanctae Sedis* (41 vols., Romae, 1865–1908), XXX (1897–1898), 77–78 (hereafter cited as *ASS*); Schneider, *Die neuen Buechergesetze der Kirche* (Mainz, 1900), pp. 17–18 (hereafter cited as *Buechergesetze*); *Acta et Decreta Sacrorum Conciliorum Recentiorum Collectio Lacensis* (7 vols., Friburgi Brisgoviae, 1870–1892), VII, 874, 883, 1017–1020 (hereafter cited as *Coll. Lac.*).

[43] *Fontes*, n. 632. The new constitution expressly mentioned that it abrogated all former law on precensorship, except the constitution "*Sollicita ac Provida*" of Benedict XIV.

gregis" on December 8, 1907. Since the modernists fully utilized the press to disseminate their doctrines, Pius strengthened the precensorship regulations as follows:

> Nec tamen pravorum librorum satis est lectionem impedire ac venditionem; editionem etiam prohiberi oportet. Ideo edendi facultatem Episcopi severitate summa impertiant.—Quoniam vero magno numero ea sunt ex Constitutione *Officiorum*, quae Ordinarii permissionem ut edantur postulent, nec ipse per se Episcopus praecognoscere universa potest; in quibusdam dioecesibus ad cognitionem faciendam censores ex officio sufficienti numero destinantur. Huiusmodi censorum institutum laudamus quam maxime: illudque ut ad omnes dioeceses propagetur non hortamur modo sed omnino praescribimus. In universis igitur curiis episcopalibus censores ex officio adsint; qui edenda cognoscant: hi autem e gemino clero eligantur, aetate, eruditione, prudentia commendati, quique in doctrinis probandis improbandisque medio tutoque itinere eant. Ad illos scriptorum cognitio deferatur, quae ex articulis XLI et XLII memoratae Constitutionis venia ut edantur indigent. Censor sententiam scripto dabit. Ea si faverit, Episcopus potestatem edendi faciet per verbum *Imprimatur*, cui tamen praeponetur formula *Nihil obstat*, adscripto censoris nomine.—In Curia romana, non secus ac in ceteris omnibus, censores ex officio instituantur. Eos, audito prius Cardinali in Urbe Pontificis Vicario, tum vero annuente ac probante ipso Pontifice Maximo, Magister sacri Palatii apostolici designabit. Huius erit ad scripta singula cognoscenda censorem destinare. Editionis facultas ab eodem Magistro dabitur nec non a Cardinali Vicario Pontificis vel Antistite eius vices gerente, praemissa a censore, prout supra diximus, approbationis formula, adiectoque ipsius censoris nomine.—Extraordinariis tantum in adiunctis ac per quam raro prudenti Episcopi arbitrio, censoris mentio intermitti poterit. —Auctoribus censoris nomen patebit nunquam, antequam hic faventem sententiam ediderit; ne quid molestiae censori exhibeatur vel dum scripta cognoscit, vel si editionem non probarit.—Censores e religiosorum familiis nunquam eligantur, nisi prius moderatoris provinciae vel, si de Urbe agatur, moderatoris generalis secreto sententia audiatur: is autem de eligendi moribus, scientia et doctrinae integritate pro officii conscientia testabitur.—Religiosorum moderatores de gravissimo officio monemus numquam sinendi aliquid a suis subditis typis edi, nisi prius ipsorum et Ordinarii facultas intercesserit.—Postremus edicimus et declaramus, censoris titulum, quo quis ornatur, nihil valere prorsus nec unquam posse afferri ad privatas eiusdem opiniones firmandas.
>
> His universis dictis, nominatim servari diligentius praecipimus, quae articulo XLII Constitutionis *Officiorum* in haec verba edicuntur: *Viri e clero saeculari prohibentur quominus, absque praevia Ordinariorum venia, diaria vel folia periodica moderanda suscipiant*. Qua si qui venia perniciose utantur, ea, moniti primum, priventur.—Ad sacerdotes quod attinent, qui *correspondentium* vel *collaboratorum* nomine vulgo veniunt, quoniam frequentius evenit eos in ephemeridibus vel

> commentariis scripta edere modernismi labe infecta; videant Episcopi ne quid hi peccent, si peccarint moneant atque a scribendo prohibeant. Idipsum religiosorum moderatores ut praestant gravissime admonemus: qui si negligentius agant, Ordinarii auctoritate Pontificis Maximi provideant.—Ephemerides et commentaria, quae a catholicis scribuntur, quoad fieri possit, censorem designatum habeant. Huius officium erit folia singula vel libellos, postquam sint edita, opportune perlegere: si quid dictum periculose fuerit, id quamprimum corrigendum iniungat. Eadem porro Episcopis facultas esto, etsi censor faverit.[44]

A Council of Vigilance (*Consilium a Vigilantia*) was also to be established in every diocese.[45]

The foregoing regulations were reaffirmed by Pius X in the Motu proprio "*Sacrorum antistitum*," dated September 1, 1910,[46] many of which were incorporated in the Code of Canon Law.

(15) Legislation Enacted in the Code of Canon Law (1918)

The Code of Canon Law completely reorganized the legislation concerning the precensorship of books. Pre-Code law had always given primary consideration to the prohibition of books, and precensorship was treated as an adjunct. In the new law, however, the primary consideration is given to precensorship in Title XXIII, "*De praevia censura librorum eorumque prohibitione*," of Part IV, "*De Magisterio ecclesiastico*," of the Third Book, "*De Rebus*," of the Code of Canon Law. Canons 1384-1394 constitute the sole law on precensorship; all pre-Code law is abrogated. Hence, the Tridentine Rules, the "*Sollicita ac provida*" of Benedict XIV, and the "*Officorum ac Munerum*" of Leo XIII have been completely supplanted. Since the promulgation of the Code, several documents have been issued by the Holy See. These will be added in their proper places in the commentary.

Article III. Summary of Legislation Before *Officiorum ac Munerum* (1897)

In order to show the changes effected by Leo XIII, it may be helpful to summarize the general legislation in force when Leo XIII issued the constitution "*Officiorum ac Munerum*."

(1) Precensorship was required for the printing of all books and writings, but especially for books on sacred matters. The same rule held for the publication of manuscript copies of books or writings of any kind.

(2) These works had to be submitted to the authority in the place where the book was to be printed: namely, in Rome, to the Cardinal Vicar and the Master of the Sacred Palace, or to some other person specially appointed by

[44] N. 44, IV—*Fontes*, n. 680.

[45] N. 44, VI—*Fontes*, n. 680.

[46] *Fontes*, n. 689.

the Pope; outside the city of Rome, to the bishop or another specially appointed by him, and to the Inquisitor of the place.

(3) Regulars were bound to obtain, besides the approval of the bishop and the inquisitor, the permission of their superiors, who were to examine the books according to the norms of their institute.

(4) The examiners were to be men of outstanding learning, piety, and integrity of morals, well versed in the subject-matter of the book under consideration, not given to favoritism, partisanship or aversion, but zealous solely for the glory of God and the good of souls. The author was not to know which censor was chosen. If the author was a regular, the censor could not be a member of the same institute, but had to be selected from another institute.

(5) The proper authorities were obliged to examine the book and togive their approbation in writing, signed with their personal signature, without delay, and gratis.

(6) Two complete copies of the manuscript, both signed by the author, had to be submitted for precensorship. After precensorship, one copy was returned to the author, who then had the work printed. The other copy was kept either by the examiner (according to Rule Ten) or by the bishop (according to the Instruction of Clement VIII) or inquisitor, who rechecked the printed copy with the manuscript before allowing the divulgation of the work.

(7) Anyone residing in the Papal States was forbidden to send his works elsewhere to be printed, unless he had approval for that procedure. If this person resided in Rome, the permission, including an examination and approval of the work, had to be obtained from the Cardinal Vicar and the Master of the Sacred Palace; if he resided elsewhere in the Papal states, that of the local ordinary was sufficient.

(8) The following had to be printed in the front of the work:
(a) The name, surname and native land of the author; if it was not known who was the author, or if for a just reason the bishop or inquisitor deemed it advisable that the name of the author be withheld, then the name of the one who examined and approved the work had to be clearly indicated;
(b) the report of the censor;
(c) the approbation of the bishop and of the inquisitor of the place of printing, or that of the Cardinal Vicar and of the Master of the Sacred Palace if the work was printed in Rome. If the author resided in the Papal states and the book was printed elsewhere, it was also required that the approval of the author's own local ordinary be printed;
(d) the permission of his own superior, if the author was a Regular;
(e) the name of the printer, the place and year of printing. This latter had to be noted in the front and the back of the book.

(9) After the printing of the book was completed, it was forbidden to offer the book for sale, or in any way to publish it, before the printed copy had been submitted to the proper authority for comparison with the approved manuscript copy and permission to sell or publish it had been given. This permission could be given only after it had been ascertained that the printer did not deviate in the least from the copy approved by the censor.

(10) Printers and booksellers were bound to promise under oath, before the bishop or inquisitor, or in Rome before the Master of the Sacred Palace, that they would fulfill their duty sincerely, faithfully and in a Catholic manner, and to observe all the laws of the Church governing their business.

(11) Vigilance and control over the sale, distribution, and use of books was to be exercised as follows:

(a) In every diocese and city all printing establishments and bookshops were to be visited frequently by men specially appointed for this by the bishop or his vicar general, and by the inquisitor;

(b) every bookseller was obliged to produce a catalogue of the books offered for sale; this list was to be signed by the appointees mentioned above; no other books were allowed to be kept, sold, or distributed in any way;

(c) if books were brought in from another place or a new public bookshop was set up, the fact had to be reported to the same appointed persons; the books, when brought in from elsewhere, could not be given in any way to others without the previous permission of the aforesaid persons, unless it was well known that the books were already permitted to all;

(d) the books left by a deceased person, or at least a list of them had to be submitted to the aforementioned persons, and permission to use or in any way to transfer them to others had to be obtained.

(12) Penalties:

(a) Those who printed books or writings of any kind or had them printed, or those who published manuscripts without previous examination and approval incurred the censure of excommunication by that very fact, and were subject to a fine of 100 ducats; printers became liable to suspension from printing for a year and to the confiscation of the books printed without approval;

(b) the proper authorities were bound to give their approbation without delay and gratis, under penalty of excommunication. Apparently this penalty was of a *ferendae sententiae* character;

(c) those who violated the regulations mentioned in number (11) (b) (c) (d) were liable to punishment by the bishop and inquisitor.

ARTICLE IV. PRECENSORSHIP IN THE UNITED STATES (1829-1884)

Precensorship of books engaged the attention of the Fathers of the First Provincial Council of Baltimore, as well as of the three Plenary Councils of Baltimore.

(1) The First Provincial Council of Baltimore (1829)

The Fathers of the First Provincial Council of Baltimore (1829) showed their concern about catechisms and prayerbooks edited without precensorship:

> Quoniam multa incommoda jam orta sunt, et in posterum oritura videntur ex eo quod in diversis hujus Provinciae Dioecesibus diversi catechismi et libri precum adhibeantur, privata auctoritate editi, et quoniam uniformitas in iis maxime optanda est; curent Episcopi ut illi tantum catecheseos libri usurpentur, qui cum eorum approbatione editi fuerint, aliis quibuscumque posthabitis . . . Moneant insuper fideles ut a precum libellis, qui sine Ordinarii approbatione a privatis quibuscumque in lucem editi circumferuntur, abstineant.[47]

(2) The First Plenary Council of Baltimore (1852)

The First Plenary Council of Baltimore (1852) legislated about the appointment of diocesan censors:

> Consulendum episcopis, ut in suis quisque dioecesibus unum aut plures sacerdotes scientia theologiae insignes designent, qui examini subjiciant libros precum, aut aliter ad religionem pertinentes, priusquam ab Ordinario aut vicario ejus generali approbatione fidelibus commendentur. Optandum etiam ut praxis aliorum quam Ordinarii loci ubi hujusmodi libri publici iuris fiunt, approbationem petendi in desuetudinem abeat.[48]

(3) The Second Plenary Council of Baltimore (1866)

The Fathers of the Second Plenary Council of Baltimore (1866) renewed the protest of the First Provincial Council against uncensored prayerbooks. They also embodied the eighth decree of the First Plenary Council in their legislation, and added the following:

> Quod decretum iterum confirmamus, atque ita ampliamus, ut omnes Episcopos obligandi vim habeat, in quorum dioecesibus sint praela aut typographea Catholica.[49]

The same Council legislated concerning Catholic newspapers:

---

[47] Decretum XXXIII—*Concilia Provincialia Baltimori habita ab anno 1829 usque ad annum 1849* (ed. altera, Baltimori, 1851), p. 83; *Coll. Lac.*, III, 146.

[48] Decretum VIII—*Concilium Plenarium Totius Americae Septentrionalis Foederatae, Baltimori habitum anno 1852* (Baltimori, 1853), p. 46.

[49] Decretum 503—*Concilii Plenarii Baltimorensis II Acta et Decreta* (2. ed., Baltimorae, 1868), p. 255.

Id omnibus notum et manifestum esse volumus, nullam a nobis Ephemeridem pro Catholica agnosci, quae non Ordinarii approbationem prae se ferat . . .

. . . Patres hujus Concilii Plenarii profitentur atque declarant, approbationem Ordinarii, quae de more Foliis Catholicis datur, nihil aliud sibi velle, quam judicare Episcopum nihil a scriptoribus contra fidem et mores proferri, spem quoque bonam se habere nihil in posterum proferendum, eosque esse redactores quorum scripta ad aedificationem utilia esse possint: Episcopum vero neque posse neque debere respondere ac rationem reddere de iis universe, quae in hujusmodi Foliis habentur, sed de iis tantum, quae vi officii sui docendo, monendo, jubendo, aut vetando in vulgus ediderit, et quibus sua ipse manu subscripserit . . . [50]

(4) The Third Plenary Council of Baltimore (1884)

The Fathers of the Third Plenary Council of Baltimore (1884) again discountenanced uncensored prayerbooks, and took the occasion to state the law on precensorship in clear terms:

Libri precatorii, quorum infinitus prope est numerus, saepius a scriptoribus imperitis concinnati, a vera et salubri orandi norma quam Ecclesia in sacra liturgia proponit, longius in dies abire videntur. Praecipimus ergo ut Episcopi examinatorum synodalium aut viri alicujus docti et pii censurae subjiciant omnes hujusmodi libros. Nec audeant typographi in lucem illos edere, aut Sacram Scripturam, catechismos, narrationes miraculorum, folia orationum, et generatim omnes libros de fide et moribus ex professo tractantes, quin prius censurae debitae subjecti et licentia Ordinarii eos typis mandandi rite muniti fuerint, ut lectores sciant nihil in eis reperiri quod fidei aut moribus repugnet. Idem statuimus de novis hujusmodi librorum editionibus.[51]

---

[50] *Ibid.*, nn. 506, 508, pp. 256–257. The pastoral letter issued by the Fathers of the Council to the clergy and laity contains further remarks on this topic. Cf. *Op. cit.*, pp. cxv–cxvi; *Coll. Lac.*, III, 535–537; 1261–1263.

[51] Decretum 220—*Acta et Decreta Concilii Plenarii Baltimorensis Tertii A.D. MDCCCLXXXIV* ([Reimpressio] Baltimorae, 1894), pp. 120–121.

PART TWO
CANONICAL COMMENTARY

CHAPTER IV

THE CHURCH'S RIGHT AND DUTY OF PRECENSORSHIP (CANON 1384, §1)

Title XXIII (can. 1384-1405) of the Third Book of the Code deals with the precensorship (1384-1394) and prohibition of books (1395-1405). Canon 1384 is prefatory to the other canons of the title, for in it the Church asserts its right to precensorship and prohibition of books. The text of the canon reads:

> Ecclesiae ius est exigendi ne libros, quos ipsa iudicio suo antea non recognoverit, fideles edant, et a quibusvis editos ex iusta causa prohibendi.

A glance at the text of this canon reveals that the law merely asserts that the Church has the right of precensorship, and that it makes no effort to prove that claim. This is not surprising, for the law finds it unnecessary to advance arguments for principles which are effectively and properly demonstrated elsewhere. In a dissertation of this kind, however, it may be useful to outline the manner in which the Church vindicates this right for itself, and to refer to the sources upon which it draws in so doing. A second article will be devoted to explaining the extent of this right and the limited use of that right. A third article will treat of the norms of interpretation pertinent to the law on precensorship. A fourth article will summarize the entire chapter.

Article I. The Existence of the Right and Duty of Precensorship

A first argument for the existence of the right of precensorship may be called the argument based on the natural law, and may be stated as follows: Every individual, every legitimate society, possesses the right to protect itself from harm. The Church, therefore, enjoys the right to protect itself from harm. The exercise of this right entails the use of means necessary, one of which is the precensorship of books. The spread of pernicious books may be halted not merely by the prohibition of books already published, but also by precensorship of books before publication. There is no call here to question that certain books are harmful to the Church and to its members.

This argument is taken from the tract on public ecclesiastical law, where it is proved that the Church is a completely self-contained society. In this tract the function of precensorship is often cited as an example of the Church's right to protect itself from harm.[1]

A second argument may be called the argument based on the supernatural mission of the Church, and may be presented as follows: The divine mission of the Church is to guide men to their eternal salvation. The Church is to accomplish this not merely by offering its sacraments to the faithful and instructing them in the body of its doctrine and in its code of morals, but also by preserving them from erroneous doctrines and evil practices. In the realm of the printed word, precensorship is both useful and necessary. It should be evident, then, that in view of its supernatural mission, the Church possesses the right and duty to precensor books. This principle is amply developed in the tract on apologetics or fundamental theology.[2]

Over and above the fact that the Church has the right to precensorship, it can also be demonstrated that the Church has the duty to precensor works. The Code itself gives evidence of this by placing the canons on precensorship under the general heading of the teaching magisterium of the Church. Canon 1322, §1, applies with full force to the precensorship of books:

> Christus Dominus fidei depositum Ecclesiae concredidit, ut ipsa, Spiritu Sancto iugiter assistente, doctrinam revelatam sancte custodiret et fideliter exponeret.

Viewed in this light, precensorship protects the deposit of faith and morals for the faithful. This argument is developed quite extensively by Pernicone, when he considers the prohibition of books.[3] It applies equally as well to the precensorship of books.

---

[1] Ottaviani, *Institutiones Iuris Publici Ecclesiastici* (2. ed., 2 vols., Romae: Typis Polyglottis Vaticanis, 1935–[1936]), I, 78–88 (hereafter cited as *Institutiones*); Coronata, *Ius Publicum Ecclesiasticum* (2. ed., Taurini: Marietti, 1934), pp. 25–26; Cappello, *Summa Iuris Publici Ecclesiastici* (3. ed., Romae: Apud Aedes Universitatis Gregorianae, 1932), pp. 67–69; Cavagnis, *Institutiones Iuris Publici Ecclesiastici* (3. ed., 3 vols., Romae, [1896]), I, nn. 71–84 (hereafter cited as *Institutiones*); Berutti, *Institutiones*, IV, 415–416; Goodwine, "Problems Respecting the Censorship of Books," *The Jurist* (Washington, D. C., 1941—), X (1950), 154–155 (5–6). A double pagination is given, the first of which indicates the pages as found in *The Jurist*, and the second (enclosed in parentheses) indicates the pages as found in the reprint issued by the *School of Canon Law*, The Catholic University of America, Washington, D. C., [1950].

[2] De Groot, *Summa Apologetica de Ecclesia Catholica ad mentem S. Thomae Aquinatis* (3. ed., Ratisbonae, 1906), pp. 53–54; Schultes, *De Ecclesia Catholica Praelectiones Apologeticae* (Parisiis, 1925), pp. 82–86; Lercher, *Institutiones Theologiae Dogmaticae* (4 vols., Oeniponte, 1924–1930), I, 386–393; Hilgers, "Censorship of Books," *The Catholic Encyclopedia* (15 vols., Index, and Supplement, New York, 1907–1922), III, 526 (hereafter cited as *CE*).

[3] *Prohibition*, pp. 11–20.

It is not necessary here to answer the many current objections raised by non-Catholics against the precensorship of books by the Church. It is alleged that by exercising this function the Church violates human liberty, insults man's intelligence, fears and conceals truth, prejudges an issue in its own favor, retards the progress of science and scholarship, etc., etc. All these charges stem from a failure to understand, or a deliberate disregard of, the nature and mission of the Catholic Church and the purpose of precensorship. Pernicone and others have met these objections well.[4]

Article II. The Extent and Use of the Right of Precensorship

All canonists and moralists admit that the Church not only claims, but also possesses the right to impose precensorship. This right is so extensive and all-inclusive that the Church could demand precensorship for all writings. *De iure*, there can be no absolute freedom of the press for Catholics.[5]

De facto, however, there is a certain freedom of the press. The Church does not use its right to the fullest extent. The Church prescribes precensorship only for certain matters, only for certain persons, and only for certain functions. Since this is a question of positive law, all that is not mentioned either explicitly or implicitly in the law is free from precensorship.[6]

A. Limitations Concerning the Matter to be Submitted

In certain fields, e.g., in the reproduction of official books and texts (canons 1387-1391), the Church exercises special care by reserving the granting of permission to publish these works to the authorities in Rome. In ordinary religious fields, e.g., regarding works on faith and morals, books of private devotion, holy pictures, etc. (canon 1385, §1), the Church prescribes precensorship by any one of three designated local ordinaries. In all other matters, e.g., concerning works on profane subjects (1386, §1), no precensorship is required at all.

B. Limitations Concerning Persons

The very first limitation concerning persons is found in canon 1384, §1, which states that the Church has the right to impose precensorship on the faithful (*fideles*). Obviously, the Code is not legislating for infidels, for they are not subject to the Church as yet. However, when the term "faithful" is considered, just how is that word to be understood? At certain times the Code uses that term to mean all baptized persons, and at other times the Code uses that term to mean only those baptized persons who adhere to the Catholic Church. All baptized persons are subjects of the Church, but not

---

[4] *Prohibition*, pp. 21–26; Ottaviani, *Institutiones*, I, 137–138; Cavagnis, *Institutiones*, I, n. 120; III, n. 15; Gagnon, *La Censure*, pp. 1–20.

[5] Goodwine, "Problems," *The Jurist*, X (1950), 153 (4).

[6] *Ibid.*, 157 (8).

all are members; all baptized persons, however, who adhere to the Church are not only subjects but members as well.

The Code itself offers no clew as to how this term is to be understood. Authors are divided in their opinions, some holding that it must be restricted to mean Catholics alone, others holding that the term means both Catholics and non-Catholics.[7] Those who hold the restrictive view (that Catholics alone are bound by this law) claim that non-Catholics are *exempt* from this law, while those who hold the extended view (that all baptized persons, whether Catholic or not, are bound by this law) claim that non-Catholics are usually *excused* from observing the law because of their ignorance of it, or, if they are aware of the law, they consider themselves as not bound to the laws of the Catholic Church. It is generally admitted that the intrinsic probability favors the opinion that "faithful" must be accepted in its extended meaning, though it is also admitted that the opinion which holds the restricted view is a probable opinion, at least by reason of extrinsic authority.[8]

For the matter contained in canon 1385, §1, however, all persons are obliged to precensorship, even the laity. All, too, must observe the regulations enacted in canons 1387-1391, in as far as they apply. For these matters, all ranks of the clergy are included. No exception is made in favor of cardinals, bishops, and other ordinaries.[9]

---

[7] Authors who hold the restrictive view are Leitner, *Handbuch des katholischen Kirchenrechts* (5 vols., Regensburg-Muenchen, 1918–1927), V, 589; Augustine, *A Commentary on the New Code of Canon Law* (8 vols., St. Louis, 1918–1922), VI (*Administrative Law*, 1921), 428 (hereafter cited as *Commentary*).

Authors who hold the extended view are Gillet, "De censura librorum," *Jus Pontificium* (Romae, 1921–1940), XI (1931), 57; Moersdorf, *Die Rechtssprache des Codex Juris Canonici* (Goerres-Gesellschaft zur Pflege der Wissenschaft im katholischen Deutschland, Veroeffentlichungen der Sektion fuer Rechts- und Staatswissenschaft, Heft 74, Paderborn: F. Schoeningh, 1937), p. 129; Vermeersch-Creusen, *Epitome Iuris Canonici cum commentariis ad scholas et usum privatum* (6. ed., 3 vols., Mechliniae-Romae: H. Dessain, 1933–1946), II, 501–502 (hereafter cited as *Epitome*); Ayrinhac, *Administrative Legislation in the New Code of Canon Law* (New York, 1930), p. 274 (hereafter cited as *Admin. Legisl.*); Blat, *Commentarium*, III, partes 2–6, 327; Cocchi, *Commentarium*, VI, 147; Gagnon, *La Censure*, pp. 75–78.

[8] McCloskey (*The Subject of Ecclesiastical Law*, The Catholic University of America Canon Law Studies, n. 165 [Washington, D. C.: The Catholic University of America Press, 1943], pp. 105–162) has thoroughly investigated the problem of baptized non-Catholics as subjects of ecclesiastical laws. On page 153 he comes to the conclusion mentioned in the text of this work.

[9] Canon 1401 mentions that cardinals, bishops and other ordinaries are not bound by the ecclesiastical law concerning the prohibition of books. It makes no similar exemption in regard to precensorship. As a matter of fact, bishops and cardinals residing in Rome (i.e., those who are not a local ordinary there) observe the requirement of obtaining the *Imprimatur* of the local ordinary of Rome. Cf. Vermeersch, *De Prohibitione et Censura Librorum Dissertatio canonico-moralis* (4. ed., Romae, 1906), p. 136 (hereafter cited as *De Prohibitione*); Dilgskron, "De revisione," *Anal. Eccl.*, IV (1896), 474.

In regard to Orientals, it is a general rule that they are not bound by the law of the Code.[10] Canon 1384, §1, asserts the right of the Church to exercise precensorship, and hence, by its very nature, binds all Catholics, both Latin and Oriental. All the rest of the canons on precensorship are disciplinary laws. These do not bind Orientals.[10a] The fact that these laws preserve and safeguard faith and morals would lead one to conclude that similar laws would be appropriate for Orientals.[10b] At most, it might be argued that Orientals who live in Latin territories are bound by the law of the Code because these matters concern public order, and are founded on the presumption of a common danger. Orientals who live in their own territories are not bound by them.[11]

The diocesan clergy and all religious who wish to write works on profane topics, or who wish to write for or manage periodicals, are obliged to obtain special permission to engage in that type of work. A reason for this requirement seems to be that the clergy and religious are usually assigned to particular offices or works and ordinarily would lack the time necessary to engage in these tasks. A superior might not wish to grant sufficient leisure time for certain types of extraneous work. An assignment to a work is the permission to engage in it. The laity do not need such special permission.

However, if a priest, bishop or cardinal is also a local ordinary, then his own *Imprimatur* is sufficient, even though the work be printed or published outside his own territory. Cf. Coronata, *Institutiones Iuris Canonici ad usum utriusque cleri et scholarum* (5 vols., Taurini: Marietti, 1928–1936), II (ed. 1931), 318–319 (hereafter cited as *Institutiones*); Augustine, *Commentary*, VI, 439; Beste, *Introductio*, p. 698. Some writers, unduly attached to the pre-Code law, hold that a local ordinary would still be required to obtain the *Imprimatur* for his own work from the local ordinary of the place of printing, e.g., Sipos, *Enchiridion Iuris Canonici* (Pécs, 1926), p. 712 (hereafter cited as *Enchiridion*); Eichmann, *Lehrbuch des Kirchenrechts* (2. ed., Paderborn, 1926), p. 465. (hereafter cited as *Lehrbuch*).

[10] "Licet in Codice iuris canonici Ecclesiae quoque Orientalis disciplina saepe referatur, ipse tamen unam respicit Latinam Ecclesiam, neque Orientalem obligat, nisi de iis agatur, quae ex ipsa rei natura etiam Orientalem afficiunt."—Canon 1.

[10a] There is, however, an undated declaration issued by the Sacred Congregation for the Oriental Church in which it is stated that Orientals are bound not only by canon 1396 but also by canon 1399.—*AAS*, XXXVI (1944), 25. Orientals are, therefore, obliged to submit for precensorship the writings mentioned in canon 1399, 5°.

[10b] A law prescribing precensorship of all writings does exist for the Orientals. It was first enacted for the Greek Melchites by Benedict XIV (Ep. encycl. "*Demandatum*," 24 dec. 1743, §21—*Fontes*, n. 338) and later extended to all Orientals by Leo XIII (Litt. ap. "*Orientalium dignitas*," 30 nov. 1894—*Fontes*, n. 627).

[11] Gagnon, *La Censure*, pp. 78–79.

C. Limitations Concerning Functions

The Code forbids the *publication* of works unless they have been precensored.[12] There is a double aspect of the prohibition to publish without precensorship. Negatively, it forbids the publication until precensorship has occurred. It is a conditional prohibition, which ceases upon the fulfillment of the prescribed function. Until that function (examination, judgment and permission to publish) has occurred, it is illicit to publish a work that requires precensorship. Similarly, if the permission to publish has been denied after the examination and judgment, it is still illicit to publish. The publication, in this latter instance, is forbidden by the general law because the condition has not yet been fulfilled. However, the local ordinary may add a particular prohibition of his own, over and above refusing permission to publish. This general negative prohibition concerns the publication and all subsequent acts, e.g., the distribution of the work. Any preparatory act, e.g., the writing, editing and even the printing of a work, is not forbidden. It is sufficient if permission is obtained before publication. There is danger in printing a work before securing permission, especially the financial risk of not being allowed to publish the work, but the law is clear: only the publication is forbidden.

Positively, the law requires that the permission be sought, and the precensorship be performed before the work is published. It is not required that the local ordinary seek those who intend to publish; but those who intend to publish are obliged to submit their works for precensorship, if and when that is prescribed. The persons on whom this obligation rests are the principals involved in the publication. It is possible that one or several of the following be the principals, e.g., the author, editor, printer, publisher, or even an interested third party, e.g., the person who is sponsoring a work, or paying for it. This obligation rests upon all *in solidum*, so that if one obtains it, all the rest are free to proceed to the publication. It is permissible to begin printing a work, as long as there exists the intention to comply with the law by submitting the work for precensorship before publication. Since the permission to publish is obtained by way of a rescript, it may be obtained without the knowledge of the principals, or through the agency of others for the principals.

---

[12] From the very beginning of the history of the legislation concerning precensorship, the emphasis was laid on the *printing* of works without examination and permission. Thus, Innocent VIII, const. "*Inter Multiplices,*" 17 nov. 1487—Voulliéme, *Buchdruck*, p. LXXXIX; Leo X, const. "*Inter Sollicitudines,*" 4 maii, 1515—*Fontes*, n. 68. During the nineteenth century, however, the printing of a work was no longer identified with its publication, which often took place elsewhere than at the printery. Hence, Pope Leo XIII made the change in his const. "*Officiorum ac munerum,*" 27 ian. 1897—*Fontes*, n. 632. This is now found in the Code.

If a non-Catholic, i.e., one not subject to the law of the Church, is involved in publishing the work, then those who are Catholic are still bound to obtain the permission to publish. Thus, a Catholic writer who publishes a work through a non-Catholic publishing firm, or a Catholic who publishes works for non-Catholics, would be obliged to obtain this permission.

One should here recall that moral personalities or societies often operate as publishing firms, printeries, etc. Even an author is identifiable with a moral personality, e.g., a religious institute which publishes its constitutions or rules. In this case, the person or persons responsible for the society or the moral personality are obliged to submit the work for precensorship. This may be the individual in whom the power is vested, or the board of officers, or the joint-owners, or the members of the corporation, firm, partnership, institute, etc., in brief, those persons in whom resides the authority to make the decision to publish.

Article III. Norms of Interpretation

The canons on the precensorship of books are to be interpreted according to the ordinary rules of interpretation. Hence, the law must be understood according to the meaning of the terms used, considered in their text and context; and if a doubt remains, recourse should be had to parallel passages in the Code, if there be such, to the purpose and circumstances of the law, and finally to the mind of the legislator.[13] When there is the problem of seeking the meaning of the present law from the pre-Code law, the norms of canon 6 must be applied. If there is still doubt, and there exists a possibility of a restricted and extended meaning, the following norms may help:

(a) A law which imposes an obligation or enacts a restriction (e.g., canons 1385, §3; 1386-1392) is to be interpreted strictly;[14]

[13] Canon 18.

[14] Canon 19. It is generally accepted that the laws of precensorship are to be interpreted strictly. The following authors mention that fact explicitly, e.g., Crnica, *Commentarium theoretico-practicum Codicis Iuris Canonici* (2 vols., Sibenik: Typis Typographiae "Kacic", 1940–1941), I, 32 (hereafter cited as *Commentarium*); Van Hove, *De Legibus Ecclesiasticis*, Commentarium Lovaniense in Codicem Iuris Canonici, Vol. I, tom. II, (Mechliniae-Romae: H. Dessain, 1930), p. 313 (hereafter cited as *De Legibus*); Ubach, *Theologia Moralis Codici Iuris Canonici accomodatum* (2. ed., 2 vols., Bonis Auris: Apud "Sociedad San Miguel" Sarimento, 1935), I, 554 (hereafter cited as *Theol. Moral.*); Vromant, *Ius Missionariorum—Introductio et Normae Generales* (Louvain: Museum Lessianum, 1934), p. 137, n. 1 (hereafter cited as *Introductio*).

It must be remarked that some pre-Code authors of note held that the laws concerning the censorship and prohibition of books were favorable laws, and therefore were to be interpreted broadly, e.g., Suarez, *Opera Omnia* (2. ed., 28 vols., Parisiis, 1856–1878), XII (*Tractatus de fide theologica*, disp. XX, sect. 2, n. 10), 502; Alphonsus de Ligorio, *Theologia Moralis* (ed. Heilig, 10 vols. in 5, Mechliniae, 1852), X (Appendix: Dissertatio de justa prohibitione et abolitione librorum nocuae lectionis, cap. V, n. VIII), 247; Arndt, *Commentarii*, pp. 120–

(b) a law which grants power or authority to permit publications of writings (e.g., canons 1385, §§2-3; 1386, §1; 1388-1391) must be interpreted broadly, since it does not impose a burden or restrict a right;

(c) a law which enacts penalties, as well as the penalties themselves, the actions or omissions which constitute the delictual act, and the persons subject to the penalty—all these are to be interpreted strictly.[15]

ARTICLE IV. SUMMARY

The Church has the right of precensorship. This may be proved in two ways. On purely natural grounds, the Church, as a legitimate society, has the right to protect itself from harm. In the supernatural sphere, the Church has been commissioned to help men attain eternal salvation. An important means in the fulfillment of this charge is the precensorship of publications. The duty of the Church to exercise precensorship arises primarily from the teaching magisterium of the Church.

Although the Church could demand precensorship for all writings, it does not do so. Certain fields, e.g., writings on profane topics, are completely free of precensorship. Thus, there is *de facto* a limited freedom of the press. *De iure*, however, there cannot be an absolute freedom of the press for Catholics. The law on precensorship binds all the "faithful," i.e., those baptized persons who are members of the Church. It is probable that those

---

121; J.V. (in a review of Vermeersch's *De prohibitione et censura librorum*)—*Nouvelle Revue Théologique* (Paris, 1869—), XXX (1898), 110 (hereafter cited as *NRT*); Van Ruymbeke, "De la prohibition des livres," *NRT*, XXXVI (1904), 142; Planchard, "L'Index," *Revue théologique francaise* (Paris, 1896—), II (1897), 159 (hereafter cited as *RTF*); Van Coillie, *Commentarius in constitutionem SSmi. Dni. Leonis XIII OFFICIORUM AC MUNERUM* (Brugis, 1899), n. 10 (hereafter cited as *Commentarius*). After the Code: Gagnon, *La Censure*, pp. 64–67.

The following pre-Code authors, however, held that the laws of precensorship and of the prohibition of books were odious laws, and therefore were to be interpreted strictly, e.g., Hollweck, *Das kirchliche Buecherverbot* (2. ed., Mainz, 1897), p. 20 (hereafter cited as *Buecherverbot*); Périès, *L'Index: commentaire de la constitution apostolique "Officiorum"* (Paris, 1898), p. 55 (hereafter cited as *L'Index*); Schneider, *Buechergesetze*, pp. 45–46; Piat, "Commentaire de la constitution OFFICIORUM AC MUNERUM de Sa Sainteté le Pape Léon XIII sur la prohibition et la censure des livres et des décrets généraux qui l'accompagnent," *NRT*, XXX (1900), 479; Pennacchi, *ASS*, XXX (1897–1898), 81, 163–164, 210; Vermeersch, *De Prohibitione*, pp. 20–24; Ciolli, *Commento breve della Costituzione leonina riguardo ai libri proibiti* (2. ed., Roma, 1906), 4 (hereafter cited as *Commento*); Genicot, *Institutiones Theologiae Moralis* (4. ed., 2 vols., Lovanii, 1904), I, 451; Wernz, *Ius Decretalium* (6 vols. in 10, Prati, 1908–1915), III, (2. ed., 1908), 116; [Heiner], "Welchem Bischofe steht die Approbation eines Buches rechtlich zu?" *Archiv fuer katholisches Kirchenrecht* (Innsbruck, 1857–1861; Mainz, 1862—), LXXVIII (1898), 187 (hereafter cited as *AKKR*).

[15] Canon 19; canon 6, 5°; canon 2219, §1.

baptized persons who are not members of the Church are not bound. Orientals are bound by the law enacted in canon 1384, §1, which is doctrinal, but not by the remaining canons, which are disciplinary.

Negatively, the law of precensorship forbids the publication of works until precensorship has been performed and until the authority has given permission for publication. Positively, the law commands that subjects seek precensorship for their writings from the proper authorities, that the authorities perform the precensorship and grant or refuse permission to publish according to the norms of the Code.

Laws of interpretation require that the obligation of precensorship must be interpreted strictly, since it restricts rights; the power to grant permission must be interpreted broadly; and the laws which enact penalties, as well as the penalties themselves, must be interpreted strictly.

CHAPTER V

TERMINOLOGY (CANON 1384, §2)

The Code devotes the second paragraph of canon 1384 to terminology. This is easily understandable, for the field of writing, publishing and censorship of books employs a vocabulary quite exclusively its own. As a general rule, canonists and moralists are familiar with those terms; but it is also known that much misunderstanding has resulted from a faulty use of this specialized terminology. Hence, it will be most advantageous to preface the commentary of the law of precensorship with a special chapter in which the terms will be investigated. They will be given as they are used ordinarily, and, if there is a technical usage, as they are employed by canonists and moralists.

There are three distinct groups of terms: (1) terms designating the *matter* submitted for precensorship; (2) terms designating the *persons* who seek or perform precensorship; (3) terms designating the *functions* performed before, after, or in the act of precensorship. Each group will be investigated in turn.

Article I. Terms Designating the Matter Submitted for Precensorship

Only the more important terms designating the matter submitted for precensorship are listed in this group. Some of these terms are quite general, e.g., a manuscript, work, writing, publication. Others are more particular and specific, e.g., sheet, page, leaf, folio, folder, leaflet, pamphlet, booklet, book, volume, periodical, newspaper, magazine, review, edition, issue, printing, impression, reprint, offprint, picture, image, slides, films. Each will be treated in turn.

A. General Terms Designating the Matter Submitted for Precensorship

(1) *A manuscript* is "an author's copy of his work in handwriting or typewriting; a written or typewritten document of any kind as distinguished from a printed copy."[1] Originally the word manuscript meant only a hand-

[1] By permission; from *Webster's New Collegiate Dictionary*, copyright, 1949, 1951, by G. & C. Merriam Co. The definitions given in this chapter are taken largely from two standard American dictionaries, namely, *Webster's New Collegiate Dictionary* just quoted, and *The New College Standard Dictionary* published by Funk and Wagnalls Company (New York, copyright 1947), as well as from the *A. L. A. Glossary of Library Terms* published by The American Library Association (Chicago, copyright 1943), with the kind permission of the respective publishers to reprint copyright material. The references to Funk and Wagnalls *New College Standard Dictionary* will be abbreviated as *FW* with the citation of the page. The *A. L. A. Glossary of Library Terms* will hereafter be cited as *A. L. A. Glossary*. The terms defined in the text of this chapter are used by the canonists and moralists in the common, usual sense, unless the contrary is indicated.

written copy (not necessarily a holograph), but today it is used for a typewritten copy as well. A printed copy is not called a manuscript.

(2) A *work* is that which is the product of labor, especially mental labor, e.g., a book, treatise, poem, a musical composition, etc. A work may be in any stage of divulgation, whether merely in manuscript or typewritten form, in printed or in published form.[2]

(3) A *writing* is any composition, especially a literary production, once it has been handwritten, typewritten, printed or published.[3]

(4) A *publication* is any work that is published, i.e., sold publicly, or distributed gratis, or at least offered for general sale or distribution.[4]

B. Particular Terms Designating the Matter Submitted for Precensorship

(1) A *sheet* is "a broad piece of paper; esp., a single piece of any of the sizes prepared for writing on or printing on;"[5] hence, a newspaper, or a leaf of a book.[5a]

(2) A *page* is "one side of a leaf of a book, manuscript, letter, etc."[6]

(3) A *leaf* is "a part of a book or folded sheet containing two pages, one on each side."[7]

(4) A *folio* is "a sheet of paper folded once or of a size adapted to folding once; a book, or the like, composed of sheets folded but once."[8] Daily newspapers are folios. Many leaflets and folders are folios.

(5) A *folder* is "a time-table or other printed paper so made that it may be readily folded or readily spread out."[9]

---

[2] Adapted from FW 1284.

[3] Cf. FW 1353. Canonists usually cite examples to show that the word *writing* applies to works in any form or size, e.g., Vermeersch, *De Prohibitione*, p. 33; De Meester, *Compendium*, III, pars 1, 256; Wernz-Vidal, *Ius Canonicum*, IV, pars 2, 133; Pennacchi, *ASS*, XXX (1897–1898), 289; Seraphinus a Loiano, *Institutiones Theologiae Moralis ad normam Iuris Canonici* (5 vols., Taurini: Marietti, 1934–1942), II, 628 (hereafter cited as *Institutiones*); Claeys Bouuaert-Simenon, *Manuale*, III, 132. Some writers are inconsistent in their attempt to exclude very small works, e.g., Beste, *Introductio*, p. 696; Ferreres, *Compendium Theologiae Moralis* (10. ed., 2 vols., Barcinone, 1919), I, 406 (hereafter cited as *Compendium*); Arregui, *Summarium Theologiae Moralis* (13. ed., Westminster, Md.: The Newman Bookshop, 1944), p. 275 (hereafter cited as *Summarium*).

[4] Adapted from FW 946.

[5] By permission; from *Webster's New Collegiate Dictionary*, copyright, 1949, 1951, by G. & C. Merriam Co.

[5a] FW 1076. See also *A. L. A. Glossary*, p. 126.

[6] By permission; from *Webster's New Collegiate Dictionary*, copyright, 1949, 1951, by G. & C. Merriam Co.

[7] By permission; from *Webster's New Collegiate Dictionary*, copyright, 1949, 1951, by G. & C. Merriam Co. See also *A. L. A. Glossary*, p. 79.

[8] FW 455. See also *A. L. A. Glossary*, pp. 60–61.

[9] FW 455. According to the *A. L. A. Glossary* (p. 60) it is "a publication consisting of one sheet of paper folded into two or more leaves, but not stitched or cut. The pages of a two-leaf folder are in the same sequence as those of a book, but a folder of three or more leaves

(6) A *leaflet* is, "in a limited sense, a publication of from two to four pages printed on a small sheet folded once, but not stitched or bound, the pages following in the same sequence as in a book; in a broader sense, a small thin pamphlet."[10]

(7) A *pamphlet* is, "in a restricted technical sense, an independent publication consisting of a few leaves of printed matter stitched together but not bound; usually enclosed in paper covers."[11] At times a pamphlet is called a booklet.

(8) A *booklet* is "a small book, usually with paper covers; or a pamphlet."[12] The single issues of many periodicals are booklets.

(9) A *book* is a collection of sheets bound together, especially a printed and bound volume.[13] Canonists, however, define a book as a [printed][14]

---

has its printed matter so imposed that when the sheet is unfolded the pages on one side of the paper follow one another consecutively."

[10] *A. L. A. Glossary*, p. 79. It is also called a folder.

[11] ". . . While independent in the sense that each pamphlet is complete in itself it is a common custom to issue pamphlets in series, usually numbered consecutively."—*A. L. A. Glossary*, pp. 96–97.

[12] *A. L. A. Glossary*, p. 18. Canonists describe a booklet (*libellus*) as a volume smaller in size than a book but consisting of at least a few pages: e.g., De Meester, *Compendium*, III, pars 1, 256; Ubach, *Theol. Moral.*, I, 555; Vermeersch, *De Prohibitione*, p. 33; Wernz-Vidal, *Ius Canonicum*, IV, pars 2, 133; Coronata, *Institutiones*, II, 317. The last mentioned author quotes Santamaria (*Comentarios al Código canónico*, IV, 288) as requiring eight pages as a minimum for a booklet; Berutti (*Institutiones*, IV, 421) gives 50 small pages as the minimum.

[13] Adapted from FW 136.

[14] Older canonists were almost unanimous in holding that manuscript volumes were books, e.g., Suarez, *Opera Omnia*, XII, 501–502; Castro-Palaus, *Opus Morale de Virtutibus et Vitiis Contrariis* (ed. nova, 3 vols., Lugduni, 1700), tom. I, tract. IV, disp. II, punct. X, §1, n. 3; Lugo, *Disputationes Scholasticae et Morales* (ed. nova . . . accurante J.B. Fournials, 8 vols., Parisiis, 1890–1894), Disp. XXI, n. 39 (hereafter cited as *Disputationes*); Lacroix, *Theologia Moralis seu ejusdem in H. Busenbaum Medulam Commentaria a Zacharia, S.J., elucidata atque vindicata* (2. ed., 4 vols., Parisiis, 1874), III, 339 (hereafter cited as *Theol. Moral.*); Reiffenstuel, *Ius Canonicum Universum* (5 vols. in 7, Parisiis, 1864–1870), Lib. V, tit. VII, n. 39; Schmalzgrueber, *Ius Ecclesiasticum Universum* (5 vols. in 12, Romae, 1843–1845), Lib. V, tit. VII, n. 30; Alphonsus de Ligorio, *Theologia Moralis*, Lib. VII, n. 293; Konings, *Theologia Moralis* (7. ed., 2 vols., Neo-Eboraci, 1892), II, 336–337; Heymans, *De ecclesiastica librorum aliorumque scriptorum in Belgio prohibitione disquisitio* (Bruxellis, 1849), n. 278.(hereafter cited as *Disquisitio*); De Brabandere, *Juris Canonici et Juris Canonico-Civilis Compendium* (3. ed., 2 vols., Brugis, 1882), II, 490 (hereafter cited as *Compendium*); Ballerini-Palmieri, *Opus theologicum morale* (2. ed., 7 vols., Prati, 1892–1894), II, 844; Schneider, *Buechergesetze*, p. 162; Van der Velden, *Principia Theologiae Moralis* (2. ed. a Piato Montensi emendata, 2 vols. in 3, Parisiis, 1875–1884), II, 617–618; Piat, *NRT*, XXX (1898), 47 and XXXIII (1901), 23; Augustine, *Commentary*, VI, 431; Arndt, *Commentarii*, pp. 119–121. Arndt included manuscripts when speaking of censorship, but excluded them when speaking of penalties (p. 216). The opposite view was held by Tamburinus, *Explicatio Decalogi* (2 vols., Monachii, 1659), II, cap. I, §VII, nn. 14–16. Lacroix (*Theol. Moral.*, VII, 339) also mentions Viva, Sylvius, Azor and Barbosa as being of the same opinion.

volume[15] having a certain bulk,[16] and a certain unity of content.[17] Although there was, and still is, considerable disagreement concerning the bulk of a book, the most common opinion is that of Schmalzgrueber (1663-1735), who held that a work becomes a book when it consists of about ten folios, i.e., 40 pages in folio size, 80 pages in quarto, 160 pages in octavo, or 320 pages

---

Modern canonists hold that manuscript volumes are not books, e.g., Hollweck, *Die kirchlichen Strafgesetze* (Mainz, 1899), p. 172 (hereafter cited as *Strafgesetze*); Gabriel de Varceno, *Compendium Theologiae Moralis* (4. ed., 2 vols., Augustae Taurinorum, 1876), I, 336 (hereafter cited as *Compendium*); Bucceroni, *Institutiones Theologiae Moralis* (5. ed., 2 vols., Romae, 1908), II, 368 (hereafter cited as *Institutiones*); Goepfert, *Moraltheologie* (5. ed., 3 vols., Paderborn, 1905–1906), I, 355–356; Hilarius a Sexten, *Tractatus de censuris ecclesiasticis cum appendice de irregularitate* (Moguntiae, 1898), p. 111 (hereafter cited as *Tractatus*); Vermeersch, *De Prohibitione*, pp. 32–33; Lehmkuhl, *Theologia Moralis* (12. ed., 2 vols., Friburgi, 1914), II, 680; De Meester, *Compendium*, III, pars 1, 309; Chelodi, *Ius Canonicum de Delictis et Poenis et de Iudiciis Criminalibus* (5. ed. a P. Ciprotti, Vicenza: Società Anonima Tipografica, 1943), p. 79 (hereafter cited as De *Delictis et Poenis*); Coronata, *Institutiones*, IV, 305; Cappello, *Tractatus Canonico-Moralis de Censuris iuxta Codicem Iuris Canonici* (3. ed., Taurinorum Augustae: Marietti, 1933), p. 216 (hereafter cited as *De Censuris*); Boudinhon, *La Nouvelle Législation de l'Index* (2. ed., Paris, 1925), pp. 298–299 (hereafter cited as *Nouv. Législ.*); Wernz-Vidal, *Ius Canonicum*, IV, pars 2, 133. As far as can be ascertained, the change of opinion was occasioned by the necessity of giving a strict interpretation to the censures listed in the constitution of Pius IX, "*Apostolicae Sedis*," 12 oct. 1869, §1, n. 2—*Fontes*, n. 552. Almost all modern commentators follow the explanation of the pertinent section of that constitution given in *Constitutio APOSTOLICAE SEDIS Pii Papae IX qua censurae latae sententiae limitantur annotationibus seu commentariis illustrata* (Claromon Ferrandi,1881), p. 38 (hereafter cited as *Constitutio*).

Some modern authors maintain that a volume must be printed (*typis impressum*) before it is a book, e.g., Sipos, *Enchiridion*, p. 711; Cocchi, *Commentarium*, VI, 148; Noldin-Schmitt, *Summa Theologiae Moralis* (27. ed., 3 vols., Oeniponte-Lipsiae: F. Rauch, 1940–1941), II, 641 (hereafter cited as *Summa*); Claeys Bouuaert-Simenon, *Manuale*, III, 368; Tummulo-Iorio, *Compendium Theologiae Moralis* (5. ed., 2 vols. & Suppl., Neapoli: D'Auria, 1934–1936), Suppl. (*De Censuris, Prohibitione Librorum, Irregularitatibus, Indulgentiis*), p. 804 (hereafter cited as *De Censuris*); Cappello, *De Censuris*, p. 215; Gougnard, *Collationes Theologicae* (2 vols., Mechliniae: H. Dessain, 1932–1936), II, 102 (hereafter cited as *Collationes*); Chelodi, *De Delictis et Poenis*, p. 79. Others deny that it need be printed, and would allow other methods of reduplication or multiplication, e.g., Vermeersch, *De Prohibitione*, p. 32; Coronata, *Institutiones*, II, 315.

[15] Hilarius a Sexten, *Tractatus*, p. 111; Pennachi, *ASS*, XXX (1897–1898), 163; Vermeersch, *De Prohibitione*, p. 28; Beste, *Introductio*, p. 696; De Meester, *Compendium*, III, pars 1, 255; Tummulo-Iorio, *De Censuris*, p. 803; Wernz-Vidal, *Ius Canonicum*, IV, pars 2, 132; Coronata, *Institutiones*, II, 315; Salucci, *Il Diritto Penale Secondo il Codice di Diritto Canonico* (2 vols., Subiaco, 1926–1930), II, 28 (hereafter cited as *Diritto*); Augustine, *Commentary*, VI, 431; Schneider, *Buechergesetze*, p. 162.

[16] Older canonists frequently extended the meaning of the word *book* to mean even small writings, e.g., Suarez, *Opera Omnia*, XII, 502; Reiffenstuel, *Ius Canonicum Universum*, Lib. V, tit. VII, nn. 40–45; Farinacius, *De Haeresi*, Quaestio CLXXX, nn. 30–31 (cited by Reiffenstuel, *l.c.*); Lacroix, *Theol. Moral.*, III, 377; Bouix, *De Curia Romana*, p. 531; Van der Velden, *Principia*, II, 618, who cites Diana and the Salmanticenses as holding the same view. This extended meaning was still held after the appearance of the Constitution "*Apos-*

in sextodecimo.[18] A less common, but current, opinion holds that Schmalzgrueber's rule is a general approximation, but that common usage applies the term to writings of much smaller size, so much so that only very small booklets, pamphlets, and the like would not be considered books.[19]

The Code of Canon Law, in canon 1384, §2, states that in title XXIII, the word *book* means every single piece of matter that is published, regardless of its size, unless the contrary be evident:

---

tolicae Sedis" in 1869 by Gury-Ballerini, *Compendium Theologiae Moralis* (12. ed., 2 vols., Prati, 1894), II, 802; Van der Velden, *Principia*, II, 618, who cites Daris (*Tractatus de Censuris*, p. 141) and Formisano (*Commentaria*, p. 33) as holding the same view.

Others, however, excluded smaller works from the meaning of books, e.g., Lugo, *Disputationes*, XXI, nn. 33–38, who cites Sanchez, Duardus, Laymann and Sousa as holding the same opinion; Tamburinus, *Explicatio Decalogi*, Lib. II, cap. I, §VII, n. 10; Castro-Palaus, *Opus Morale*, Tom. I, Tract. IV, disp. II, punct. X, §1; Schmalzgrueber, *Jus Ecclesiasticum Universum*, Lib. V, tit. VII, nn. 53–55, who cites Herinx and Wiestner as holding the same view.

At the present time, the common opinion holds that the book must be of some sizeable bulk, e.g., Hilarius a Sexten, *Tractatus*, p. 11; Vermeersch, *De Prohibitione*, p. 28; Goepfert, *Moraltheologie*, I, 355; Ojetti, *Synopsis Rerum Moralium et Iuris Pontificii* (3. ed., 3 vols. & Index, Romae, 1909–1914), I, 712 (hereafter cited as *Synopsis*); Schneider, *Buechergesetze*, pp. 145, 162; Boudinhon, *Nouv. Législ.*, p. 298; Augustine, *Commentary*, VI, 431; Ayrinhac, *Admin. Legisl.*, p. 275; Sipos, *Enchiridion*, p. 711; Beste, *Introductio*, p. 696; Claeys Bouuaert-Simenon, *Manuale*, III, 368; De Meester, *Compendium*, III, pars 1, 255; Coronata, *Institutiones*, II, 315; Wernz-Vidal, *Ius Canonicum*, IV, pars 2, 132; Ubach, *Theol. Moral.*, I, 555; Gagnon, *La Censure*, pp. 84–85.

[17] Older canonists did not require unity of content for a book, e.g., Hilarius a Sexten, *Tractatus*, p. 111; Bucceroni, *Institutiones*, II, 368. It seems that there was little need to discuss the problem before the appearance and wide diffusion of newspapers and periodicals in the nineteenth century. Modern canonists and moralists, however, are quite unanimous in demanding unity of content, e.g., Vermeersch, *De Prohibitione*, pp. 29–30; Goepfert, *Moraltheologie*, I, 355; Ojetti, *Synopsis*, I, 712; Boudinhon, *Nouv. Législ.*, p. 298; Ayrinhac, *Admin. Legisl.*, p. 275; De Meester, *Compendium*, III, pars 1, 255; Claeys Bouuaert-Simenon, *Manuale*, III, 368; Vermeersch-Creusen, *Epitome*, III, 319; Coronata, *Institutiones*, II, 315; Noldin-Schmitt, *Summa*, II, 638; Seraphinus a Loiano, *Institutiones*, II, 627; Ubach, *Theol. Moral.*, I, 555; Beste, *Introductio*, p. 696; Sipos, *Enchiridion*, p. 711; Wernz-Vidal, *Ius Canonicum*, IV, pars 2, 132; Ferreres, *Compendium*, I, 406; Tummulo-Iorio, *De Censuris*, p. 803; Cocchi, *Commentarium*, VI, 148; Cappello, *De Censuris*, p. 215; Aertnys-Damen, *Theologia Moralis secundum doctrinam S. Alfonsi de Ligorio Doctoris Ecclesiae* (14. ed., 2 vols., Taurinorum Augustae: Marietti, 1944), II, 747 (hereafter cited as *Theol. Moral.*); Gougnard, *Collationes*, II, 102; Gagnon, *La Censure*, pp. 85–86.

Even at the present time, however, commentators do not specify very clearly just what that unity of content entails. Some demand that the whole book treat of the same topic, or at least have the same common tendency or purpose, e.g., Vermeersch, *De Prohibitione*, pp. 28–31; Ojetti, *Synopsis*, I, 712; Augustine, *Commentary*, VI, 431; De Meester, *Compendium*, III, pars 1, 255; Vermeersch-Creusen, *Epitome*, III, 319; Beste, *Introductio*, p. 696; Sipos, *Enchiridion*, p. 711; Cocchi, *Commentarium*, VI, 148; Wernz-Vidal, *Ius Canonicum*, IV, pars 2, 132; Gougnard, *Collationes*, II, 102.

> Quae sub hoc titulo de libris praescribuntur, publicationibus diariis, periodicis et aliis editis scriptis quibuslibet applicentur, nisi aliud constet.[20]

The binding of several pamphlets into one volume does not constitute a book, even though it have the required bulk, unless it also have the required unity of content, e.g., Vermeersch, *De Prohibitione*, p. 29; Goepfert, *Moraltheologie*, I, 355; Coronata, *Institutiones*, II, 315; Ubach, *Theol. Moral.*, I. 555; Beste, *Introductio*, p. 696; Sipos, *Enchiridion*, p. 711; Cappello, *De Censuris*, p. 216.

Individual sections of a large work, when published separately, are usually not books in themselves; though, when they reach the required bulk, they may constitute a book, provided they have the required unity of content; and they constitute a book even before they are bound. Thus, Lehmkuhl, *Theologia Moralis*, II, 680; Piat, *NRT*, XXX (1898), 48; Augustine, *Commentary*, VI, 431; Coronata, *Institutiones*, II, 315; De Meester, *Compendium*, III, pars 1, 255; Vermeersch, *De Prohibitione*, pp. 29–30; Beste, *Introductio*, p. 696.

It is possible to have several distinct volumes, each dependent upon the others in such a way that they constitute one single work, e.g., the four volumes of Ojetti's *Synopsis*. Similarly, it is possible to have several distinct volumes by one author, all treating of the same topic, but each constituting a book in its own right, e.g., Van Hove's series on the first book of the Code of Canon Law, namely, *Prolegomena*, *De Legibus Ecclesiasticis*, *De Consuetudine—De Temporis Supputatione*, *De Rescriptis*, *De Privilegiis—De Dispensationibus*.

As a rule, periodicals and newspapers are not books, because they lack the required bulk, or particularly because they lack the required unity of content. However, some could easily meet the requirements of books, especially those which are more scientific, and have progressive pagination.

[18] *Jus Ecclesiasticum Universum*, Lib. V, tit. VII, n. 55. It seems that Castro-Palaus (*Opu. Morale*, Tom. I, Tract. IV, disp. II, punct. X, §1, nn. 4–5) was the first to propose this norm, Modern adherents of this view are Pennacchi, *ASS*, XXX [1897–1898], 163 527; Goepfert; *Moraltheologie*, I, 355; Augustine, *Commentary*, VI, 431; Ayrinhac, *Admin Legisl.*, p. 275, Claeys-Bouuaert-Simenon, *Manuale*, III, 368; Coronata, *Institutiones*, II, 315; Noldin-Schmitt, *Summa*, II, 638; Seraphinus a Loiano, *Institutiones*, II, 627; Beste, *Introductio*, p. 696; Sipos, *Enchiridion*, p. 711; Ferreres, *Compendium*, I, 406; Hilarius a Sexten, *Tractatus*, p. 111; Vermeersch, *De Prohibitione*, p. 28. Pennacchi (*ASS*, XXX, [1897–1898], 163) held that a work of 8 or 9 folios would be a book, while Dilgskron (*Anal. Eccl.*, IV [1897], 227) held that a volume of less than 5 or 6 folios would not be a book. Vermeersch-Creusen (*Epitome*, III, 319) hold that a book, to be such, must contain about 250 octavo pages.

[19] Lugo, *Disputationes*, XXI, n. 38; Schneider, *Buechergesetze*, p. 162; Vermeersch, *De Prohibitione*, pp. 28–29; De Meester, *Compendium*, III pars 1, 255; Tummulo-Iorio, *De Censuris*, p. 804; Ubach, *Theol. Moral.*, I, 555; Boudinhon, *Nouv. Législ.*, p. 298; Wernz-Vidal, *Ius Canonicum*, IV pars 2, 132; Lehmkuhl, *Theologia Moralis*, II, 680; Aertnys-Damen, *Theol. Moral.*, II, 747; Cocchi, *Commentarium*, VI, 148; Cerato, *Censurae Vigentes ipso facto a Codice Iuris Canonici Excerptae*, (2. ed., Patavii, 1921), p. 215 (hereafter cited as *Censurae*); Gagnon, *La Censure*, p. 85.

[20] In view of this official, technical, extended meaning, the opinion of those canonists who exempt small writings (e.g., folders, etc.) is no longer tenable. Such an opinion was still held by Ferreres, *Compendium*, I, 406; Arregui, *Summarium*, p. 275; Beste, *Introductio*, p. 696. It is undoubtedly true that there is such a thing as smallness of matter. It is also admissible that the old adage may sometimes apply, "*De minimis non curat praetor.*"

Hence, the presumption is that the term is used in its extended sense, and the contrary must be proved. In case of doubt, one must follow the presumption in favor of the extended meaning.[21]

In the field of Sacred Scripture, the term *book* is used for each and every unit of the Old and the New Testament. Thus, it is said that there are 72 books in the Bible, despite the fact that some of them are no more than a page or two in length.[22]

(10) A *volume* is "a collection of printed sheets bound together, whether a single work, a part of a work, or more than one work; a book, esp., that part of an extended work bound together in one cover."[23]

(11) A *periodical* is "a publication, usually a weekly, monthly, or quarterly magazine, appearing at regular intervals."[24] The term is not generally applied to newspapers, whether daily, semiweekly, or weekly; but it is used for magazines, reviews, bulletins, etc. In canonical parlance, the terms "*publicationes diariae*" and "*diaria*" mean newspapers, journals, especially, those issued daily.[25] "*Publicationes periodicae*" are publications which appear at regular intervals but less frequently than daily; such as, semiweeklies, weeklies, semimonthlies, quarterlies, or annuals.[25a] "*Folia periodica*" are

[21] Bouscaren-Ellis make a statement which seems to imply that in case of doubt the restricted meaning is to be followed, e.g.: "If any particular canon can reasonably be interpreted as applying only to books in the strict sense, it should be so interpreted (cf. c. 1384, §2, *nisi aliud constet;* cc. 15, 19)."—*Canon Law, A Text and Commentary* (Milwaukee: Bruce Publishing Co., [1946]), p. 706 (hereafter cited as *Canon Law*). Further discussion will be found below in Chapter VI, article II, D, pp. 87–91.

[22] Conc. Trident., sess. IV, *de canonicis scripturis.* The documentary history of the canon may be found, briefly, in Schroeder, *Canons and Decrees of the Council of Trent* (St. Louis: B. Herder, 1941), pp. 17, n. 4, and 296, n. 4.

[23] By permission; from *Webster's New Collegiate Dictionary,* copyright, 1949, 1951, by G. & C. Merriam Co. Also confer *A. L. A. Glossary* (p. 147) for a more extensive description of the term *volume* both in the bibliographical and in the material sense.

[24] FW 873. According to the *A. L. A. Glossary* (pp. 99, 85, 117) a *periodical* is "a publication with a distinctive title intended to appear in successive (usually unbound) numbers or parts at stated or regular intervals and, as a rule, for an indefinite time; each part generally contains articles by several contributors"; a *magazine* is "a periodical for general reading, containing articles on various subjects by different authors, and generally fiction and poetry"; a *review* is "a periodical publication primarily devoted to critical articles and reviews of new books."

[25] Pennacchi, *ASS,* XXX (1897–1898), 344; Van Coillie, *Commentarius,* p. 64; Cappello, *De Curia Romana,* I, 286; Vermeersch, *De Prohibitione,* p. 107; Beste, *Introductio,* p. 695; Blat, *Commentarium,* III, partes 2–6, 327, 335; De Meester, *Compendium,* III, pars 1, 261; Sipos, *Enchiridion,* p. 711; Wernz-Vidal, *Ius Canonicum,* IV, pars 2, 165; Augustine, *Commentary,* VI, 441.

[25a] Beste, *Introductio,* pp. 695–696; Blat, *Commentarium,* III, partes 2–6, 327; Sipos, *Enchiridion,* p. 711.

periodical publications issued in the form of folded sheets; as, the various weekly newspapers or diocesan weeklies like *The Register*, *Our Sunday Visitor*, etc. "*Libelli periodici*" are periodical publications issued in pamphlet or booklet form, though many of them reach the size of books and meet all the requirements of books in the strict canonical sense.[25b] Although these terms are mentioned by the Code in canons 1384, §2, and 1386, their distinction is of little practical importance today, since these publications are governed by the same regulations.

(12) An *edition* is "1. The form in which a literary work is published; as, a single-volume *edition*. 2. The whole number of copies of a work published at one time; as, the first *edition* of a work;—disting. from *impression*. 3. One of the several issues of a newspaper for a single day."[26]

(13) An *issue* is "the whole quantity emitted at one time";[27] or, an edition, as of a newspaper, [27a] an impression, a printing.[27b]

(14) An *impression* comprises "all the copies of a work printed at one time: especially, an unaltered reprint from standing type or from plates, as distinguished from an *edition*."[28] Sometimes an impression is called a *printing*.[28a]

(15) A *print* is an impression with ink from type, plates, etc.; any printed matter or printed publication, as, a newspaper, pamphlet, or the like; a printed picture.[29] A work is said to be *in print* when it is printed, or published, or when it is still available from the publisher in printed form. It is said to be *out of print* when it is no longer on sale, or procurable from the publisher, the edition being exhausted or withdrawn.[30]

(16) A *reprint* is a new printing, without material alteration, from new or original type or plates, as, a new edition, a new impression, a new issue,

---

[25b] Pennacchi, *ASS*, XXX (1897–1898), 344; Cappello, *De Curia Romana*, I, 286; Vermeersch, *De Prohibitione*, p. 108; Augustine, *Commentary*, VI, 441; Coronata, *Institutiones*, II, 321.

[26] By permission; from *Webster's New Collegiate Dictionary*, copyright, 1949, 1951, by G. & C. Merriam Co. In reference to the second meaning, an edition comprises "all the impressions of a work printed at any time or times from one setting of type, including those printed from stereotype or electrotype plates from that setting (provided, however, that there is no substantial change in or addition to the text, or no change in make-up, format, or character of the resulting book). A facsimile reproduction constitutes a different edition."—*A. L. A. Glossary*, p. 51.

[27] By permission; from *Webster's New Collegiate Dictionary*, copyright, 1949, 1951, by G. & C. Merriam Co.

[27a] FW 633.

[27b] Cf. *A. L. A. Glossary* (pp. 75–76, 92) for a more lengthy description of the term *issue*.

[28] FW 595. See also *A. L. A. Glossary*, p. 71.

[28a] For other meanings of the term *printing*, see FW 931.

[29] Adapted from FW 931.

[30] FW 931; *A. L. A. Glossary*, pp. 71, 95.

an offprint, or a facsimile reprint;[31] or more, specifically, a reissue of a work long out of print, or by some other person than the original publisher.[31a]

(17) An *offprint* is "an impression of an article, chapter, or other portion of a larger work, printed from the type or plates of the original and separately issued, sometimes with one or more additional pages or leaves."[32]

(18) A *picture* is "a surface representation of an object or scene, as by a painting, drawing, engraving, or photograph."[33]

(19) A *slide* is "a plate of glass or other transparent material on which is a picture to be projected, as by a magic lantern."[34]

(20) A *film* is "a thin, flexible, transparent sheet of cellulose nitrate or acetate or similar material coated with a light-sensitive emulsion, used for taking photographs";[35] a filmstrip; a motion picture.

Article II. Terms Designating the Persons Who Seek or Perform Precensorship

In this classification, one set of persons is concerned with the composition, manufacture and distribution of the work, namely, the author, writer, compiler, editor, translator, printer, publisher, book-seller; one person, the precensor, actually performs the precensorship; and a third group is obligated to provide officials for that task, namely, the competent authority, the local ordinary, and the major superior. Each will be taken in turn.

A. Persons Who Compose, Manufacture and Distribute Publications

(1) An *author* is the original writer who composes a book, article, poem, or the like, as distinguished from a translator, editor, or compiler.[36] Canon-

---

[31] *A. L. A. Glossary*, pp. 115–116, 55.

[31a] Cf. FW 993. See also *A. L. A. Glossary* (p. 116) for the meaning of the terms *reprint edition* and *republication*.

[32] *A. L. A. Glossary*, p. 93. Perhaps the term is also taken in a wider meaning as any "reproduction or separate printing of an article or paragraph [etc.] printed in some publication."—FW 819.

[33] FW 888. When it is reproduced by any printing process, it is called a *print*.—*A. L. A. Glossary*, p. 105.

[34] By permission; from *Webster's New Collegiate Dictionary*, copyright, 1949, 1951, by G. & C. Merriam Co.

[35] By permission; from *Webster's New Collegiate Dictionary*, copyright, 1949, 1951, by G. & C. Merriam Co.

[36] FW 82. In a broader sense an author is "the maker of the book or the person or body immediately responsible for its existence. Thus, a person who collects and puts together the writings of several authors (compiler or editor) may be said to be the author of a collection. A corporate body may be considered the author of publications issued in its name or by its authority."—*A. L. A. Glossary*, p. 8.

ists also use this term to designate the person who is the composer of the present form of a work, e.g., a translator, an editor, etc. In regard to paintings, the painter or designer is the author.[37]

(2) A *writer* is "1. One who writes. 2. One who practices writing as an occupation, as an author, journalist, etc."[38]

(3) A *compiler* is "one who produces a work by collecting and putting together written or printed matter from the works of various authors; also, one who chooses and combines into one work selections or quotations from one author."[39]

(4) An *editor* is one who prepares for publication material not originally composed by himself; such as, manuscripts, copy, a work or collection of works or articles written by others. The editorial labor may consist in any one or several of the following functions: the mere preparation of the matter for the printer; the compilation and arrangement of the material; the collation, restoration, emendation, or revision of the text; the addition of an introduction, notes, or other critical matter.[40] The editor (reviser) of a previous edition of a work is the author only of the material which contributes, but is sometimes called the author of the whole.[40a] Furthermore, an editor is one who has charge of a publication (e.g., a newspaper, periodical, book of reference) or of a special department of such a publication (e.g., a newseditor); that is, one who directs its policies and supervises the selection, preparation and arrangement of the material to be published.[41] It is important, however, to remember that the Code, in title XXIII and in canon 2318, uses the words "*edere*" and "*editor*" in the sense of "publishing" and "publisher" respectively.

(5) A *translator* is one who gives the equivalent of a work by rendering it into his own or another language.[42]

---

[37] Blat, *Commentarium*, V, 206; Cocchi, *Commentarium*, VIII, 233; Coronata, *Institutiones*, IV, 310; Cerato, *Censurae*, p. 70; Beste, *Introductio*, p. 961; Cappello, *De Censuris*, p. 345; Pistocchi, *I Canoni Penali del Codice Ecclesiastico Esposti e Commentati* (Torino-Roma, 1925), p. 39 (hereafter cited as *Canoni*); Salucci, *Diritto*, II, 35: Gagnon, *La Censure*, p. 82.

[38] By permission; from *Webster's New Collegiate Dictionary*, copyright, 1949, 1951, by G. & C. Merriam Co.

[39] *A. L. A. Glossary*, p. 35.

[40] *A. L. A. Glossary*, p. 51; FW 369.

[40a] E.g., one who prepares a special edition of the books of the Bible.—Blat, *Commentarium*, V, 206. See also *A. L. A. Glossary*, p. 8.

[41] FW 369; *Webster's New Collegiate Dictionary*, p. 261.

[42] Adapted from FW 1241. According to the *A. L. A. Glossary* (p. 142) a translator is "one who renders from one language into another, or from an older form of a language into the modern form, more or less closely following the original."

(6) A *printer* is "the person, or firm, by whom a book [or other material] is printed, as distinguished from the publisher and the bookseller by whom it is issued and sold."[43]

(7) A *publisher* is "the person, firm, or corporate body undertaking the responsibility for the issue of a book or other printed matter to the public,"[44] either directly or through various channels of distribution, gratuitously or for a price. It is immaterial whether the person, firm, or corporate body makes a business of publishing printed matter or not. It may happen that a publisher is also a printer, though that is not at all necessary. Many modern publishers let out all their printing to other firms. The financial costs of a publication may be borne by the author, the publisher, or by a third party; hence, that is not a component part of the definition of a publisher. At times, the author undertakes the issuance of his own work to the public; he thereby acts as his own publisher. The Latin word "*editor*" is the most common equivalent of our English "publisher."[45]

(8) A *bookseller* is one who vends books, and the like, made available to the public by a publisher.

B. The Person Who Performs the Precensorship

A *censor* is an official examiner of manuscripts who is empowered to prohibit their publication if they are offensive to government or good morals.[46] In canonical parlance a censor is an official designated to examine writings and pass judgment upon them according to certain ecclesiastical standards. A censor does not positively approve or prohibit a work unless such power has been specially committed to him. Ordinarily it is his task to decide simply whether or not the writing conforms to ecclesiastical norms. A censor

[43] *A. L. A. Glossary*, p. 105. FW 931 gives the following more extensive definitions: "1. One engaged in the trade of typographical printing; one who sets type or runs a printing-press; specifically, a compositor. 2. One who owns a printing establishment and employs printers. 3. One who prints, stamps, impresses, or transfers copies of anything as a business."

[44] *A. L. A. Glossary*, pp. 108–109.

[45] Canonists have produced a most extensive divergence of opinion in their attempts to define a publisher, and have concocted numerous unreliable criteria. Some hold that a publisher is a person who, acting in his own name, employs a printer to print a work, and pays the expenses of the printing, e.g., Cappello, *De Censuris*, pp. 214–215; Chelodi, *De Delictis et Poenis*, p. 79. Others hold that the publisher is the person who bears the cost of the work, e.g., Blat, *Commentarium*, V, 205–206. Others hold that a publisher is one who prints and disseminates a book, e.g., Beste, *Introductio*, p. 961; Tummulo-Iorio, *De Censuris*, p. 745. Others claim that a publisher is one who, acting his in own name, has the work printed at his own expense, and assumes the responsibility of putting it into general circulation, e.g., Pistocchi, *Canoni*, p. 29; Salucci, *Diritto*, II, 28; Coronata, *Institutiones*, IV, 304, 310.

The following subscribe to the opinion given in the text: Cocchi, *Commentarium*, VIII, 231; Claeys Bouuaert-Simenon, *Manuale*, III, 368; Aertnys-Damen, *Theol. Moral.*, II, 747; Vermeersch-Creusen, *Epitome*, III, 319; Sipos, *Enchiridion*, p. 715; Cerato, *Censurae*, p. 147.

[46] Adapted from FW 194.

who is commissioned to review a work before publication may be called a *precensor*, whose work terminates in the formation of the judgment "*Nihil* [*aliquid*] *obstat quominus imprimatur*."

C. The Persons Who Provide Precensorship

(1) An *authority* is one who has power to permit or refuse permission for publication of writings. Some authorities also may approve or prohibit published works.

(2) The *local ordinary* is an ecclesiastical superior who is the competent authority in a given territory.[47] The local ordinary of the author is the ecclesiastical superior in that territory where the author has a domicile or a quasi-domicile; or, where the author happens to be staying, if he has not any fixed abode. The local ordinary of the place of publication is the ecclesiastical superior of the territory in which the publishing firm is situated or has its business address. The local ordinary of the place of printing is the ecclesiastical superior of the territory in which the printing establishment is situated.[48]

(3) A *proper local ordinary* (canon 1385, §2) of an author is the local ordinary of the place of the author's domicile or quasi-domicile, or of the place where the author happens to be staying, if he has not any fixed abode. In the case of diocesan clerics, the proper local ordinary of the author is the local ordinary of the diocese in which the cleric is incardinated, and also the local ordinary of any other place in which the cleric legitimately has a domicile or a quasi-domicile, even though he might not be incardinated in that diocese. In the case of religious, the proper local ordinary of the author is the local ordinary of the territory in which is situated the religious house to which the religious is attached, or, if the religious is legitimately residing elsewhere, the local ordinary of the diocese in which he possesses a domicile or a quasi-domicile.[49]

---

[47] Canon 198, states: §1. "In iure nomine *Ordinarii* intelliguntur, nisi quis expresse excipiatur, praeter Romanum Pontificem, pro suo quisque territorio Episcopus residentialis, Abbas vel Praelatus *nullius* eorumque Vicarius Generalis, Administrator, Vicarius et Praefectus Apostolicus, itemque ii qui praedictis deficientibus interim ex iuris praescripto aut ex probatis constitutionibus succedunt in regimine, pro suis vero subditis Superiores maiores in religionibus clericalibus exemptis.

§2. Nomine autem *Ordinarii loci* seu *locorum* veniunt omnes recensiti, exceptis Superioribus religiosis."

[48] It is not correct to say that the competent authority is the local ordinary of the printer or of the publisher. The printer or publisher may reside in a diocese other than that where the firm is situated. More will be said about this in the commentary on canon 1385, §2.

[49] More will be said about the proper local ordinary in the commentary on canon 1385, §2.

(4) A *major superior* is one of the higher superiors of religious, to the exclusion of the local superior.[50]

Article III. Functions Performed Before, After, or in the Act of Precensorship

Of the various functions, some are connected with the composition, manufacture and distribution of works, and are performed before actual censorship, e.g., to write, to edit, to translate, to print, and, sometimes, to publish. Other functions pertain to the ecclesiastical authorities and are performed after censorship, e.g., to grant or refuse permission to publish, to positively approve or condemn a work. Still others pertain to the censor himself and are performed in the very act of censorship, e.g., to examine a writing and to pass judgment on it. Each will be treated in the order given above. This indeed involves an inversion of the temporal order, but designedly so, in order to allow the function of censorship to come last in the treatment.

A. Functions Performed Before Censorship

The first set of functions pertains to the composition, manufacture and distribution of the work.

(1) To *write* means to compose or produce in writing, especially to be the author of a work.[51]

(2) To *edit* means to prepare matter for publication by compiling, arranging, emending, etc; to prepare a special edition of a work; to oversee, conduct, or have charge of a publication, as, to edit an encyclopedia, a newspaper, or a periodical.[52]

(3) To *translate* means to give the sense or equivalent of a work in a language different from the original or a previous version.[53]

(4) To *print* means "to strike off an impression or impressions of, from type, or from stereotype, electrotype, or engraved plates, or the like."[54] In a less strict sense, to print means to reproduce by any modern mechanical process, whether manual or motorized, e.g., by planographic printing (lithography, photolithography, offset or photo-offset printing), or by

[50] ". . . veniunt nomine . . . *Superiorum maiorum*, Abbas Primas, Abbas Superior Congregationis monasticae, Abbas monasterii sui iuris, licet ad monasticam Congregationem pertinentis, supremus religionis Moderator, Superior provincialis, eorundem vicarii aliique ad instar provincialium potestatem habentes."—Canon 488, 8°.

[51] Adapted from FW 1353.

[52] Adapted from FW 369. It is important to recall that the Latin word "*edere*" means to publish. The Code, in canon 1386, §1, uses the word "*moderari*" as the Latin equivalent for the editing or managing of a newspaper or periodical.

[53] Adapted from FW 1241.

[54] By permission; from *Webster's New Collegiate Dictionary*, copyright, 1949, 1951, by G. & C. Merriam Co.

any similar process, as is done on Multigraph machines, Mimeograph machines, etc.[54a]

(5) To *publish* means to make copies of a work available to the general public, e.g., by selling them, by distributing them gratis, or at least by offering them for sale or free distribution.[55] First of all, to publish means *to make copies of a work available*. It does not mean the making of the original manuscript available, but copies thereof. In and of themselves even typewritten copies would suffice, but, in consequence of the impracticality of producing sufficient copies, there is little likelihood that this method will be used to any appreciable extent. The ordinary method of reduplication is printing, either by means of type or any other modern equivalent.[56]

It is not required that a publisher do his own printing. If a publisher does his own printing he both prints (*imprimere*) and publishes (*edere*). Many printers are not publishers, e.g., if after printing and binding a work they surrender it to others who engage in the business of distributing it.

[54a] FW 931; *A. L. A. Glossary*, pp. 84, 88, 93, 100, 102. Transcription by hand is not printing.—Cf. Coronata *Institutiones*, II, 315; Claeys Bouuaert-Simenon, *Manuale*, III, 132; Sipos, *Enchiridion*, p. 711; Seraphinus a Loiano, *Institutiones*, II, 628; Vermeersch-Creusen, *Epitome*, II, 503; Haring, *Grundzuege des katholischen Kirchenrechtes* (3. ed., 2 vols., Graz, 1924), 371 (hereafter cited as *Grundzuege*).

The following consider all modern methods of reduplication as printing, e.g., De Meester, *Compendium*, III, pars 1, 255; Lehmkuhl, *Theologia Moralis*, II, 760; Cocchi, *Commentarium*, VI, 147–148; Sipos, *Enchiridion*, p. 711; Van Coillie, *Commentarius*, p. 88; Schneider, *Buechergesetze*, p. 145; Vermeersch, *De Prohibitione*, pp. 32–33; Ayrinhac, *Admin. Legisl.*, p. 275; Coronata, *Institutiones*, II, 315; Vermeersch-Creusen, *Epitome*, II, 503; Beste, *Introductio*, p. 696; Marc-Gestermann-Raus, *Institutiones*, I, 854; Claeys Bouuaert-Simenon, *Manuale*, III, 132; Boudinhon, *Nouv. Législ.*, p. 273; Seraphinus a Loiano, *Institutiones*, II, 628; Wernz-Vidal, *Ius Canonicum*, IV, pars 2, 133; Tummulo-Iorio, *De Censuris*, pp. 816–817. In this sense, even typewriting is classed as printing by Beste, *Introductio*, p. 696; Seraphinus a Loiano, *Institutiones*, II, 628; Claeys Bouuaert-Simenon, *Manuale*, III, 132; Cocchi, *Commentarium*, VI, 148; De Meester, *Compendium*, III, pars 1, 256; Anon., "Les nouveautes du Codex, Censure des Livres et Index," *L'Ami du Clergé* (Langres, 1879—1939, 1947—), XXXIX (1922), 115–116 (hereafter cited as *L'Ami*).

[55] Goodwine, *The Jurist*, X (1950), 155–156 (6–7); Jombart, *DDC*, III, 157; Gagnon, *La Censure*, pp. 89–90.

[56] Van Coillie, *Commentarius*, p. 88; Schneider, *Buechergesetze*, p. 145; Vermeersch, *De Prohibitione*, pp. 32–33; Ayrinhac, *Admin. Législ.*, p. 275; Coronata, *Institutiones*, II, 315; Vermeersch-Creusen, *Epitome*, II, 502; Marc-Gestermann-Raus, *Institutiones*, I, 854; Sipos, *Enchiridion*, p. 711; Boudinhon, *Nouv. Législ.*, p. 273; Wernz-Vidal, *Ius Canonicum*, IV, pars 2, 133; Berutti, *Institutiones*, IV, 418; Gagnon, *La Censure*, p. 89; Jombart, *DDC*, III, 157; Goodwine, *The Jurist*, X (1950), 155 (6). The following include reduplication by typewriter: De Meester, *Compendium*, III, pars 1, 256; Beste, *Introductio*, p. 696; Claeys Bouuaert-Simenon, *Manuale*, III, 132; Seraphinus a Loiano, *Institutiones*, II, 628; *L'Ami*, XXXIX (1922), 115–116. Noldin-Schmitt (*Summa*, II, 641) seem to require the work to be printed from type.

Conversely, some publishers are not printers, e.g., if they "let out" the printing of their works to other firms.[57]

Actual diffusion of the copies is not required for publication. A work is said to be published when the date, which the publisher has set as the date of publication, has arrived. At that date the publisher expects to have sufficient copies on hand to meet demands, and it is then that he releases the copies of the work to the general public.[58] The advance distribution of complimentary copies, e.g., to reviewers, etc., does not affect the date of publication. American law considers publication in the same manner as outlined above.[59]

Secondly, publication means the making of a work *available to the general public*. In a certain sense, the work must be surrendered to the public domain.[60] In relinquishing the private rights over a work, an author and

[57] Sources are mentioned in the previous division under the word "publisher."

[58] Ayrinhac, *Admin. Legisl.*, p. 275; Beste, *Introductio*, p. 696; Augustine, *Commentary*, VI, 432; Cerato, *Censurae*, p. 148; Claeys Bouuaert-Simenon, *Manuale*, III, 133; Cocchi, *Commentarium*, VI, 147; Coronata, *Institutiones*, II, 315; De Meester, *Compendium*, III, pars 1, 255; Gagnon, *La Censure*, p. 90; Marc-Gestermann-Raus, *Institutiones*, I, 825; Ubach, *Theol. Moral.*, I, 556–557; Vermeersch-Creusen, *Epitome*, III, 319; Wernz-Vidal, *Ius Canonicum*, IV, pars 2, 133; Boudinhon, *Nouv. Législ.*, p. 273; Pernicone, *Prohibition*, pp. 81–82; Tummulo-Iorio, *De Censuris*, p. 245.

[59] Whitman, "Literary Property," *Cyclopedia of Law and Procedure* (40 vols., New York, 1901–1913), XXV, 1495 (hereafter cited as *CLP*); Wetmore, "Copyright," *CLP*, IX, 920; Howell, *The Copyright Law* (Washington, D. C.: The Bureau of National Affairs Inc., 1942), p. 192; Wittenberg, *The Protection and Marketing of Literary Property* (New York: J. Messner Inc., 1937), pp. 11–12, 37 (hereafter cited as *Protection*).

[60] The Code uses the words "*edere*" (can. 1384; 1385, §1; 1386, §1; 1387–1392), "*publicare*" (can. 1399, 1°), "*publici iuris facere*" (can. 1385, §2; 1390; 2318, §1; 1781; 1819; 2083, §2), and "*in diariis scribere* [*conscribere*]" (can. 1386, §§1–2). The terms "*edere*" and "*divulgare*" (which is often used by commentators) and also "*in diariis scribere* [*conscribere*]" denote a transferral from the state of being unknown to the state of being known. Cf. Vermeersch, *De Prohibitione*, p. 33; Van Coillie, *Commentarius*, p. 88; Pennacchi, *ASS*, XXX (1897–1898), 103; Beste, *Introductio*, p. 696; Claeys Bouuaert-Simenon, *Manuale*, III, 133; Vermeersch-Creusen, *Epitome*, II, 502, and III, 266; Chelodi, *De Delictis et Poenis*, p. 79; Cerato, *Censurae*, p. 148; Marc-Gestermann-Raus, *Institutiones*, I, 825, 854; Cocchi, *Commentarium*, VIII, 231; Goodwine, *The Jurist*, X (1950), 155–156 (6–7).

The terms "*publicare*" and "*publici iuris facere*" denote a transferral from the state of exclusive private ownership to the state of public availability. Cf. Vermeersch, *De Prohibitione*, p. 33; Van Coillie, *Commentarius*, p. 88; Lehmkuhl, *Theologia Moralis*, II, 760; De Meester, *Compendium*, III, pars 1, 255; Marc-Gestermann-Raus, *Institutiones*, I, 854; Seraphinus a Loiano, *Institutiones*, II, 628; Vermeersch-Creusen, *Epitome*, II, 502; Cocchi, *Commentarium*, VI, 147; Blat, *Commentarium*, III, partes 2–6, 327; Ubach, *Theol. Moral.*, I, 556–557; Coronata, *Institutiones*, II, 315; Wernz-Vidal, *Ius Canonicum*, IV, pars 2, 133; Ayrinhac, *Admin. Legisl.*, p. 275; Augustine, *Commentary*, VI, 432; Anon., "De novarum Constitutionum editione et vi," *Periodica de Religiosis et Missionariis* (Brugis, 1905–1919); *Periodica de Re Canonica et Morali utilia praesertim Religiosis et Missionariis* (Brugis, 1920–1927); *Periodica de Re Morali, Canonica, Liturgica* (Brugis, 1927–1936; Romae, 1937—), VII (1914), (8) (hereafter cited as *Periodica*).

publisher do not necessarily surrender all claim to that work. They may still retain property rights over the manuscript as a material object, and also the rights reserved to the author or proprietor by statutory or copyright laws.[61] However, these claims do not affect the surrender of copies of the work to the public domain, so that they may be procured by all. The mere fact that some works are specialized, or highly technical, or advertized only among select circles, does not alter the fact that they are obtainable by all. In some cases, however, the author or distributor so limits the distribution of a work that it is available only to a select group, to a designated few, not for the general public; it does not matter if occasionally the work reaches a few outside the group. Canonists generally admit that such a restricted distribution is not a publication in the strict sense of the word.[62]

---

[61] Noldin-Scmitt, *Summa*, II, 364–365; Seraphinus a Loiano, *Institutiones*, III, 52–53; Vermeersch, *Quaestiones de Iustitia* (2. ed., Brugis, 1904), 317–328; Ballerini-Palmieri, *Opus Theologicum Morale*, III, 51–52; Genicot-Salsmans, *Institutiones Theologiae Moralis* (14. ed., 2 vols., Buenos Aires: Dedebec, Ediciones Desclée, De Brouwer, 1939), I, 404–406 (hereafter cited as *Institutiones*); Whitman, *CLP*, XXV, 1488–1501; Wittenberg, *Protection*, pp. 11–12.

[62] Vermeersch, *De Prohibitione*, p. 82; De Meester, *Compendium*, III, pars 1, 255; Claeys Bouuaert-Simenon, *Manuale*, III, 132; Vermeersch-Creusen, *Epitome*, II, 502; Marc-Gestermann-Raus, *Institutiones*, I, 825, 854; Wernz-Vidal, *Ius Canonicum*, IV, pars 2, 133; Seraphinus a Loiano, *Institutiones*, II, 628; Cochi, *Commentarium*, VI, 148; Ubach, *Theol. Moral.*, I, 556–557; Genicot-Salsmans, *Institutiones*, I, 385; Coronata, *Institutiones*, II, 315; Haring, *Grundzuege*, II, 371; Beste, *Introductio*, p. 696; Ayrinhac, *Admin. Legisl.*, p. 275; Bouscaren-Ellis, *Canon Law*, p. 706; Noldin-Schmitt, *Summa*, II, 641; Berutti, *Institutiones*, IV, 418; Gagnon, *La Censure*, p. 89; Goodwine, *The Jurist*, X (1950), 155 (6); Jombart, *DDC*, III, 157. The classical example given by the authors is that of a professor who has his lecture notes printed or mimeographed or reduplicated in some other manner and distributed, even in bound form, to his students. It is also held that writings intended for the exclusive use of the members of a particular religious institute are not published in the strict sense, e.g., the Constitutions and Rules, commentaries on them, manuals of prayers, ceremonies and customs, printed circular letters and communications of the superiors addressed to their subjects. Beste, *Introductio*, p. 696; Berutti, *Institutiones*, IV, 418; Gagnon, *La Censure*, p. 89; Marc-Gestermann-Raus, *Institutiones*, I, 854; Vermeersch, *Periodica*, VII (1914), (8); Hartl, "Imprimatur," *ThPrQs*, LXVI (1913), 488; Anonymous, "The Approval of Pictures and Prayers," *Ecclesiastical Review*, LXXXIX (1933), 190–192; Goodwine, *The Jurist*, X (1950), 155 (6). Woywod ("Printing of Books and Pamphlets as Manuscript without Ecclesiastical Approbation," *The Homiletic and Pastoral Review* [New York, 1900—], XXXVI [1935–1936], 970–971 [hereafter cited as *HPR*]), however, holds such writings are subject to the precensorship of the local ordinary. According to Goodwine (*loc. cit.*) the usual *Parish Bulletin* is destined, not for the general public, but for a select group.

Pernicone (*Prohibition*, pp. 81–82) gives a workable criterion: "Usually a work is published by means of *printing*. When the typewriter, lithography, polygraph, mimeograph, photography, handwriting or any other process is used to multiply copies of a work, the work is usually intended not for the general public, but for a restricted number of persons, for a private group, such as the pupils of a professor, the members of a family, etc. In this case the writing is not considered *published* and, therefore, does not come under the present book legislation. The same is true of the original copy or the manuscript, strictly so called.

It is not required for publication that a work be put up for sale. It is quite immaterial whether the distribution occur for a price, or gratis.[63] In American law a work is considered published in both instances, whether it is put up for sale, or whether it is offered to the public by gratuitous distribution.[64] Similarly, it is not required that the publisher bear the cost of the work. There are several different kinds of contractual arrangements whereby the burdens and returns on a work are distributed among the author, the publisher, the printer, or even an interested third party.[65] American law does not require that the publisher bear the expenses.[66]

B. Functions Performed After Precensorship

Functions of the ecclesiastical authorities are usually performed after censorship.

(1) *The granting or refusing of permission to publish.* In either case, the action is composite. When the permission is granted, the act of warranting the publication implicitly includes the act of the competent authority whereby he makes the judgment of the censor his own, together with the express declaration of the authority that this work may be published. When the permission is refused, the act of denying permission implicitly includes the act of the competent authority whereby it makes the judgment of the cen-

---

Nevertheless, if by any of the above means a work is made accessible to all promiscuously, then that work, even though not printed, is considered published." Italics are in the original.

Very often such restricted works will bear the words "*Private Printing*," "*Printed as manuscript*," "*For private use*," "*For private circulation only*." However, the expedient of printing such an expression on the title page, or elsewhere, does not exempt the work from precensorship if it is really published, though it be distributed widely through other channels than the regular book trade.

[63] Ayrinhac, *Admin. Legisl.*, p. 203; Claeys Bouuaert-Simenon, *Manuale*, III, 133; Woywod, "Printing of Books and Pamphlets as Manuscripts without ecclesiastical approbation,", *HPR*, XXXVI (1935–1936), 970; Marc-Gestermann-Raus, *Institutiones*, I, 825; Cerato, *Censurae*, pp. 148–149; Jombart, *DDC*, III, 157; Beste, *Introductio*, p. 696; Pennacchi, *ASS*, XXX (1897–1898), 163; Coronata, *Institutiones*, IV, 305, who approves this view in the footnote, but seems to require the sale of the work in his commentary on canon 2318, §1.

The following take it for granted that the distribution occurs by sale: Wernz-Vidal, *Ius Canonicum*, IV, pars 2, 133; Creyghton, "Vicariatus Generalis Diocesis Osnabrugensis Decretum 4 martii 1936," *Periodica*, XXVI (1937), 549; Ubach, *Theol. Moral.*, I, 557; Boudinhon, *Nouv. Législ.*, p. 273; Genicot-Salsmans, *Institutiones*, I, 405; Anon., *Periodica*, VII (1914), (8); Augustine, *Commentary*, VIII, 295; Vermeersch-Creusen, *Epitome*, III, 319; Salucci, *Diritto*, II, 30; Pistocchi, *Canoni*, p. 29; Gougnard, *Collationes*, II, 101; Goodwine, *The Jurist*, X (1950), 155–156 (6–7).

[64] Wetmore, *CLP*, IX, 920; Howell, *The Copyright Law*, pp. 59–60.

[65] Wernz-Vidal, *Ius Canonicum*, IV, pars 2, 153; Arregui, *Summarium*, p. 270. Cappello (*De Censuris*, pp. 214–215) and Blat (*Commentarium*, V, 205–206) hold that the publisher must bear the expense of the work.

[66] Whitman, *CLP*, XXV, 1495; Wetmore, *CLP*, IX, 920; Howell, *The Copyright Law*, p. 192; Wittenberg, *Protection*, pp. 11–12.

sor his own. There is no need for an express declaration that the work may not be published. The simple notification of the fact that the work failed to pass censorship is an implicit refusal of the permit to publish. However, the authority may make an express declaration to that effect, if he sees fit to do so.

The license or permit to publish is a formal permission[67] authorizing the writer to perform an action (publication) which would be unlawful if it were done without permission. Hence, the obtaining of the permit to publish is a condition upon the fulfillment of which the action of publication becomes an act done according to the law. The granting of the permit is not a dispensation, nor a conditional release from the law, but a compliance with the law.

When the permit to publish is denied, the condition is not fulfilled, and the general prohibition, that works may not be published if they have not first obtained favorable censorship, is still obligatory. It is not necessary for the authority positively to forbid the work, though he may issue an enjoinder to that effect.

Canons 1385, §2, 1387, 1388, §§1-2, 1389, 1390, 1391, 1392 prescribe that the permission to publish may not be granted until a favorable judgment has been obtained from the censor. In other instances (canon 1386, §1) the authority may give the permission to publish without requiring an examination and favorable judgment on the work. There is some dispute whether canon 1385, §3, demands examination and judgment before permission is granted, though it is generally admitted that it does not.[68]

When the permission to publish must follow upon examination and judgment, there must be an express grant of permission in each instance. If no previous examination is required, then there need not be an express permission for every act of publication, but a general permission may suffice. In this latter case the general permission may be granted expressly or tacitly, and even may be presumed when conditions so warrant. Permission which follows upon an examination and judgment must always be express (explicitly or implicitly), and may never be tacit or presumed.[69]

[67] The Code uses various terms, e.g., "*licentia*" (can. 1385, §§2–3; 1386, §1; 1387–1389; 1394), "*consensus*" (can. 1386, §1), "*attestatio*" (can. 1390), "*approbatio*" (can. 1392), "*approbati*" (can. 1391) and "*potestas edendi*" (can. 1393, §4; 1394, §1). All these terms amount to the same thing, the formal permit to publish. Coronata (*Institutiones*, II, 315) errs in bringing the superior-subject relationship into the definition, for at times the permission may be given by a superior to one who is not his subject, according to the terms of canon 1385, §2.

[68] Fuller explanation and documentation will be given in the commentary on canon 1385, §3, and canon 1386, §1.

[69] Seraphinus a Loiano, *Institutiones*, II, 627; Vermeersch-Creusen, *Epitome*, II, 509; Wernz-Vidal, *Ius Canonicum*, IV, pars 2, 131; Coronata, *Institutiones*, II, 315–316; Cocchi, *Commentarium*, VI, 148; De Meester, *Compendium*, III, pars 1, 256–257.

The authority competent to grant these permissions is outlined in canons 1385-1392. Canon 1385, §2, evinces the general rule, and gives the option of procuring this permission from the proper local ordinary of the author, or the local ordinary of the place of publication, or the local ordinary of the place of printing. Canons 1387-1391 require permission from the Holy See under the conditions specified therein.

Religious are bound by these canons. They are also bound by the special requirements contained in canons 1385, §3, and 1386, §1. Since these canons do not distinguish, the permission may be granted by major superiors of all institutes, clerical or lay. It is not an exercise of jurisdiction.

(2) *The positive approval or condemnation of a work.* Over and above the granting of permission to publish a work, it is possible that the local ordinary wish to recommend a work in a special way, which he can accomplish by means of a positive approval. Similarly, over and above the refusal of permission to publish, the local ordinary may wish to take more stringent measures to curb a work, and this he may do by means of a condemnation. The permission or refusal of permission attaches primarily to the person in reference to the act of publishing. The approval or the condemnation attaches primarily to the work and its contents.

The *Imprimatur* is a negative approval, and means nothing more than that the work has been examined and found to contain nothing contrary to ecclesiastical standards. A positive approval guarantees, or at least testifies to, the merit of the work in question. There are various grades of approval, successively implying a greater degree of authority, e.g., the simple approval (*nihil obstat*), the approval of a text as genuine, the approval of a work as official, the approval of a work as exclusive of all other works, etc.[70]

The refusal of the permit to publish is the simplest form of rejection. It does not necessarily mean that the contents of the work are contrary to faith or morals; it means merely that the work is untimely at the present moment, or that the reproduction of official texts is faulty. Various degrees of condemnation may be found in the various theological treatises.[71] A positive condemnation means that the doctrine is not free from error. It automatically renders that work forbidden. The simple prohibition of a work, however, does not render that work condemned. A work may be forbidden because of flagrant typographical errors in the reproduction of important official documents, despite the fact that none of the errors amount to a doctrinal mistake. It is also possible that the prohibition attaching to a condemned work may be lifted while the condemnation of the work re-

[70] The basis for these distinctions is found in Cicognani, *Canon Law* (tr. O'Hara-Brennan, 2. ed., Reprint, Westminster, Md., The Newman Bookshop, 1948), pp. 132–134.

[71] Quilliet (*DTC*, II, 2103–2113) expresses these very well.

main, e.g., a qualified Catholic may be given permission to read a heretical book for the purpose of refuting it.[72]

C. Functions Performed in the Act of Censorship

The term *censorship* derives from the verb "to censor," which means to examine and judge a work.[73] This double operation is called censorship. In canonical parlance, however, the term has taken on any number of shades of meaning.

(1) In its usual[74] acceptation, censorship means the examination and judgment of a work according to ecclesiastical standards.[75] Hence, the examination and judgment may be:

(a) Either antecedent or subsequent to the date of publication.[76] The chief characteristic of antecedent censorship is preventive, whereas of subsequent censorship the chief characteristic is repressive.

(b) Either obligatory or voluntary, depending on the presence or absence of compulsion in the performance of this function.[77]

---

[72] The distinction between works that are condemned (*damnati*) and works that are forbidden (*prohibiti*) seems to be sufficiently indicated in canon 1396. It is expressly mentioned by Wernz-Vidal, *Ius Canonicum*, IV, pars 2, 127; Beste, *Introductio*, p. 694.

[73] Adapted from FW 194.

[74] The word *usual* is taken here as canonists employ it when commenting on canon 18, i.e., in its less technical and less scientific but more popular usage. Cf. Beste, *Introductio*, p. 80; Jone, *Commentarium in Codicem Iuris Canonici* (Paderborn: F. Schoeningh, 1950), I, 37 (hereafter cited as *Commentarium*).

[75] Just what that examination entails will be treated under canon 1393, §2.

[76] The Code uses the term "*censura*" three times in title XXIII. Twice (in the rubrics before canons 1384 and 1385) the adjective "*praevia*" is added. In canon 1385, §1, the use of the verb "*praecesserit*" makes it evident that antecedent censorship is meant.

In older canonical usage, however, the term "*censura*" was often used to designate subsequent censorship. Cf., e.g., Benedictus XIV, const. "*Sollicita ac provida*," 9 iul. 1753, §§3–4—*Fontes*, n. 426; Pius X, encycl. "*Pascendi*," 8 sept. 1907—*Fontes*, n. 680. All censorship involved in the prohibition of books is subsequent censorship.

In still other documents the term means both antecedent and subsequent censorship. Cf., e.g., Leo XIII, const. "*Officiorum ac munerum*," 27 ian. 1897, Decreta Generalia—*Fontes*, n. 632. Canonists use the term in this wide meaning, e.g., Regatillo, *Institutiones*, II, 111–112; Naz, *Traité de Droit Canonique* (ed. R. Naz, 4 vols., Paris: Letouzey et Ané, 1948–49), III (*Lieux et Temps Sacrés, Culte Divin, Magistère, Bénéfices Ecclésiastiques, Biens Temporels de L'Eglise*, [1948]), 161 (hereafter cited as *Traité*). Putnam, a non-Catholic, uses the term in this meaning throughout *The Censorship of the Church of Rome*.

[77] The term is used to mean obligatory censorship alone by Aichner-Friedle, *Compendium Iuris Ecclesiastici* (12. ed., Brixinae, 1915), p. 543 (hereafter cited as *Compendium*). As far as could be ascertained, the term is not used to designate voluntary censorship alone. It is used quite commonly, however, to designate both voluntary and obligatory censorship, particularly in secular writings, e.g., throughout the symposium on "The Censorship of Books" in *Nineteenth Century and After* (London, 1877—), CV (1929), 433–450, in which the following writers participated: Lord Darling, Havelock Ellis, Stephen Foot, E. M. Forster, Virginia Woolf, Carrol Romer and Viscount Brentford, who added further comments on the same topic in the same periodical, Vol. CVI (1929), 207–211.

(c) Either official or unofficial, depending on the legal authority of the person who performs the function.[78]

(d) Either ecclesiastical or civil, depending upon the character of the official censorship.[79]

(e) Either favorable or unfavorable, depending upon the nature of the contents of the work, and how it squares up with ecclesiastical standards.[80]

The Nihil Obstat

A favorable judgment is called a "*Nihil Obstat.*" These are the opening words of a formula usually printed in works to signify that the examination has resulted in such an issue. The complete formula reads "*Nihil [aliquid] obstat ex parte ecclesiae quominus hoc scriptum imprimatur et edatur.*" The *Nihil Obstat* means that a work may be read without [notable] danger to the faith.

---

[78] The term is used widely for official censorship alone. Other terms for official censorship are: public, legal, judicial, authorized, authoritative, administrative, authentic, etc. Cf. Cappello, *Summa Iuris Canonici in Usum Scholarum Concinnata* (2. ed., 3 vols., Romae: Apud Aedes Universitatis Gregorianae, 1932–1940), II, 420 (hereafter cited as *Summa*); Regatillo, *Institutiones*, II, 110; Blat, *Commentarium*, III, pars 4, 326; Beste, *Introductio*, p. 696; Jone-Adelman, *Moral Theology* (2. ed., Westminster, Md.: The Newman Bookshop, 1946), p. 282; Coronata, *Institutiones*, II, 315.

As far as could be ascertained, the term is not used for unofficial censorship alone. Other terms for unofficial censorship are: private, unauthorized, extrajudicial, doctrinal, scientific, etc.

The correlatives public and private have been used extensively, but in view of the disadvantages connected with the use of the term "public" in this matter the terms official and unofficial are to be preferred.

[79] At the present time ecclesiastical censorship is performed by censors, i.e., officials appointed for that task. In mediaeval times, however, the faculties of universities often exercised this function. Even Popes sent their manuscripts to the universities for scrutiny, e.g., to the University of Paris, or of Cologne. Bouix (*De Curia Romana*, p. 382) held that such censorship was official ecclesiastical censorship. It seems rather that it was semi-official, i.e., it was requested and accepted by the Church, but it did not necessarily imply that it was the official verdict of the Church.

Civil censorship is found in many fields, e.g., in the postal regulations forbidding the dissemination of immoral literature through the mails. In times of war, mail that enters or leaves the country, save certain privileged communications, is subjected to censorship. Cf. Alpert, "Judicial Censorship of Obscene Literature," *Harvard Law Review* (Cambridge, 1887—), LII (1938–1939), 40–76; Keating, "Civil Censorship, Theory and Practice," *The Month* (London, 1864—), CLIX (1932), 239–249.

[80] Canon 1385, §1, presupposes that a favorable judgment has been obtained. When speaking of antecedent censorship, Naz (*Traité*, III, 161) uses the term "censorship" exclusively for that which results in a favorable judgment, whereas when speaking of subsequent censorship he uses the same term exclusively for that which results in an unfavorable judgment. The mere fact that a work is examined, either antecedently or subsequently to its publication, does not predetermine the outcome of that examination. Antecedent censorship may result in an unfavorable judgment, and subsequent censorship may result in a favorable judgment. Some authors use the term "censorship" to include both, e.g., Wernz-Vidal, *Ius Canonicum*, IV, pars 2, 127; Thouvenin, "Index," *DTC*, VII, 1572; Berutti, *Institutiones*, IV, 415.

It is an official declaration that the work contains nothing contrary to faith or morals, that it will not disrupt ecclesiastical discipline, or that it conforms to official texts. It is not to be construed as a positive recommendation or endorsement of the contents of the book.[81] It is a negative approval, which merits credence, because it is given by a competent ecclesiastical authority, and is an act of the authentic teaching magisterium of the Church, and enjoys the presumption of being correct. Still, it does admit of contrary proof.[82]

(2) In a wider meaning, *censorship* is often used to mean not only the various concepts as explained above, but also the action which follows upon the conclusion of the examination and judgment, that is, the grant or refusal of permission to publish.[83] Others use the term *censorship* to include the

---

[81] Augustine, *Commentary*, VI, 433; Sipos, *Enchiridion*, p. 712; Coronata, *Institutiones*, II, 315; Cance, *Le Code de Droit Canonique* (2. ed., 3 vols., Paris, 1929), III, 156 (hereafter cited as *Le Code*); Cappello, *Summa*, II, 420; Vermeersch, *De Prohibitione*, p. 130; Blat, *Commentarium*, III, partes 2–6, 326.

At times, it may be prudent to append a statement to the effect that the views expressed remain the author's own, even though the work bears the *Imprimatur*, though this fact should be self-evident. It appears that such a practice has been adopted for all works in the Archdiocese of New York. Cf. Goodwine, *The Jurist*, X (1950), 183 (34).

The Code still uses the word "*approbatio*," e.g., in canon 1392. This was used consistently in pre-Code law. Cf., e.g., Leo X (in Conc. Lateranen. V) "*Inter Sollicitudines*," 4 maii 1515, §2—*Fontes*, n. 68; Conc. Trident., sess. IV, *de editione et usu sacrorum librorum;* Regulae Indicis: Regula X—*Fontes*, n. 426; Clemens VIII, instr. "*Ad fidei catholicae*," 17 oct. 1595—*Fontes*, n. 426; Leo XIII, const. "*Officiorum ac munerum*," 25 ian. 1897, nn. 30, 35, 37, 44—*Fontes*, n. 632. It is the accepted opinion today, just as it was then, that this approval is nothing more than the negative approval explained above. Cf. Dilgskron, *Anal. Eccl.*, IV (1896), 472; Bouix, *De Curia Romana*, p. 567; De Brabandere, *Compendium*, II, 514; Bonal, *Institutiones Theologiae ad usum Seminariorum* (17. ed., 6 vols., Tolosae, 1891), I, 645–646 (hereafter cited as *Institutiones*); Schneider, *Buechergesetze*, p. 130; Vermeersch, *De Prohibitione*, p. 130; Pruemmer, *Manuale*, p. 484; Cance, *Le Code*, III, 156; Coronata, *Institutiones*, II, 315; Goodwine, *The Jurist*, X (1950), 178 (29), 183 (34).

[82] Cappello, *Summa*, II, 420; Wernz-Vidal, *Ius Canonicum*, IV, pars 2, 130. Vermeersch (*De Prohibitione*, p. 130) states that a bishop may prohibit a work which has received the *Imprimatur* of another bishop, should he deem it necessary to do so. Davis (*Moral and Pastoral Theology* [3. ed., 4 vols., New York: Sheed and Ward, 1938], II, 445 [hereafter cited as *Theology*]) and Beste (*Introductio*, p. 701) cite a number of examples where books had received the *Nihil Obstat* and *Imprimatur* from several bishops, were recommended by prominent ecclesiastics, and were finally condemned by the Holy Office. Cf. *Acta Apostolicae Sedis, Commentarium Officiale* (Romae, 1909—), XIV (1922), 193 (hereafter cited as *AAS*); *AAS*, XXX (1938), 318.

[83] Some authors use the term "censorship" to mean that examination which terminates in the grant of the *Imprimatur*, e.g., Blat, *Commentarium*, III, partes 2–6, 333; Cappello, *Summa*, II, 420–422; Claeys Bouuaert-Simenon, *Manuale*, III, 132–133; Coronata, *Institutiones*, II, 315.

Other authors use the term "censorship" to mean that examination which terminates in the refusal of permission to publish, and still others admit that the term is used for either positive approval or positive condemnation of a work.[84]

(3) In its widest meaning, *censorship* is often used to denote all the concepts given above, together with several other pertinent and relevant concepts, e.g., the obligation of submitting works for examination, the rules for performing the function of a censor, the obligation of obtaining a simple permission to write, even when censorship is not demanded, etc. In brief, the term means the complete supervision of the press with a view to preventing or suppressing abuses thereof, and, as such, includes the whole body of laws governing the publication of any type of writing.[85]

Precensorship

Since the term *censorship of books* is often understood as the examination and condemnation of books against faith or morality,[86] it is necessary to stress the distinction between the censorship performed prior to publication (*censura praevia*) and the censorship exercised after the publication or distribution of a work (*censura repressiva*). For this purpose a new term will be used, namely, *precensorship*, by which is understood the antecedent, obligatory, official, eccesiastical examination and judgment of books, whether that judgment be favorable or unfavorable. In a wider sense, it will include the granting or refusing of permission to publish. In its widest sense, it will also take in the whole body of the Church's norms governing the publication of any kind of writing and the performance of antecedent censorship.

---

eventuality, e.g., Vermeersch-Creusen, *Epitome*, II, 503; Claeys Bouuaert-Simenon, *Manuale*, III, 132; De Meester, *Compendium*, III, pars 1, 256; Wernz-Vidal, *Ius Canonicum*, IV, pars 2, 131; Seraphinus a Loiano, *Institutiones*, II, 627.

[84] Some authors mention that censorship is the cause, and prohibition is the effect, e.g. Augustine, *Commentary*, VI, 454; Pennacchi, *ASS*, XXX (1897–1898), 96; Thouvenin, *DTC*, VII, 1572. Pruemmer, one of the many who uses terms loosely, was the most unfortunate of all in his choice of disparate terms for correlative ideas and also of correlative terms for disparate ideas, when he wrote: "Solet distingui duplex censura librorum: altera praevia, altera repressiva. Censura praevia est examen libri edendi et consistit in eius approbatione vel reprobatione. Censura repressiva est prohibitio libri iam editi."—*Manuale*, p. 483.

[85] Gregory XVI was the first pontiff to use the term "*censura*" in a papal document in this extremely wide meaning, in his const. "*Mirari vos*," 15 aug. 1832—*Fontes*, n. 482. The Code itself uses the term in a very broad sense in the rubric preceding canon 1384. Authors also use the term in this fashion, e.g., Wernz-Vidal, *Ius Canonicum*, IV, pars 2, 131; Gagnon, *La Censure*, p. xii, n. 13 and pp. 60, 69; Hilgers, *CE*, III, 519; Hilgenreiner, "Buecherzensur," *Lexikon fuer Theologie und Kirche* (10 vols., Freiburg im Breisgau: Herder & Co., 1930–1938), II, 605 (hereafter cited as *Lexikon*); De Brabandere, *Compendium*, II, 514.

[86] Cf. FW 194.

CHAPTER VI

PUBLICATIONS FOR WHICH PRECENSORSHIP IS REQUIRED (CANON 1385, §1)

In view of the fact that the Code specifies those works which require precensorship, it will be the purpose of this chapter to determine accurately which works must be submitted, and which works need not be submitted. Only that matter need be submitted which is mentioned in the law. The law mentions two broad classes of material: (1) Works which may be published according to the ordinary rules of precensorship (canon 1385, §1); (2) works which may be published only after an observance of special rules of precensorship (canons 1387-1391). Only the first group will be treated in this dissertation, for the second has already been given sufficient treatment in another dissertation.[1]

Canon 1385, §1, covers the entire field of ordinary precensorship in three simple divisions: (1) Books of Sacred Scripture, and their annotations and commentaries; (2) works on religion and morals; (3) holy pictures. Each grouping will be treated in turn, and a summary will conclude the chapter.

Article I. Books of Sacred Scripture and Their Annotations and Commentaries (Canon 1385, §1, 1°)

The regulation of precensorship for scriptural works is found in three places in the Code: canons 1385, §1, 1°; 1385, §1, 2°; and 1391. The broadest is that found in canon 1385, §1, 2°, which states that all books pertaining to Sacred Scripture must be submitted for precensorship. Canon 1385, §1, 1°, makes explicit mention of the actual texts of Sacred Scripture, as well as annotations and commentaries on the text. Canon 1391 enacts special regulations regarding the preparation of vernacular translations for publication, and partially overlaps with canon 1385, §1, 1° or 2°. For the present it will be sufficient to treat only of canon 1385, §1, 1°, which reads as follows:

> Nisi censura ecclesiastica praecesserit, ne edantur etiam a laicis: 1°. Libri sacrarum Scripturarum vel eorumdem adnotationes et commentaria.

It is easily understandable why the Church should demand precensorship for the publication of the text of Sacred Scripture. The Church relies on the

---

[1] Sonntag, *Censorship of Special Classes of Books*, The Catholic University of America Canon Law Studies, n. 262 (Washington, D. C.: The Catholic University of America Press, 1947).

inspired word as one of the sources of revelation, given for the instruction and edification of men. Incorrect, faulty, or adulterated texts could do much harm, even though the errors be unintentional, and much more so if they be malicious.

Even when the genuine text is had, it is not always easy to discern the genuine meaning of the inspired word. The original languages are a barrier in themselves, for the Scriptures were written in places and circumstances so different from our own. History records the ruin of many who were misled by private and unhappy interpretations. Christ committed to the Church alone the authority to guard the true sense of Sacred Scripture, which it does by demanding the precensorship of the texts and all annotations and commentaries thereof. Each of these, then, will be given individual treatment.

A. Books of Sacred Scripture (*Libri Sacrarum Scripturarum*)

Ordinarily the term "book" means a volume of some bulk (about 160 pages), and connotes a certain unity of content. In scriptural language, however, a book means each and every unit of the entire Bible, i.e., the 45 units of the Old Testament and the 27 units of the New.[2] Some of these units are scarcely two pages in length, e.g., the Third Epistle of St. John, and yet each is called a book. It is evidently the meaning of the law that each and every book of the Bible be submitted for precensorship, even though it be very small. Even parts of books, e.g., pericopes, must be submitted for precensorship if they are published separately.[3]

Canon 1385, §1, 1°, is concerned primarily with the genuine text of the Bible, and, since it makes no distinction, applies equally to all texts, no matter in what language they are produced.[4] The precensorship of texts will consist in the comparing of the text with the original (e.g., the Hebrew, the Aramaic, the Greek) in the case of the publication of the original

---

[2] Conc. Trident., sess. IV, *de canonicis scripturis.*

[3] Augustine, *Commentary,* VI, 434; Coronata, *Institutiones,* II, 315; Cance, *Le Code,* III, 156; Beste, *Introductio,* p. 697; Nevin, "Censorship of Books," *Australasian Catholic Record* (Sidney, 1924—), II (1925), 50 (hereafter cited as *ACR*); Wernz-Vidal, *Ius Canonicum,* IV, pars 2, 133; Genicot-Salsmans, *Institutiones,* II, 560; Blat, *Commentarium,* III, partes 2–6, 331; Vermeersch-Creusen, *Epitome,* III, 319; Goodwine, *The Jurist,* X (1950), 157–158 (8–9).

With reference to the applying of penalties it must be remembered that smallness of matter may excuse a person from incurring the excommunication. This will be treated under the commentary on canon 2318, §2.

[4] Augustine, *Commentary,* VI, 434; Claeys Bouuaert-Simenon, *Manuale,* III, 133; Nevin, *ACR,* II (1925), 50; Wernz-Vidal, *Ius Canonicum,* IV, pars 2, 133; Cance, *Le Code,* III, 156; Coronata, *Institutiones,* II, 316. A few writers exclude modern vernacular translations, claiming that they are treated under canon 1391, e.g., Beste, *Introductio,* p. 697; De Meester, *Compendium,* III, pars 1, 257; Ubach, *Theol. Moral.,* I, 557. Canon 1391 merely gives special regulations to be observed in the precensorship of vernacular translations of the Scriptures.

texts, in as far as that is possible; or in the comparing of it with an ancient text, e.g., the Septuagint, the Itala, the Peshitto, etc.; or in the comparing of it with the Vulgate; or in the comparing of a translation with the version from which it is translated.[5]

In consequence of the fact that the Vulgate text was approved as authentic for the entire Church, and imposed as the official text for public ecclesiastical usage, special rules and regulations were issued for the safeguarding of that text. Some of these detailed regulations concerned the actual text; others, the usage of annotations and variant readings in lateral or lower margins; others, the making of different Latin translations, even for private use, etc. Since these purely disciplinary laws were not mentioned either explicitly or implicitly in the Code, they are no longer to be considered in force, in view of canon 6, 6°.[6]

In 1943, Pope Pius XII issued an important encyclical, "*Divino afflante Spiritu*,"[7] in which he mentions that, although the Vulgate remains the authentic and juridic text for the Church, it need not be regarded as the most critical in each and every instance. In doctrinal matters the authority of the Vulgate is supreme and exclusive, but there is no obligation to adhere to the text of the Vulgate when more critical texts are available.[8]

According to canon 1399, 5°, books of the Bible that are published without an *Imprimatur* are forbidden books. According to canon 2318, §2, an editor and publisher who has such a book printed incurs an excommunication not reserved to anyone.

B. Annotations and Commentaries (*Adnotationes et Commentaria*)

Annotations and commentaries are those works which are composed as an aid in the understanding of the unadorned text of the Bible. These, too, must be submitted for precensorship.

Annotations are brief explanatory comments which accompany and elucidate words, phrases, or passages of the sacred text. The term includes all that was formerly understood by the two words "gloss" and "scholion."

---

[5] Cance, *Le Code*, III, 156; Augustine, *Commentary*, VI, 434; Beste, *Introductio*, p. 697; Coronata, *Institutiones*, II, 316; Claeys Bouuaert-Simenon, *Manuale*, III, 133; De Meester, *Compendium*, III, pars 1, 257; Wernz-Vidal, *Ius Canonicum*, IV, pars 2, 133; Nevin, *ACR*, II (1925), 50.

[6] An excellent account of the pre-Code legislation may be found in Hoepfl, *Beitraege zur Geschichte der Sixto-Klementinischen Vulgata*, Biblische Studien, XVIII Band, 1–3 Heft (Freiburg im Breisgau, 1913), pp. 1–237 (hereafter cited as *Beitraege*). Also cf. Mangenot, "Septante, Version des," *DB*, V, 1640. The accepted critical edition of the Vulgate is *Biblia Sacra Vulgatae Editionis* (ed. Hetzenauer, Oeniponte, 1906). Cf. also the decision of the Pontifical Biblical Commission concerning the printing of variant readings.—*AAS*, XIV (1922), 27.

[7] 30 sept. 1943—*AAS*, XXXV (1943), 297–325.

[8] *AAS*, XXXV (1943), 309–310. Cf. also Gasquet, "Revising the Vulgate," *The Dublin Review* (London, 1836—), CXLIII (1908), 264.

Glosses are brief notes explaining the meaning of rare, obsolete or foreign words in the text, and were usually printed in lateral margins. Scholia are short comments explaining a difficult or obscure passage of the text, e.g., variant readings, verbal difficulties, unknown persons, places or things, grammatical, historical, archeological, geographical, exegetical difficulties, doctrinal problems, dogmatic and ascetical implications, etc. All glosses and scholia are now called annotations.[9]

Annotations have three characteristics which distinguish them from other forms of biblical exegesis: (1) They are explanations distinct from the inspired text itself; (2) annotations are restricted to more difficult parts, and hence there is no intention of forming a complete, connected, or continuous explanation of the text; thus, they differ from commentaries; (3) annotations are brief comments on individual words or passages, and thus differ from exegetical dissertations, which are large commentaries on a small text, or more complete, systematic, and even exhaustive expositions.[10]

Commentaries are longer expositions by which the entire text, or designated portions of the text, are interpreted and explained. These expositions need not be closely systematized or organized, nor need they be complete or exhaustive treatises. It is not required that they comment on the whole Bible, or even on a whole book of the Bible. Ordinarily they comment on the text, advancing from verse to verse, using the text as a framework around which the comments are grouped.[11]

Hence, the words *annotations* and *commentaries* in the present law include all exegetical or expository works, those which were formerly called glosses and scholia, as well as paraphrases, exegetical dissertations and commentaries properly so called. These must be submitted for precensorship in virtue of canon 1385, §1, 1°. Other scriptural works, such as dissertations, biblical novels, etc., will be treated under canon 1385, §1, 2°, with those works which pertain to Sacred Scripture, but are not annotations or commentaries.

---

[9] Grannan, *A General Introduction to the Bible* (4 vols., St. Louis, 1921), IV, 176 (hereafter cited as *Introduction*); Ubaldi, *Introductio in Sacram Scripturam ad usum scholarum Pont. Seminarii Romani et Collegii Urbani de Propaganda Fide* (5. ed., 3 vols., Romae, 1901), III, 371 (hereafter cited as *Introductio*); Hoepfl, *Introductionis in Sacros Utriusque Testamenti Libros Compendium* (4. ed., 3 vols., Romae: Editiones A. Arnodo, 1935–1940), I, 524–525 (hereafter cited as *Compendium*); Augustine, *Commentary*, VI, 434; Ayrinhac, *Admin. Legisl.*, p. 278; Beste, *Introductio*, p. 698; Coronata, *Institutiones*, II, 316.

[10] Grannan, *Introduction*, IV, 172, 174, 179–180; Ubaldi, *Introductio*, III, 358, 370.

[11] Vigouroux, "Commentaires de l'Ecriture," *DB*, II, 877; Augustine, *Commentary*, VI, 435; Beste, *Introductio*, p. 697; Coronata, *Institutiones*, II, 311, 316; Nevin, *ACR*, II (1925), 50; Schneider, *Buechergesetze*, p. 176; De Meester, *Compendium*, III, pars 1, 315; Boudinhon, *Nouv. Législ.*, p. 320; Gagnon, *La Censure*, p. 97.

It is quite immaterial if the annotations and commentaries are published with the sacred text, or without it. The latter is sometimes done. The word *vel* in the text of the canon means that they are to be submitted, even if they are published alone. It is also immaterial how long or extensive, or how short, the annotations and commentaries are. The size of the publication is not considered. It is also to be noted that not only the first editions, but also new editions, translations, etc., by the same author or by another, are subject to the law of precensorship according to the norm of canon 1392.[12]

Annotations and commentaries published without having been precensored automatically fall into the class of forbidden books, as is enacted in canon 1399, 5°. An author or publisher who prints such works automatically incurs an excommunication not reserved to anyone, according to the terms of canon 2318, §2.[13]

Article II. Works on Religion and Morals (Canon 1385, §1, 2°)

The second large class of works to be submitted for precensorship is listed here under the general heading of works on religion and morals (canon 1385, §1, 2°). It is the broadest of the three classes, and in itself comprises three subdivisions. It will be seen that, for various reasons, this class of works meets with the greatest divergence of opinion among canonists. The text of the law is as follows:

> 1385, §1: Nisi censura ecclesiastica praecesserit, ne edantur . . . 2° Libri qui divinas Scripturas, sacram theologiam, historiam ecclesiasticam, ius canonicum, theologiam naturalem, ethicen aliasve huiusmodi religiosas ac morales disciplinas spectant; libri ac libelli precum, devotionis vel doctrinae institutionisque religiosae, moralis, asceticae, mysticae aliique huiusmodi, quamvis ad fovendam pietatem conducere videantur; ac generaliter scripta in quibus aliquid sit quod religionis ac morum honestatis peculiariter intersit.

The very text indicates the three groups: A. Books on the religious and moral branches of knowledge; B. books and booklets on the more immediately practical aspects of religion; C. writings that contain anything of special interest to religion and morals. The matter of each group will be treated in turn. This will be followed by a special consideration: D. the meaning of "book" in canon 1385, §1, 2°, and E. the problem of periodicals.

[12] Blat, *Commentarium*, III, partes 2–6, 331; Pistocchi, *Canoni*, p. 40; Salucci, *Diritto*, II, 36; Augustine, *Commentary*, VI, 435; Coronata, *Institutiones*, II, 316; Ayrinhac, *Admin. Legisl.*, p. 278; Nevin, *ACR*, II (1925), 50; De Meester, *Compendium*, III, pars 1, 315; Vermeersch-Creusen, *Epitome*, III, 319; Cerato, *Censurae*, p. 71.

[13] Beste, *Introductio*, pp. 960–961; Cappello, *De Censuris*, p. 347; Cerato, *Censurae*, p. 71; Cocchi, *Commentarium*, VIII, 232; Coronata, *Institutiones*, IV, 311; De Meester, *Compendium*, III, pars 1, 315; Vermeersch-Creusen, *Epitome*, III, 319; Woywod, *A Practical Commentary on the Code of Canon Law* (3. ed., 2 vols., New York, 1929), II, 470 (hereafter cited as *Commentary*).

A. Books on the Religious and Moral Branches of Knowledge

In general, this class includes all books on the Church and its mission here on this earth, whether these are considered in their more theoretical or more practical aspects. The text of the law indicates the following divisions: (1) Sacred Scripture; (2) Sacred Theology; (3) Church History; (4) Canon Law; (5) Natural theology and ethics; (6) Other religious and moral branches of knowledge. The first four are properly called theological branches, the next two are properly called philosophical branches, while the last is all-inclusive.

(1) Books Pertaining to Sacred Scripture

The first field is that of Sacred Scripture, which includes the following subdivisions:

(a) Editions of the text of Sacred Scripture, whether it be the original text, one of the ancient versions, or any recent or modern text or translation. It is quite immaterial whether the whole text, or only a part of it, be reproduced.[14]

(b) Books of biblical exegesis, i.e., expositions, explanations, paraphrases, annotations, commentaries, dissertations, homilies, etc. It is quite immaterial whether these works are strictly scientific and historical, or more popular, ascetical or mystical in design.[15]

(c) Books of biblical introduction, which furnish information useful and necessary for a proper understanding of the Scriptures, i.e., discussion and proofs for the human and divine origin of the Bible, its history, the integrity of the entire Bible or any book thereof, the true sense of the text, etc.

---

[14] In spite of the fact that this class receives individual mention in canon 1385, §1, 1°, it is also included under works that pertain to Sacred Scripture. The historical development of each section of these laws shows that they overlap. Cf. Pennacchi, *ASS*, XXX (1897–1898), 303; Schneider, *Buechergesetze*, p. 144; Hurley, *A Commentary on the Present Index Legislation* (Dublin, 1907, and New York, 1908), p. 208 (hereafter cited as *Commentary*); Anon., *L'Ami*, LII (1935), 88–89; Coronata, *Institutiones*, II, 316; Goodwine, *The Jurist*, X (1950), 158–159 (9–10).

[15] Pennacchi, *ASS*, XXX (1897–1898), 303; Schneider, *Buechergesetze*, p. 144; Hurley, *Commentary*, p. 208; Ayrinhac, *Admin. Legisl.*, p. 278; Blat, *Commentarium*, III, partes 2–6, 332; Beste, *Introductio*, p. 698; Gagnon, *La Censure*, p. 98; Coronata, *Institutiones*, II, 316; Cance, *Le Code*, III, 157; Boudinhon, *Nouv. Legisl.*, p. 275; *L'Ami*, LII (1935), 89. The Holy Office has condemned the proposition that "the ecclesiastical law prescribing precensorship for books pertaining to Scripture does not apply to those who devote themselves to the scientific criticism or the scientific exegesis of the books of the Old and the New Testament."—S.C.S.Off., decr., 4 iul. 1907—*Fontes*, n. 1283.

Augustine (*Commentary*, VI, 435) ruled out exegetical works in this section for the reason that he considered them already included under canon 1385, §1, 1°.

Biblical introduction also furnishes answers to difficulties and objections by having recourse to its auxilliary sciences, e.g., to biblical philology, geography, history, archeology, etc.[16]

(d) Books of biblical criticism, whether *textual*, i.e., those that judge the text, point out or detect errors according to historical norms, reproduce the original as far as possible, or *higher criticism*, i.e., determining by literary and historical methods the human credibility and human authority of the books, and whether they are genuine or not. This would include those works which discuss the Bible, as well as those which attempt to formulate principles of biblical criticism.[17]

(e) Books on all other biblical studies, treatises, works, etc., whose subject-matter is the Bible or any part of it, e.g., bible histories, history of biblical revelation, biblical theology, history of the religion of Israel, biblical archeology, biblical biography, polemical works on scriptural problems, dictionaries and encyclopedias of the Bible, etc. Works of this last class are included only if they have reference to the Bible, and not if they are merely profane archeology, history, the study of Greek, Hebrew, etc.[18]

(2) Books Pertaining to Sacred Theology

The second field is that of Sacred Theology, perhaps the broadest of all the classes in this section of the canon. However, the field is limited to sacred theology, for natural theology is given special mention later on. As such, this field would cover:

(a) Books on fundamental and dogmatic theology, i.e., the more theoretic aspects of religion.[19]

---

[16] Hurley, *Commentary*, p. 208; Ayrinhac, *Admin. Legisl.*, p. 278; Augustine, *Commentary*, VI, 435; Beste, *Introductio*, p. 698; Blat, *Commentarium*, III, partes 2–6, 332; Coronata, *Institutiones*, II, 316; Boudinhon, *Nouv. Législ.*, p. 275; Cance, *Le Code*, III, 157; *L'Ami*, LII (1935), 88; Hoepfl, *Compendium*, I, 2; Cornely-Knabenbauer, *Historia et Critica Introductio in V.T. Libros Sacros*, Cursus Scripturae Sacrae Pars Prior (2. ed., 3 vols. in 4., Parisiis, 1894–1897), I, 11–14; Grannan, *Introduction*, I, xviii; Mangenot, *DB*, III, 914; Gagnon, *La Censure*, p. 98.

[17] Ayrinhac, *Admin. Legisl.*, p. 279; Augustine, *Commentary*, VI, 435; Beste, *Introductio*, p. 698; Hurley, *Commentary*, p. 208; Hoepfl, "Critique Biblique," *DBS*, II, 175–177; Grannan, *Introduction*, II, 5, 52.

[18] Boudinhon, *Nouv. Législ.*, p. 275; Cance, *Le Code*, III, 157; *L'Ami*, LII (1935), 88; Gagnon, *La Censure*, p. 98.

[19] Lercher, *Institutiones*, II, v, xviii; Van Noort, *Tractatus*, pp. xi-xii; Augustine, *Commentary*, VI, 435; Ayrinhac, *Admin. Legisl.*, p. 279; Blat, *Commentarium*, III, partes 2–6, 332; Coronata, *Institutiones*, II, 316; Boudinhon, *Nouv. Législ.*, p. 275; Hurley, *Commentary*, p. 208; Schneider, *Buechergesetze*, p. 144; Pennacchi, *ASS*, XXX (1897–1898), 503; Nevin, *ACR*, II (1925), 51; *L'Ami*, LII (1935), 88–89; Gagnon, *La Censure*, p. 99.

(b) Books on moral theology, i.e., the more immediately practical aspects of religion. Ethics is given special mention later.[20]

(c) Books on ascetical and mystical theology, i.e., those branches which deal with the perfection of human activity in relation to man's final end.[21]

(d) Books on pastoral theology, i.e., all such works as deal with the care of souls. Pastoral care is to be taken in its broadest sense, e.g., to include confessional and marriage guidance, catechetics, sacred eloquence, liturgics, etc.[22]

(3) Books Pertaining to Ecclesiastical History

The third field covers the entire branch of ecclesiastical history. All ecclesiastical histories are included, whether they are in the form of simple chronicles or annals, or, more precisely, in the form of methodical narratives which are given proper interpretation. It is immaterial whether the books treat the history of the entire Church, functioning from century to century, over the entire world, or whether they treat more particular phases of that history, e.g., the ecclesiastical history of a single country, province, diocese, parish, etc. It would also include the history of religious orders, monasteries, convents, etc.

Biographies, as such, are not ecclesiastical history in the strict sense of the word. However, some biographies do pertain to ecclesiastical history because of the career and influence of the person involved in the life of the Church. It is quite immaterial whether that influence was good or bad. Hence, it is not only the lives of saints who leave their mark in ecclesiastical

---

[20] Scheeben, *Handbuch der katholischen Dogmatik* (4 vols., Freiburg im Breisgau, 1873–1897), I, 4 (hereafter cited as *Handbuch*); Lercher, *Institutiones*, II, xvii; Van Noort, *Tractatus*, p. xii; Tanquerey, *Synopsis Theologiae Moralis et Pastoralis* (4. ed., 3 vols., Neo-Eboraci, 1910–1912), I, xxii–xxiii (hereafter cited as *Synopsis*); Vermeersch, *Theologiae Moralis Principia, Responsa, Consilia* (4. ed., 4 vols., Romae: Apud Aedes Universitatis Gregorianae, 1944–1948), I, 1–9 (hereafter cited as *Theol. Moral.*); Merkelbach, *Summa Theologiae Moralis* (3 vols., Parisiis: Desclée, De Brouwer, et Soc., 1931–1936), I, 11–12 (hereafter cited as *Summa*); Seraphinus a Loiano, *Institutiones*, II, 1–4; Noldin-Schmitt, *Summa*, I, 2–5; Genicot-Salsmans, *Institutiones*, I, 4; Ubach, *Theol. Moral.*, I, 1–3; Gagnon, *La Censure*, p. 99.

[21] Tanquerey, *The Spiritual Life*, A Treatise on Ascetical and Mystical Theology (2. ed., Tournai: Soc. of St. John the Evangelist, Desclée & Co., 1932), pp. ix-xvi, 2–6; Farges, *The Ordinary Ways of the Spiritual Life* (New York, 1927), pp. 2–14; Poulain, *The Graces of Interior Prayer*, a Treatise on Mystical Theology (London, 1910), pp. 1–6; Gagnon, *La Censure*, p. 99.

[22] Schneider (*Buechergesetze*, p. 144) appears to be the only canonist who expressly includes pastoral theology under the term sacred theology in this canon. Even though it might not be sacred theology in its strictest sense, it certainly is one of the moral or religious branches of knowledge. Matters which pertain to this branch are discussed in Scheeben, *Handbuch*, I, 4; Lercher, *Institutiones*, II, xvii; Genicot-Salsmans, *Institutiones*, I, 7; Ubach, *Theol. Moral.* I, 2; Seraphinus a Loiano, *Institutiones*, I, 4; Merkelbach, *Summa*, I, 12; Vermeersch, *Theol. Moral.*, I, 4–6; Pruemmer, *Manuale Theologiae Moralis*, (2–3. ed., 3 vols., Friburgi Brisgoviae,

history, but the lives of heresiarchs and sinners as well. However, once a person has broken with the Church, the independent history of the heretic or heretical sect is no longer part of true ecclesiastical history of the Catholic Church.

Secular events do not come under the realm of ecclesiastical history unless they bear upon the Church and influence its progress; otherwise they are merely profane history. It is not required that the ecclesiastical history intend to point the way to a better life. If it merely intends to inform, that is sufficient. These works may be popular or scientific.[23]

(4) Books Pertaining to Canon Law

The fourth field is that of canon law, which is to be taken in its broadest sense. Hence it includes not only human ecclesiastical law, but also divine law, which is not enacted but approved by the Church. It means not only the general law for the entire Church, but also particular law for any group within the universal Church.[24]

1923), I, 4 (hereafter cited as *Theol. Moral.*); Noldin-Schmitt, *Summa*, I, 4–5; Gatterer, *Katechetik oder Anleitung zur Kinderseelsorge* (4. ed., Innsbruck: F. Rauch, 1931), pp. 4–6; Boudinhon, *Nouv. Législ.*, p. 275; Wintersig, "Pastoralliturgik," *Jahrbuch fuer Liturgiewissenschaft* (Muenster in Westf., 1921—), IV (1924), 153–167 (hereafter cited as *JLW*); Schubert, "Die Zukunft der Pastoraltheologie," *Theologie und Glaube* (Paderborn, 1909—), XVI (1924), 119–129 (hereafter cited as *TuG*); Schubert, "Neubau der Liturgik," *TuG*, XIX (1927), 238–254.

[23] Alzog, *History of the Church* (tr. by F.J. Pabisch-T.S. Byrne, 3 vols., New York, [1912]), I, 5–11: Scheeben, *Handbuch*, I, 4; Schneider, *Buechergesetze*, pp. 144–145; Boudinhon, *Nouv. Législ.*, p. 275; Blat, *Commentarium*, III, partes 2–6, 332; *L'Ami*, LII (1935), 88–89; Pennacchi, *ASS*, XXX (1897–1898), 503; Coronata, *Institutiones*, II, 316; Augustine, *Commentary*, VI, 435–436; Nevin, *ACR*, II (1925), 51; Hurley, *Commentary*, p. 209; Gagnon, *La Censure*, pp. 99–100; Vermeersch, *De Prohibitione*, p. 142.

[24] For a comparison of the various meanings attached to the terms "ecclesiastical law," "canon law," "public law," etc., cf. Heiner, *Katholisches Kirchenrecht* (2. ed., 2 vols., Paderborn, 1897), I, 12–13; Ottaviani, *Institutiones*, I, 4–13; Lijdsman, *Introductio*, I, 13–17; Van Hove, *Prolegomena*, pp. 30–34; Vermeersch-Creusen, *Epitome*, I, 16–18; Cicognani-Staffa, *Commentarium ad librum primum Codicis iuris canonici* (2. ed., 2 vols., Romae: Ex Officina Typographica Romana "Buona Stampa," 1939; vol. II, Romae: Apud Custodiam Librariam Pontificii Instituti Utriusque Iuris, 1942), I, 45–47; Bargilliat, *Praelectiones Juris Canonici* (37. ed., 2 vols., Parisiis, 1923–1924), I, 3–4 (hereafter cited as *Praelectiones*); Michiels, *Normae Generales Iuris Canonici* (2 vols., Lublin, 1929), I, 9–11 (hereafter cited as *Normae*); Blat, *Commentarium*, I, 15; Saegmueller, *Lehrbuch des katholischen Kirchenrechts* (3. ed., 2 vols., Freiburg im Breisgau, 1914), I, 10 (hereafter cited as *Lehrbuch*); Wernz-Vidal, *Ius Canonicum*, I, 69–77; Beste, *Introductio*, pp. 9–10; Cappello, *Summa*, I, 4, 32; Maroto; *Institutiones Iuris Canonici* (2 vols., Romae-Madrid, Vol. I, 3. ed., 1921; Vol. II, 1919), I, 33–34 (hereafter cited as *Institutiones*); Goyeneche, *Iuris Canonici Summa Principia* (2 vols., Roma: Tip. Pol. "Cuore di Maria," Vol. I, Pro Manuscripto; Vol. II, 1938), I, 12 (hereafter cited as *Principia*); Soglia, *Institutiones Juris Publici Ecclesiastici* (5. ed., Paris [1853]), pp. 2–9 (hereafter cited as *Institutiones*); De Brabandere, *Compendium*, I, 3–4; Craisson, *Manuale Totius Iuris*

Hence canon law would include the following:

(a) Public ecclesiastical law, both divine and human;[25]

(b) Current ecclesiastical law of the Church, universal or particular, written or unwritten, enacted or accepted by competent authority;[26]

(c) Juridical norms which are not laws properly so-called, e.g. statutes, decrees, precepts, rescripts, privileges, dispensations, judicial sentences, etc.;[27]

(d) History of canon law, its institutes, sources, development and influence on modern law;[28]

(e) History of the science of canon law, that is, history of its schools, of the methods of teaching the subject; and the study of the more important writings on canon law.

Therefore, not only all writings on ecclesiastical law, whether scientific or popular, but also all editions of the text of ecclesiastical laws and of other enactments of ecclesiastical authority, whether universal or particular, past or present, must be submitted for precensorship, e.g., editions of the papal encyclicals, papal bulls and other papal documents, or collections thereof; collections of the decisions of the Pontifical Commission for Interpreting the Code; collections or editions of the decrees, decisions and instructions of the Sacred Congregations; collections or editions of the deci-

---

Canonici (7. ed., 4 vols., Paris, 1885), I, 3–4; De Meester, *Compendium*, I, 3; Santi-Leitner, *Praelectiones Juris Canonici* (4. ed., 5 vols. in 3, Neo Eboraci, 1904–1905), I, 1 (hereafter cited as *Praelectiones*); Pennacchi, *ASS*, XXX (1897–1898), 503; Claeys Bouuaert-Simenon, *Manuale*, I, 3–5; Laemmer, *Institutionen des katholischen Kirchenrechts* (Freiburg im Breisgau, 1886), p. 6; Augustine, *Commentary*, I, 2, 4; Aichner-Friedle, *Compendium*, pp. 7–9; Pruemmer, *Manuale*, p. 2; Sipos, *Enchiridion*, p. 6; Ayrinhac, *General Legislation in the New Code of Canon Law* (New York, 1923), p. 21; Chelodi-Ciprotti, *Jus Canonicum de Personis* (3. ed., Vicenza: Società Anonima Tipografica, 1942), p. 13 (hereafter cited as *De Personis*); Solieri, *Iuris Publici Ecclesiastici Elementa* (Romae, 1900), pp. 25–29 (hereafter cited as *Elementa*); Cavagnis, *Institutiones*, I, n. 20; Vecchiotti, *Institutiones Canonicae* (16. ed., 3 vols., Augustae Taurinorum, 1876), I, 2, 12–16 (hereafter cited as *Institutiones*); Boudinhon, *Nouv. Législ.*, p. 276.

[25] Blat, *Commentarium*, III, partes 2–6, 332; Boudinhon, *Nouv. Législ.*, p. 276; Gagnon, *La Censure*, p. 100.

[26] Schneider, *Buechergesetze*, p. 145; Boudinhon, *Nouv. Législ.*, p. 276; Pennacchi, *ASS*, XXX (1897–1898), 503; Gagnon, *La Censure*, p. 100. Liturgical law, that is, the regulation of public worship and of the liturgy is truly a part of canon law.—Van Hove, *Prolegomena*, p. 25; Boudinhon, *Nouv. Législ.*, p. 276; *L'Ami*, LII (1935), 88–89. The greater part of liturgical law, however, pertains to a special branch, called "liturgy."—Claeys Bouuaert-Simenon, *Manuale*, I, 4, note (2).

[27] Michiels, *Normae*, I, 11; Goyeneche, *Principia*, I, 12; Maroto, *Institutiones*, I, 3; Cicognani, *Ius Canonicum primo studii anno in usum auditorum excerpta* (Romae: Ex Officina Typographica Ausonia, 1925), p. 47; Van Hove, *Prolegomena*, pp. 24–25.

[28] Schneider, *Buechergesetze*, p. 145; Boudinhon, *Nouv. Législ.*, p. 276; *L'Ami*, LII (1935), 88–89; Blat, *Commentarium*, III, partes 2–6, 332; Gagnon, *La Censure*, p. 100.

sions of Sacred Roman Rota; editions of the laws and statutes enacted at ecumenical councils, provincial councils, diocesan synods, or the like; editions of the approved constitutions of religious institutes; collections of privileges and indults, etc. Canon 1385, §1, 2°, contains the general rule, while special norms for certain matters are given in canons 1387-1390.[28a] Permission of the Holy See is required for the publication of reprints or translations of the Code of Canon Law.[29]

(5) Books Pertaining to Natural Theology and Ethics

The fifth field departs from the field of theology proper and takes up two branches from the realm of philosophy, natural theology (theodicy) and ethics. These are of the utmost importance for theology, because they show the substratum of reason in conjunction with the faith.

Theodicy is the branch which treats of God from the viewpoint of reason unaided by faith. Ethics is the branch which treats of the morality of human conduct as determined by human reason, unaided by faith or revelation. This includes general ethics and also special ethics, e.g., sociology, human relations, etc. It is duly to be remembered, however, that many Catholic philosophers publish incomplete texts in ethics because they prefer to have certain ethical problems treated from the theological viewpoint.[30]

The fact that the law selects these two philosophical branches and omits mention of the others allows us to conclude that the others, in themselves, are not matter for precensorship. Thus, logic, epistemology, ontology, psychology and cosmology are not included. However, certain problems in these fields, e.g., the problem of the soul in psychology, or the problem of the origin of matter in cosmology, are points of particular interest to religion, and for that reason may be subject to precensorship, as will be seen later.[31]

(6) Books Pertaining to Other Religious and Moral Branches of Knowledge

The sixth field is expressed by an all-inclusive phrase, which indicates that the former were examples of works which pertain to religion and

[28a] E.g., for collections of indulgences, for the republication of collections of decrees of the Sacred Congregations, and for reprints of liturgical books. Cf. Sonntag, *Censorship of Special Classes of Books*, pp. 1–97.

[29] The reverse side of the title page of editions of the Code contains the following official notice: "*Nemini liceat sine venia Sanctae Sedis hunc Codicem denuo imprimere aut in aliam linguam vertere.*"

[30] Donat, *Summa Philosophiae Christianae* (3. ed., 8 vols., Oeniponte, 1923–1928), VI (*Theodicea*), i; VII (*Ethica Generalis*), 1; VIII (*Ethica Specialis*), iv–viii; Bittle, *Man and Morals: Ethics* (Milwaukee, Bruce Publ. Co., [1950]), pp. 3–7, 309–313; Augustine, *Commentary*, VI, 436; Schneider, *Buechergesetze*, p. 145; Brosnahan, *Prolegomena to Ethics* (New York: Fordham University Press, 1941), p. 19; Cronin, *The Science of Ethics* (2. ed., 2 vols., New York, 1929–1930), I, 1.

[31] Pennacchi, *ASS*, XXX (1897–1898), 504.

morals. All other branches of knowledge are included, provided they deal with religion and morals, i.e., those whose material and formal object has ultimate reference to God. Examples are patrology, liturgy, sacred music, etc.[32]

The distinction between religion and morals is not as clear-cut as might be desired. They may be compared from various aspects. Understood in a very broad sense, religion embraces all of man's relations, direct and indirect, to God. It includes all truths, principles, and practices which have reference to God, to himself, and to his neighbor, both in theory and in practice, objectively and subjectively. Morals, taken as the principles and practice of right conduct, is a part of religion in that sense.[33] Some make the distinction that religion refers primarily to doctrine, while morals refers primarily to practice.[34]

When considered in their proper sense, religion and morals are not mutually exclusive. Religion comprises everything that enters the ambit of man's relation to God, and God's dealing with man, known from reason and revelation. Morals embraces the principles of action, and also the acts themselves, from the viewpoint of moral right and wrong, as known from

---

32 Some of the examples cited by canonists are not religious or moral branches of knowledge, but works of particular interest to religion or morals, e.g., the works on spiritism, hypnotism, astrology, etc. Other examples would fit into the classifications given above, e.g., lives of the servants of God, works on miracles, on the social sciences, etc. However, all agree that books on the other branches are meant, e.g., De Meester, *Compendium*, III, pars 1, 257; Beste, *Introductio*, p. 697–698; Vermeersch, *De Prohibitione*, p. 142; Laurentius, *Institutiones Iuris Ecclesiastici* (3. ed., Friburgi im Breisgau, 1914), p. 432 (hereafter cited as *Institutiones*); Cocchi, *Commentarium*, VI, 150; Augustine, *Commentary*, VI, 436; Cappello, *Summa*, II, 420; Genicot-Salsmans, *Institutiones*, I, 385; Ubach, *Theol. Moral.*, I, 557; Ayrinhac, *Admin. Legisl.*, p. 279; Piat, *NRT*, XXXII (1900), 468; Pennacchi, *ASS*, XXX (1897–1898), 504; Lehmkuhl, *Theologia Moralis*, II, 818; Goodwine, *The Jurist*, X (1950), 159 (10): Gagnon, *La Censure*, p. 101–102.

33 S. Thomas Aquinas, *Summa Theologica*, IIa, IIae, q. 81, art. 1—*Opera Omnia* (ed. Leonina, 16 vols., Romae, 1882–1948), IX, 177–178; Lercher, *Institutiones*, I, 2–7; Van Noort, *Tractatus de vera religione* (4. ed., Hilversum, 1923), p. 1 (hereafter cited as *De Vera Religione*); Perrone, *Praelectiones Theologicae de Virtute Religionis deque Vitiis Oppositis* (Ratisbonae, 1866), pp. 1–2; Wernz-Vidal, *Ius Canonicum*, III, 6, n. (7), 41-42; Schaefer, *De Religiosis ad normam Codicis Iuris Canonici* (4. ed., Roma: Typis Polyglottis Vaticanis, 1947), nn. 151–156 (hereafter cited as *De Religiosis*); Seraphinus a Loiano, *Institutiones*, I, 91; Merkelbach, *Summa*, I, 104–105; Noldin-Schmitt, *Summa*, I, 73; Frins, *De Actibus Humanis* (3 vols., Friburgi Brisgoviae, 1897–1911), II, 3–53, 514–544; Pruemmer, *Theol. Moral.*, I, 69; Brunsmann-Preuss, *A Handbook of Fundamental Theology* (4 vols., St. Louis: B. Herder Book Co., 1928–1932), I, 83–84; Vermeersch, *De Prohibitione*, p. 64; Claeys Bouuaert-Simenon, *Manuale*, III, 142; De Meester, *Compendium*, III, pars 1, 286.

34 Canon 1491, §2, seems to hint at such a distinction: "Episcopali vigilantiae subsunt quod spectat ad religionis magisteria, honestatem morum . . ."

reason and revelation. Taken together, they seem to cover all works, whether one considers religion objectively or subjectively.[35]

B. Books and Booklets Pertaining More Immediately to the Practice of Religion

The second large group of works mentioned in the canon is that which deals more directly with the practic of religion, i.e., those works which foster piety and mould religious conduct. The text reads:

> Nisi censura ecclesiastica praecesserit, ne edantur . . . libri ac libelli precum, devotionis vel doctrinae institutionisque religiosae, moralis, asceticae, mysticae aliique huiusmodi, quamvis ad fovendam pietatem conducere videantur . . .

The text speaks of books and booklets: (1) of prayers; (2) of devotion; (3) of religious, moral, ascetical and mystical doctrine and instruction; (4) of other considerations of a like character. Each will be taken in turn.

(1) Books and Booklets of Prayers

Books and booklets of prayers are those which contain prepared formulas of prayers addressed to God, the Father, Son and Holy Spirit, to the Blessed Virgin Mary, to the angels and saints. It is quite immaterial whether these be for private or for public (extra-liturgical) use. This group would include vernacular translations of the missal, breviary, ritual and other liturgical books, whether they have the Latin text accompanying them or not. It also includes hymns, published conjointly with prayers or alone; hymns are prayers in verse form.[36]

(2) Books and Booklets of Devotion

Books and booklets of devotion is a class which is rather difficult to define, but includes many works which are ordinarily called prayerbooks. Devotion must be taken in its broad sense, so as to include general and par-

[35] Van Noort, *Tractatus*, pp. 125–128; Seraphinus a Loiano, *Institutiones*, II, 8–9; Billot. *De Virtutibus Infusis Commentarius in Secundam Partem S. Thomae* (4. ed., Romae, 1928), p, 219, n. (2); Wernz-Vidal, *Ius Canonicum*, IV, pars 2, 164, n. (94); Boudinhon, *Nouv. Législ.* p. 18; Vermeersch, *De Prohibitione*, p. 142; Pennacchi, *ASS*, XXX (1897–1898), 504; Claeys Bouuaert-Simenon, *Manuale*, III, 134.

[36] Pennacchi, *ASS*, XXX (1897–1898), 343; Hurley, *Commentary*, p. 145; Vermeersch, *De Prohibitione*, pp. 97–98, 105; Anon., *L'Ami*, XXVI (1904), 184; Van Coillie, *Commentarius*, p. 63; Wernz, *Ius Decretalium*, III, 119, n. (74); Wernz-Vidal, *Ius Canonicum*, IV, pars 2, 134; Vermeersch-Creusen, *Epitome*, II, 504; *Theologia Mechliniensis, Tractatus de Censuris, Casibus Reservatis, Irregularitatibus et Libris Prohibitis ad usum Alumnorum Seminarii Archiepiscopalis Mechliniensis* (3. ed., Mechliniae, 1906), p. 216 (hereafter cited as *Theol. Mechlin.*); Hollweck, *Buecherverbot*, p. 52; Ayrinhac, *Admin. Legisl.*, p. 279; Beste, *Introductio*, pp. 697–698; Genicot-Salsmans, *Institutiones*, I, 385; Ubach, *Theol. Moral.*, I, 557; De Meester, *Compendium*, III, pars 1, 258; Goodwine, *The Jurist*, X (1950), 159–160 (10–11); Gagnon, *La Censure*, p. 102.

ticular devotion, substantial and accidental. Under such headings would come: (a) works which foster a prompt and ready will to do all that pertains to the service of God, whether that be in practicing virtue in general, or some particular virtue; (b) works which move the will to practice certain particular exercises of worship or devotion; (c) works which influence the will to be devoted to certain particular objects, e.g. Our Lord in the Eucharist, the Sacred Heart, Our Lady, etc.; (d) works which foster spiritual joy and consolation, and even sensible consolation to some extent; (e) works which cultivate attention of mind and fervor of heart at prayer or in the performance of acts of worship. In all these works the primary appeal is toward the will, though not excluding the appeal to the intellect.

In contrast, there is another class of works which appeals primarily to the intellect, though not exclusively so. This class would include spiritual reading books, most meditation books, spiritual conferences, lives of the saints, the Imitation of Christ, etc., and those books which present or advocate a particular devotion, e.g. the month of Mary, the devotion to the Eucharistic Heart of Jesus, etc.[37]

(3) Books and Booklets of Religious, Moral, Ascetical and Mystical Doctrine and Instruction

The third class comprises all those works which are directed primarily to the intellect, but whose nature (in itself, or by design) is doctrinal and instructional.[38] The Code mentions four different groups, distinguished by reason of their objects:

(a) Books and booklets of *religious* doctrine and instruction. This group would comprise works explanatory of religious truths that are necessary or useful for salvation, e.g., catechisms, explanations of the liturgy, of the sacraments, of the mass, of the commandments, bible histories, collections of sermons, etc. All such works, whether intended for children or adults, are included, whether they are intended to accompany oral explanation or not.[39]

(b) Books and booklets of *moral* doctrine and instruction. This group comprises all those works which treat of or explain the principles of morality, right and wrong, the morality of human acts, obligations binding in

[37] Merkelbach, *Summa*, II, 683–685; Cathrein, "Die Andacht," *Zeitschrift fuer Aszese und Mystik* (Innsbruck, 1926—), VI (1931), 233–235; Suarez, *Opera Omnia*, XIV, 139–155; Perrone, *Praelectiones*, pp. 14–18; Pruemmer, *Theol. Moral.*, II, 271–274; Schneider, *Buechergesetze*, p. 93; Vermeersch, *De Prohibitione*, p. 105; Beste, *Introductio*, p. 698; De Meester, *Compendium*, III, pars 1, 258; *L'Ami*, XXVI (1904), 186; *Theol. Mechlin.*, p. 216.

[38] Hurley, *Commentary*, p. 145; Goodwine, *The Jurist*, X (1950), 159–160 (10–11).

[39] Boudinhon, *Nouv. Législ.*, p. 183; Pennacchi, *ASS*, XXX (1897–1898), 343; Hurley *Commentary*, p. 146; Augustine, *Commentary*, VI, 436; Gagnon, *La Censure*, p. 102.

conscience, etc. It would cover works on the duties of children, of parents, of teachers, of professional men, of religious, of the clergy, of the laity, etc.[40]

(c) Books and booklets of *ascetical* doctrine and instruction. This group comprises all those works which explain the meaning of christian perfection and the means to attain it, the obstacles that will be met, the particular virtues to be practiced, the vices to be eradicated, etc.[41]

(d) Books and booklets of *mystical* doctrine and instruction. This group comprises all those works which explain the various aspects of contemplation, whether ordinary or extraordinary and infused, also the various phases of infused contemplation and the mystical phenomena which often accompany it, e.g., revelations, visions, charisms, miracles, etc. Examples of such writings are the works of St. Theresa of Avila, St. John of the Cross, etc.[42]

(4) Other Books and Booklets of a Similar Character

The final class mentioned in the law makes it evident that the previous classes were merely exemplary, and not an exhaustive listing. This final group includes all other works of a similar character which attempt to stimulate the faithful to a better life, whether these works be theoretical or practical.[43]

The law contains a phrase which emphasizes the obligation of precensorship, namely, "even though these works seem to foster piety." Actually, this phrase was carried over from the pre-Code law, which stated that these works were forbidden works if they were published without being submitted for precensorship, "even though they seemed to foster piety." Good intentions do not always supply for lack of judgment. Since the time of the promulgation of the Code of Canon Law, the Holy See has reaffirmed the importance of this law, by forbidding certain works which were free from error, but failed to correspond to forms of piety that are approved in the Church today.[44] Books which introduce new forms of devotion are forbidden

---

[40] Pennacchi, *ASS*, XXX (1897–1898), 343; Boudinhon, *Nouv. Législ.*, p. 183; Blat, *Commentarium*, III, partes 2–6, 332; Hurley, *Commentary*, p. 146.

[41] Boudinhon, *Nouv. Législ.*, p. 183; Hurley, *Commentary*, p. 146; Pennacchi, *ASS* (1897–1898), 343; Blat, *Commentarium*, III, partes 2–6, 332.

[42] Augustine, *Commentary*, VI, 436–437.

[43] Beste, *Introductio*, p. 697; De Meester, *Compendium*, III, pars 1, 258; Gagnon, *La Censure*, p. 103.

[44] Older decisions are: S.C.S.Off., decr., 13–18 ian. 1875—*ASS*, VIII (1874–1875), 269–270; decr., 3 iun. 1891—*NRT*, XXIII (1891), 382; decr., 3 apr. 1895—*NRT*, XXVII (1895), 488–489. In 1922 the Holy Office condemned a work that had already received the *Imprimatur* of a bishop: S.C.S.Off., decr., 17 mart. 1922—*AAS*, XIV (1922), 193. The history of this work is given in Beste, *Introductio*, pp. 701–702. The Holy Office acted similarly in 1938. Cf. decr., 31 aug. 1938—*AAS*, XXX (1938), 318. Cf., also, S.C.S.Off., decr., 26 maii, 1937—*AAS*, XXIX (1937), 304–305, and the monitum, 29 mart. 1941—*AAS*, XXXIII (1941), 121,

books if they have not been submitted for precensorship, in virtue of canon 1399, 5°.[45]

C. Writings Which Contain Something of Special Interest to Religion or Morals

The third general class of works mentioned in canon 1385, §1, 2°, is that class of works which contains something of special interest to religion or morals. The text reads:

> Nisi censura ecclesiastica praecesserit, ne edantur . . . ac generaliter scripta in quibus aliquid sit quod religionis ac morum honestatis peculiariter intersit.

The commentary on this section of the canon will deal with: (1) the term "writing"; (2) the "special interest."

(1) The Term "Writing"

The text of the canon uses the word "*scripta*," which means "writings" of any kind, form or size, provided they are published.[46] Accordingly, not only books, booklets, pamphlets, leaflets, even of one page, but also periodicals, newspapers and single articles in secular periodicals or newspapers, are subject to precensorship if they contain anything of special interest to religion or morals.[47]

---

and 17 apr. 1942—*AAS*, XXXIV (1942), 149. These decrees and warnings insist on the care which must be taken by bishops in appointing qualified censors for these matters.

Canonists treating of this matter are Boudinhon, *Nouv. Législ.*, p. 182; Vermeersch, *De Prohibitione*, p. 105; *L'Ami*, XXVI (1904), 186; Périès, *L'Index*, p. 120; Woywod-Smith, *A Practical Commentary on the Code of Canon Law* (revised and enlarged ed., 2 vols., Wagner: New York, 1948), II, 141 (hereafter cited as *Commentary*); Hurley, *Commentary*, p. 146; Desjardins, "La Nouvelle Constitution apostolique sur l'Index," *Etudes Religieuses des PP. Jesuites* (Paris, 1856—), LXX (1897), 215 (hereafter cited as *Etudes*); Eichmann, *Lehrbuch*, p. 464. An excellent article on the writing of devotional literature and the defects to which it is susceptible is that of Huber, "Die Pflege der Ascetik von Seiten des Clerus," *Theologisch-praktische Quartalschrift* (Linz, 1848—), LIV (1901), 49–71, 332–351, 582–605; LV (1902), 43–60, 269–279; LVI (1903), 14–37, 304–313 (hereafter cited as *ThPrQs*).

[45] Goodwine, *The Jurist*, X (1950), 160–161 (11–12).

[46] Wernz-Vidal, *Ius Canonicum*, IV, pars 2, 134; De Meester, *Compendium*, III, pars 1, 259; Ayrinhac, *Admin. Legisl.*, p. 279; Vermeersch-Creusen, *Epitome*, II, 504; Coronata, *Institutiones*, II, 317.

[47] Pennacchi, *ASS*, XXX (1897–1898), 504–505; Piat, *NRT*, XXXII (1900), 472; Van Coillie, *Commentarius*, p. 87; Périès, *L'Index*, p. 202; Hurley, *Commentary*, pp. 209–210; Vermeersch, *De Prohibitione*, p. 143; Ojetti, *Synopsis*, I, 711; Laurentius, *Institutiones*, p. 432, n. 2; Villada, "Estan sujetos los diarios a la censura eclesiastica previa?" *Razón y Fe* (Madrid, 1901—), XXIV (1909), 213–217; Villada, "Una objeción sobre la censura previa de los periódicos," *Razón y Fe*, XXIV (1909), 352–354; Wernz-Vidal, Ius Canonicum, IV, pars 2, pp. 135–136; Ferreres, *Institutiones Canonicae iuxta Novissimum Codicem* (2. ed., 2 vols., Barcinone, 1920), II, 150 (hereafter cites as *Institutiones*); Santamaria, *Comentarios al Codigo canonico*

The phrase "*in quibus aliquid sit*" signifies that precensorship is demanded, not only if the writing is concerned *principally* with a matter of special interest to religion or morals, but also if the writing contain only one page on a matter of this kind or treat it as an incidental question.[48]

(2) The "Special Interest"

The present law has the word "*peculiariter*," which is the correlative of "*communiter*," whereas the pre-Code law had the word "*specialiter*," which is the correlative of "*generaliter*." If there is any change of meaning, it is not readily apparent. The English term "special" is the best translation for both terms, in the pre-Code law as well as in the present law.

The special interest or importance arises (*a*) whenever the writing deals principally with a religious or moral subject, or (*b*) whenever it treats principally or incidentally of any other subject which either by its nature or by reason of circumstances of time, place or persons is of special interest to religion or morals.[49]

(6 vols., Madrid, 1919–1922), IV, 288 (hereafter cited as *Comentarios*); Cance, *Le Code*, III, 157; Blat, *Commentarium*, III, partes 2–6, 332–333; Cappello, *Summa*, II, 420; Marc-Gestermann-Raus, *Institutiones*, I, 853–854; Sipos, *Enchiridion*, p. 712; Berutti, *Institutiones*, IV, 421–422.

Cocchi (*Commentarium*, VI, 150) strangely holds that "*scripta*" here does not include books. Lehmkuhl (*Theol. Moral.*, II, 765) and Schneider (*Buechergesetze*, p. 146) held that the term meant "separate" writings, not articles published in periodicals or newspapers not subject to precensorship. Genicot-Salsmans (*Institutiones*, I, 386) mention that it is the practice in some countries to publish such articles without precensorship.

[48] Ayrinhac, *Admin. Legisl.*, p. 279; Vermeersch-Creusen, *Epitome*, II, 504; Beste, *Introductio*, p. 697; Coronata, *Institutiones*, II, 317; Cocchi, *Commentarium*, VI, 150; De Meester, *Compendium*, III, pars 1, 259; Sipos, *Enchiridion*, p. 712; Blat, *Commentarium*, III, partes 2–6, 333; Berutti, *Institutiones*, IV, 421; Nevin, *ACR*, II (1925), 51–52. The insertion of the words "*in quibus aliquid sit*" into the text of the law reveals the legislator's intent to strengthen the law and, thus, to rule out some of the milder pre-Code opinions. The re-phrasing is not a mere re-enactment of the old law to be interpreted according to the old law, as Goodwine (*The Jurist*, X [1950], 162–164 [13–15]) maintains. The authorities (Augustine, *Commentary*, VI, 437; Cance, *Le Code*, III, n. 95; Boudinhon, *Nouv. Législ.*, p. 275) cited in his favor by Goodwine merely state that a writing is of special interest to religion or morals only when its principal subject is a religious or moral topic. The interpretation adopted above does not make the law unworkable, since it does not claim that "every pamphlet, book, article, etc. that contained even a single line or paragraph pertaining to some religious or moral question had to be submitted to the censors." For an incidental question to be of special interest to religion or morals it would have to be of such a nature and amount as to create a proximate danger of serious harm to religion or morals or ecclesiastical discipline if that part of the writing did not conform to ecclesiastical standards.

[49] Gagnon, *La Censure*, pp. 104-108; Goodwine, *The Jurist*, X (1950), 161 (12); Claeys Bouuaert-Simenon, *Manuale*, III, 133–134; Van Coillie, *Commentarius*, pp. 86–88; *Theol. Mechlin.*, p. 227, n. 1; Pennacchi, *ASS*, XXX (1897–1898), 504–505.

The "special interest" clause has evoked a great variety of opinions on account of the indeterminateness of the verb "*interesse*."

(*a*) First, whenever the main topic of a writing deals directly with a religious or moral subject, the writing must be considered as containing something of special interest to religion or morals by the nature of the topic itself. Several reasons support this statement.

Thus, one group of authors holds that the main topic of the writing must be of a religious or moral nature, e.g., Gennari, "Circa la Nuova Disciplina sulla Proibizione e sulla Censura de'Libri," *Il Monitore Ecclesiastico* (Romae, 1876—), X, parte 1 (1897), 133 (hereafter cited as *ME*); Schneider, *Buechergesetze*, pp. 144–145; Hurley, *Commentary*, p. 210; Boudinhon, "Les Nouvelles Règles sur l'Interdiction et la Censure des Livres," *Le Canoniste Contemporain* (Paris, 1878–1922), XXI (1898), 310 (hereafter cited as CC); Boudinhon, *Nouv. Législ.*, p. 276–277; Marc-Gestermann-Raus, *Institutiones*, I, 854; Cance, *Le Code*, III, 157. The following contrast "*peculiariter*" (or "*specialiter*") with "*obiter*" or "*perfunctorie*," so that one or the other sentence, or brief passages here and there, bearing on religion or morals do not suffice to create the "special interest," e.g., Pennacchi, *ASS*, XXX (1897–1898), 505; Augustine, *Commentary*, VI, 437; Coronata, *Institutiones*, II, 317; Davis, *Moral Theology*, II, 412. They do not specify whether the main topic of the writing must deal with a religious or moral subject. This group of authors interprets the "special interest" clause of the const. "*Officiorum ac munerum*" (n. 41) and of the present canon according to the encyclical letter of Pius IX to the Papal States, dated June 2, 1848 (*Pii IX Pontificis Maximi Acta*, I, 99–101), which is the earliest source of the present text.

A second group of authors takes a different view. They deny that special interest to religion or morals arises from the mere fact that religion or morals is the main topic of the writing, and affirm that something more is necessary. Special importance for religion or morals may be had even if the main topic be not of a religious or moral nature. According to some, the special interest must come from external circumstances of time or place, e.g., Vermeersch, *De Prohibitione*, p. 143; Laurentius, *Institutiones*, p. 432, n. 3; Piat, *NRT*, XXXII (1900), 473; Ojetti, *Synopsis*, I, 711; Cocchi, *Commentarium*, VI, 150; Ubach, *Theol. Mor.*, I, 557; Claeys Bouuaert, *Selecta Capita Codicis Iuris Canonici* (Gandae, 1919), p. 97 (hereafter cited as *Capita*); Raus, *Institutiones Canonicae* (2. ed., Lugduni, Parisiis: E. Vitte, 1931), p. 555 (hereafter cited as *Institutiones*); Vermeersch-Creusen, *Epitome*, II, 504; Seraphinus a Loiano, *Institutiones*, II, 628; Noldin-Schmitt, *Summa*, II, 639; Piscetta-Gennaro, *Elementa*, II, 86. According to others, the special importance might arise also from other circumstances or reasons, e.g., Ferreres, *Institutiones*, II, 150; Ferreres, *Compendium*, I, 407–408; Wernz-Vidal, *Ius Canonicum*, IV, pars 2, 134–135.

A third group of authors admits that the special interest might arise not merely from extrinsic circumstances, but also from the nature of the subject-matter itself, e.g., Lehmkuhl, *Theologia Moralis*, II, 764; Wernz, *Ius Decretalium*, III, 131, n. (109); Ayrinhac, *Admin. Legisl.*, p. 279; De Meester, *Compendium*, III, pars 1, 259; Beste, *Introductio*, p. 697; Nevin, *ACR*, II (1925), 51–52; Genicot-Salsmans, *Institutiones*, I, 385–386; Berutti, *Institutiones*, IV, 421–422.

A fourth group combines the foregoing opinions, as is done in the text of this dissertation.

Finally, there are those who merely repeat the wording of the canon without explanation, e.g., Blat, *Commentarium*, III, partes, 2–6, 333; Sipos, *Enchiridion*, p. 712; Pruemmer, *Manuale*, p. 484; Haring, *Grundzuege*, II, 372; Tummolo-Iorio, *De Censuris*, p. 810; Woywod, *Commentary*, II, 721; Woywod, "The Law of the Code—Ecclesiastical Censorship," *HPR*, XXVIII (1927–1928), 861; Cappello, *Summa*, II, 420–421.

(i) The best interpretations of the law come from expressions of the mind of the Holy See itself.

The earliest source for canon 1385, §1, 2°, is the encyclical letter of Pius IX to the Papal States, dated June 2, 1848. After listing the subject matter, the Pope adds an official explanation:

> ". . . Censores . . . de iis tantum solliciti sint, quae Divinas Scripturas, Sacram Theologiam, Historiam Ecclesiasticam, Jus Canonicum, Theologiam naturalem, Ethicen, aliasque huiusmodi religiosas aut morales disciplinas respiciunt, ac generatim de omnibus, in quibus Religionis, vel morum honestatis speciatim intersit. *Iuxta haec igitur* statuimus atque permittimus ut in omni Ephemeridum et Librorum genere illi dumtaxat sine praevia Ecclesiastica Censura edi nequeant, qui moralis aut religiosi, uti diximus, argumenti sint; in caeteris vero ii tantum articuli, qui simile argumentum habeant, vel causam ipsam Religionis aut morum honestatis proxime attingant.[50]

In an instruction issued on Jan. 27, 1902, the Sacred Congregation for Extraordinary Ecclesiastical Affairs considered writings treating of religion, christian morals and natural ethics as subject to precensorship in virtue of n. 41 of the const. "*Officiorum ac munerum.*"[51] The reference could only have been to the "*scripta omnia*" clause of n. 41, since the first clause contained the word "*libri,*" which was understood in the strict sense.

Pius X was more explicit in the motu proprio, dated Dec. 18, 1903, in which he gave certain basic norms for "Popular Christian Action" in Italy. He stated that christian-democratic writers and all Catholic writers must submit to precensorship all writings dealing with religion, christian morals, and natural ethics, in virtue of n. 41 of the const. "*Officiorum ac munerum.*"[52] Since the word "*libri*" was interpreted strictly, the Pope must have referred to the "*scripta omnia*" clause. And the Pope based his declaration, not on the particular circumstances existing in Italy at that time, but on the fact that all Catholic writers must submit such writings to precensorship.

The Sacred Congregation of Rites declared on March 21, 1914, that episcopal permission is needed for the distribution among the faithful of printed

[50] *Pii IX Pontificis Maximi Acta*, I, 100. (Italics inserted).

[51] "Quando gli scritti democratico-cristiani trattano specialmente argomenti di religione, morale cristiana ed etica naturale, sono soggetti alla previa censura dell'Ordinario, secondo l'art. 41 della Constit. Apost. *Officiorum* . . . "—S.C. pro Neg. Eccles. Extraordin., 27 ian. 1902, n. 3—*Fontes*, n. 6416. The word "*specialmente*" does not refer to "*specialiter*" in n. 41, but to the fact that the writers promoting "christian-democratic action" in Italy wrote on sociological and economical questions and often also on matters pertaining to religion, morals and ethics.

[52] "XVII. Gli scrittori democratico-cristiani, come tutti gli scrittori cattolici, devono sottomettere alla preventiva censura dell'Ordinario tutti gli scritti, che riguardanó la religione, la morale cristiana e l'etica naturale, in forza della Costituzione *Officiorum et munerum* (art. 41)"—*ASS*, XXXVI (1903–1904), 344.

prayers to be employed for the obtaining of favors through the intercession of Servants of God.[53] Since such prayers are usually printed in leaflets, they came under the "*scripta omnia*" clause.[54]

In a decree, dated April 17, 1942, the Holy Office declared books and leaflets of piety subject to rigorous precensorship.[55] If the terms "books" and "booklets," as used in the second group listed in canon 1385, §1,2°, are to be understood in the strict sense, these leaflets of piety find a place only in the third group.

The books and booklets which narrate new apparitions, revelations, etc., or introduce new devotions, as mentioned by canon 1399, 5°, must come under the writings which are of special interest to religion or morals.[56]

Similarly, pious papers devoted to the publication of graces and favors received and offerings made at sacred shrines, etc., must be submitted for precensorship in accordance with canon 1385, as declared by the Sacred Congregation of the Council in a decree dated June 7, 1932.[57] Only the third group listed in canon 1385, §1, 2°, seems to extend to these pious papers.

All the foregoing documents lead one to conclude that the Holy See regards all writings on religious or moral topics subject to precensorship.

(ii) The text itself of canon 1385, §1, 2°, suggests the same conclusion. It exhibits a progression from the particular to the general, from the explicit enumeration of the more frequent examples to all-inclusive clauses. The third clause is a final, all-embracing statement including the two previously mentioned groups and all other writings of special importance to religion or morals. This progression from the particular to the general becomes clear from the introductory words of the last clause "*ac generaliter*," the force of which is overlooked by many authors. Hence, the three sections of canon 1385, §1, 2°, do not constitute three separate and completely distinct categories of publications. The first and second partly overlap; and they, in turn. are included in the third section.[58]

---

[53] *AAS*, VI (1914), 192; *Fontes*, n. 6398.

[54] Vermeersch, *Periodica*, VIII (1919), 26.

[55] " . . . Ut igitur haec vitentur, Ordinarii ad praeviam librorum foliorumque pietatis censuram doctos et prudentes viros deputent, qui in suo obeundo munere nedum doctrinae puritati, sed et sacri cultus gravitati consulant; iidemque Ordinarii licentiam edendi huiusmodi scripta ne concedant nisi maxima adhibita cautela."—*AAS*, XXXIV (1942), 149.

[56] Canon 1399, 5° " . . . itemque ex illis de quibus in cit. can. 1385, §1, 2°, libri ac libelli qui novas apparitiones, revelationes, visiones, prophetias, miracula enarrant, vel qui novas inducunt devotiones, etiam sub praetextu quod sint privatae, si editi fuerint non servatis canonum praescriptionibus."

[57] *AAS*, XXIV (1932), 240; "Quaedam corrigenda"—*AAS*, XXIV (1932), 461.

[58] Claeys Bouuaert-Simenon, *Manuale*, III, 133–134; Gagnon, *La Censure*, p. 107.

(iii) The conclusion that special interest to religion or morals is involved whenever the main topic of the writing is of a religious or moral nature finds support among a number of authors both before and after the Code.[59]

(*b*) Secondly, the special interest to religion or morals may also arise in the case of writings whose main topic is not of a religious or moral nature, either by reason of the nature of the subject, the manner of treatment, or by reason of external circumstances of time, place or persons.[60] Thus, certain secular subjects may be discussed from a religious or moral viewpoint, in their implications for religion, morals or the Church, e.g., economics, sociological problems, released time education, sex education in the schools, euthanasia, psychotherapy, proposed civil legislation on the taxation of religious or charitable institutions, on the liberalizing of divorce, etc. Or, a writing whose main topic is secular may also treat secondarily of a religious or moral subject, e.g., a work on geology or evolution with a discussion on the reconciliation of scientific data with the accounts narrated in the Bible; a book on medicine, with a chapter or two devoted to a discussion of the ethics of certain practices or surgical operations; or even a novel which intends, in part, to portray certain ecclesiastic characters as representative of the Church.

The importance which such writings may have for religion or morals consists in the same reasons for which the Church subjects any work to precensorship: the prevention of harm to the Church, to ecclesiastical discipline, and to religion and morals in the faithful. And if the danger is proximate, the writing is of special interest to religion and morals. This could happen if the mere publication of the writing or a mishandling of the question through inaccuracy, imprudence or lack of tact, will beget serious misunderstandings of the Church's position or doctrine, arouse bigotry and persecution, or further inflame passions and controversies already stirred up. In other words, the subject in itself or by reason of circumstances may be a ticklish question that requires most careful handling in order to forestall dangers to the Church or to the faithful.

Admittedly, there is no readily available norm by which a writer could

---

[59] E.g., Gennari, *ME, X*, parte 1 (1897), 133; Schneider, *Buechergesetze*, pp. 144–145; Hurley, *Commentary*, p. 210; Boudinhon, *Nouv. Législ.*, p. 276–277; Pennacchi, *ASS*, XXX (1897–1898), 504–505; Van Coillie, *Commentarius*, pp. 86–88; *Theol. Mechlin.*, p. 227, n. 1; Marc-Gestermann-Raus, *Institutiones*, II, 854; Cance, *Le Code*, III, 157; Claeys Bouuaert-Simenon, *Manuale*, III, 133–134; Gagnon, *La Censure*, pp. 104–108; Goodwine, *The Jurist*, X (1950), 161 (12); and probably the following: Augustine, *Commentary*, VI, 437; Coronata, *Institutiones*, II, 317; Davis, *Moral Theology*, II, 412. Wernz (*Ius Decretalium*, III, 131 [109]) stated that periodicals or magazines devoted to the edification and religious instruction of the people or of the clergy, e.g., pastoral magazines, seem to be of special importance to the Church and should be accurately precensored.

[60] Cf. the authorities cited above, in footnote 49.

judge whether or not a given writing would be of "special interest" to religion or morals. The term is somewhat indeterminate and flexible. The Holy See or local ecclesiastical authorities may issue a declaration that writings on certain matters must be submitted for precensorship because of their special bearing on religion or morals. If the ecclesiastical authorities have made no pronouncement, the writer must come to his own decision, with the counsel of others where possible. There seems to be no positive law which obliges a writer to have recourse to the local ordinary for a decision. The natural law, however, prescribes that one take the ordinary precautions against being the cause of serious harm. Hence, even in a case of doubt, prudence suggests consulting the local ordinary or submitting the writing itself for precensorship. Theoretically, the principle is easy to state: those writings which might seriously compromise the position of the Church, or endanger religion, morals or ecclesiastical discipline, must be submitted for precensorship.

D. The Meaning of "Book" in Canon 1385, §1, 2°

A glance at the text of canon 1385, §1, 2°, reveals that, in the three parts of the law, "books" occurs in the first, "books and booklets" in the second, and "writings" in the third. It is generally accepted that the term "writings" is all-inclusive, but there is wide divergence of opinion on the meaning of "books."

According to canon 1384, §2, the term "book" is to be taken in its extended meaning, i.e., so as to include all writings, unless the contrary is evident. In doubt, the presumption of law stands in favor of the extended meaning.[61] The term is not used in the extended sense when the nature of the case or the wording of the law in its text or context gives unmistakable evidence thereof.[62]

Many commentators assert that in canon 1385, §1, 2°, the word "books" must be understood in the strict sense.[63] The context, they say, gives proof

---

[61] Seraphinus a Loiano, *Institutiones*, II, 628; Vermeersch-Creusen, *Epitome*, II, 502, who state that exceptions must be proved. Bouscaren-Ellis (*Canon Law*, p. 706) reverse the presumption by saying: "If any particular canon *can reasonably be interpreted* as applying only to books in the strict sense, it *should be* so interpreted." (Emphasis added).

[62] Vermeersch-Creusen, *Epitome*, II, 502; Ayrinhac, *Admin. Legisl.*, p. 274; Sipos, *Enchiridion*, p. 711; Beste, *Introductio*, p. 696; De Meester, *Compendium*, III, pars 1, 255; Claeys Bouuaert, *Capita*, p. 97; Raus, *Institutiones*, p. 544; Cocchi, *Commentarium*, VI, 148; Berutti, *Institutiones*, IV, 418–419. Thus, in canon 1385, §1, 1°, and in canon 1390 the very nature of the case shows that the term "books" applies to certain specific units, the books of the Bible and liturgical books respectively.

[63] E.g., Vermeersch-Creusen, *Epitome*, II, 504; Coronata, *Institutiones*, II, 316–317; Wernz-Vidal, *Ius Canonicum*, IV, pars 2, 134–135; Raus, *Institutiones*, p. 544; Cocchi, *Commentarium*, VI, 150; Seraphinus a Loiano, *Institutiones*, II, 630; Piscetta-Gennaro, *Elementa*, II, 85–86; Ubach, *Theol. Moral.*, I, 557; Noldin-Schmitt, *Summa*, II, 639; Claeys Bouuaert, *Capita*, p. 97; Ferreres, *Compendium*, I, 406; Bouscaren-Ellis, *Canon Law*, p. 706; Jombart, *DDC*, III,

that the legislator did not intend the extended meaning, because the canon enumerates three categories of publications and specifies "books" for the first part, "books and booklets" for the second, and "writings" for the third. Otherwise, why should the Code make any distinction at all? If all writings are to be submitted for precensorship, then the word "book" would have been sufficient once. Hence, as this opinion claims, the general rule of understanding "books" in its extended meaning must give way.

However, another large group of commentators is not convinced by the foregoing arguments, and accordingly maintains that the general rule of canon 1384, §2, stands.[64] The nature of the writings mentioned in the first and second sections of canon 1385, §1, 2°, does not demand a strict interpretation of the term "book." Booklets and leaflets on scriptural, theological, canonical matters, etc., have been published; likewise, prayer leaflets and leaflets of devotion. Nor does the context prove the strict meaning of the term. Its advocates base their argument on the premise that, when the law mentions books and certain other forms of writings in the same text or context, the legislator intends "books" in the strict sense. "Books" are mentioned alone in the first part of canon 1385, §1, 2°. If, as most of these authors imply, the three parts of this law form three distinct and separate categories of writings by reason of the subject-matter, the first part must be viewed independently of the other two. In this hypothesis, the first part involves no intrinsic connection with the second. Though all three parts are juxtaposed in one typographical section, they could have been separated into three distinct sections without any change of meaning. Hence, there is no evidence of the legislator's intention to abandon the extended meaning in favor of the strict meaning. Canon 1399, 5°, offers a parallel case.[65] "Books" are

160; Regatillo, *Institutiones*, II, 112; Naz, *Traité de Droit Canonique*, III, 164. Blat (*Commentarium*, III, partes 2–6, 332) held that the first "books" is to be taken in its extended sense, but that the second "books" is to be interpreted strictly, because of the presence of "booklets."

The strict interpretation of "books" was universally held by commentators on n. 41 of the "*Officiorum ac munerum*" of Leo XIII, e.g., by Schneider, *Buechergesetze*, p. 145; Vermeersch, *De Prohibitione*, p. 141; Wernz, *Ius Decretalium*, III, 131, n. (109); Lehmkuhl, *Theologia Moralis*, II, 764–765; Dilgskron, *Anal. Eccl.*, V (1897), 227; Laurentius, *Institutiones*, p. 432; Ojetti, *Synopsis*, I, 712.

[64] E.g. De Meester, *Compendium*, III, pars 1, 258; Claeys Bouuaert-Simenon, *Manuale*, III, 133; Pruemmer, *Manuale*, p. 485; Beste, *Introductio*, pp. 697–698; Sipos, *Enchiridion*, p. 712; Cance, *Le Code*, III, 156; Boudinhon, *Nouv. Législ.*, p. 277; Woywod, *HPR*, XXVIII (1927–1928), 861–862; Genicot-Salsmans, *Institutiones*, I, 386; Gagnon, *La Censure*, pp. 106–107. Blat (*Commentarium*, III, partes 2–6, 332) and Berutti (*Institutiones*, IV, 418, 422) hold that the term must be taken in the extended sense in the first part, and in the strict sense in the second part because of the presence of "booklets."

[65] "Ipso iure prohibentur: . . . 5° Libri de quibus in can. 1385, §1, n. 1 et can. 1391; itemque ex illis de quibus in cit. can. 1385, §1, n. 2, libri ac libelli qui novas apparitiones, revelationes, visiones, prophetias, miracula enarrant, vel qui novas inducunt devotiones, etiam sub praetextu quod sint privatae, si editi fuerint non servatis canonum praescriptionibus."

mentioned first, then "books and booklets." The first "books" evidently refers not only to the books of the Bible but also to annotations and commentaries on them. Yet, no author has been found to limit the first "books" to the strict sense of the term so as to exempt scriptural commentaries published in booklet form from the prohibition if they have been published without precensorship. If the context in canon 1399, 5°, does not demand the strict meaning of "books" in the first part, neither does the context require it in the first part of canon 1385, §1, 2°. Hence, the term must be taken in the extended meaning determined by canon 1384, §2.

Does the use of "books and booklets" together in the second part of canon 1385, §1, 2°, prove, here at least, the legislator's intent to limit the term "books" to its strict meaning.[66] At first sight, it would appear so; otherwise, why should the canon specially mention "booklets" when "books" would have sufficed? This seems confirmed by the common interpretation given to the parallel case of "books and booklets" in canon 1399, 5°. However, the method of arguing from the mention of a smaller form of writing to the use of "books" in the strict sense is contradicted by other passages in the canons on precensorship: "*libros et imagines*," in canon 1385, §2; "*libros quoque, qui de rebus profanis tractent, edere, et in diariis, foliis vel libellis periodicis scribere vel eadem moderari*," in canon 1386, §1; "*indulgentiarum libri omnes, summaria, libelli, folia, etc.*," in canon 1388, §1; and "*libri, folii vel imaginis*", in canon 1394, §1. In these cases, the inclusion or mention of some does not argue the exclusion of other writings not mentioned. No one holds that booklets or leaflets need not be submitted for precensorship to one of the three local ordinaries mentioned in canon 1385, §2, just because the law speaks only of "books" and "images." Nor does any one maintain that the local ordinary's permission to publish need not be printed in a booklet, or on a single sheet, for the reason that canon 1394, §1, explicitly mentions only "books, leaflets or images." Therefore, the use of "books and booklets" together in the second part of canon 1385, §1, 2°, does not necessarily prove the legislator's intent to exclude pamphlets, leaflets, periodical publications or other writings not covered by the strict meaning of "books and booklets." Hence, the presence of an exception to the general rule of canon 1384, §2, is not established.[67]

Moreover, those who accept the strict interpretation of the term "books" are faced with an untoward sequel of that position, if they also deny that

[66] Blat (*Commentarium*, III, partes 2–6, 332) and Berutti (*Institutiones*, IV, 418, 422) affirm, and Wernz-Vidal (*Ius Canonicum*, IV, pars 2, 134) deny, that the term "books" can have the extended meaning in the first part and the strict meaning in second part of the same section of the canon.

[67] Cf. Gagnon, *La Censure*, p. 91.

the "special interest" group of canon 1385, §1, 2°, automatically embraces all writings dealing principally with a religious or moral topic. In the first group, all booklets, pamphlets, periodicals, leaflets, etc., are not subject to precensorship, even though they treat of dogma, morals, canon law, etc. In the second group, where "books and booklets" is found, all other smaller works of devotion would escape precensorship, e.g., pamphlets, folders, etc., which contain new private litanies, or other prayers composed and published either by competent writers, or even by incompetent and ill-informed persons, etc. In view of the intent of canon 1384, §2, it hardly seems admissible that such a large class would be exempted from precensorship.[68]

Further clarity on this question derives from a consideration of the two separate pieces of the const. *Officiorum ac munerum*, whence this unit of the Code is taken. It also explains the presence of "booklets" in the text.

The first piece is found in n. 41 of const. *Officiorum ac munerum:*

> Omnes fideles tenentur praeviae censurae ecclesiasticae eos saltem subiicere libros, qui divinas Scripturas, sacram theologiam, historiam ecclesiasticam, ius canonicum, theologiam naturalem, ethicen, aliasve huiusmodi religiosas aut morales disciplinas respiciunt, ac generaliter scripta omnia, in quibus religionis et morum honestatis specialiter intersit.[69]

The second piece of legislation is found, not in the section on precensorship, but in the section dealing with the prohibition of books. It reads:

> Libros, aut libellos precum devotionis, vel doctrinae institutionisque religiosae, moralis, asceticae, mysticae, aliosque huiusmodi, quamvis ad fovendam populi christiani pietatem conducere videantur, nemo praeter legitimae auctoritatis licentiam publicet: secus prohibiti habeantur.[70]

The term "*libellos*" had to be added in order to bring most of the devotional and popular religious instructional literature under prohibited literature if published without precensorship. Since "books" was taken strictly, writings smaller than books would otherwise have escaped the prohibition. This class of unauthorized publications is no longer forbidden by law.

Now, when the Code was published, it was found that both pieces of legislation were placed in the section dealing with precensorship. Furthermore, they were combined in such a fashion that n. 20 was inserted between the two segments of n. 41, but with the words "books and booklets" retained. The Code, however, through canon 1384, §2, superimposed the extended meaning of "books" upon the pre-Code formula incorporated into canon 1385, §1, 2°. There can be little doubt that the Code intended thereby

---

[68] Cf. Gagnon, *La Censure*, p. 107.

[69] *Fontes*, n. 632.

[70] N. 20—*Fontes*, n. 632.

to extend the law and to render it more severe by including all intended publications, of whatever size or frequency. That canon 1384, §2, admits the possibility of an exception to the extended sense of "books" creates no difficulty. The existence of one exception justifies the presence of the clause "*nisi aliud constet.*" Thus, in canon 1385, §1, 1°, the term, by its nature, means one of the units of the Bible, one of the books of Sacred Scripture. Another exception is verified in canon 1390, which treats of "liturgical books."

The term "books" in canon 1385, §1, 2°, must, therefore, be taken in the extended sense determined by canon 1384, §2, since the contrary is not evident. However, if one admits that all writings on a religious or moral topic are of special interest to religion or morals, the distinction between "books" and "booklets," between "books" and other publications, is more of an academic than a practical problem.[71]

E. The Problem of Periodicals

More conclusive evidence in favor of adopting the extended meaning of "books" in canon 1385, §1, 2°, is furnished by a consideration of the problem of periodicals. It is well known that periodicals are so varied that they comprise almost every type of publication, from the smallest leaflets to the largest books. Most periodicals appear in booklet or pamphlet form.

Before the appearance of the Constitution "*Officiorum ac munerum*" in 1897, a few canonists held that periodicals were not subject to the law of precensorship.[72] After 1897, however, some held that all periodicals were exempt from precensorship, because the editor would be of upright character.[73] Others held that professedly theological periodicals should have been submitted for precensorship, but that custom exempted them.[74] Others held that periodicals were to be submitted for precensorship only if the individual issues were large enough to be considered books.[75] A final group held that all religious periodicals were subject to precensorship, since they were included in the "*scripta omnia*" phrase of art. 41.[76]

---

[71] Goodwine, *The Jurist*, X (1950), 158–159 (9–10).

[72] Arndt, *Commentarii*, p. 293; Fessler, *Sammlung vermischter Schriften* (Freiburg, 1869), 181.

[73] Hollweck, *Buecherverbot*, p. 44, n. 3; Schneider, *Buechergesetze*, pp. 146–147.

[74] Moureau, *La Nouvelle Législation de l'Index* (Lille, 1898), p. 93 (hereafter cited as *Nouv. Législ.*); Schneider, *Buechergesetze*, p. 147; Vermeersch (*De Prohibitione*, pp. 141–142) cites Goepfert (1849–1913) as holding that such a custom existed in Germany at his time.

[75] Vermeersch, *De Prohibitione*, pp. 141–142; Genicot, *Addita*, p. 67; Planchard, *RTF*, III (1897), 393; Dilgskron, *Anal. Eccl.*, V (1897), 227.

[76] Boudinhon, *Nouv. Législ.*, pp. 276–277; Pennacchi, *ASS*, XXX (1897–1898), 511, 519; Van Coillie, *Commentarius*, p. 87; *Theol. Mechlin.*, p. 227; Genicot, *Addita*, p. 67; Ojetti, *Synopsis*, I, 711–712; Van Ruymbeke, *NRT*, XXXVI (1904), 102–103.

Some also held that articles of special interest were subject to precensorship, even though the periodicals were not.[77] Others held that in certain places a contrary legal custom exempted them from precensorship.[78] Still others held that such articles were exempt from precensorship entirely.[79]

Pope Pius X, however, ordered that, as far as possible, all periodicals and newspapers had to be censored. This was not a precensorship, but a subsequent censorship, i.e., a censor had to examine each issue as it appeared, and, if necessary, order the printing of corrections in the succeeding issue. This law held for all periodicals and papers edited by [lay?] Catholics, even though they did not treat of religion and morals.[80] Since this regulation of Pius X was not mentioned by the Code, it is no longer in force.[81] Pius X, however, had expressly mentioned (§44, IV) that article 41 was not abolished, but still had to be observed when the periodicals and articles required precensorship. His encyclical letter which imposed subsequent censorship was an additional measure.

If periodicals are subject to the law of precensorship today, it must be in virtue of canon 1385, §1, 2°, for there is no indication that they are mentioned elsewhere in the law. Those who hold the extended meaning of "books" in this canon, naturally include periodicals under the ambit of that term, some logically[82] and others expressly.[83] Those who hold the strict

[77] Pennacchi, *ASS*, XXX (1897–1898), 504–505; Périès, *L'Index*, p. 202; Planchard, *RTF* III (1897), 393; Hurley, *Commentary*, p. 210–211; Vermeersch, *De Prohibitione*, p. 144; Piat *NRT*, XXXII, (1900), 472; Laurentius, *Institutiones*, p. 432, n. 2; Villada, *Razón y Fe*, XXIV (1909), 213–217, 352–354.

[78] Van Coillie, *Commentarius*, p. 88; Vermeersch, *De Prohibitione*, (l. ed., 1897) p. 47. With reference to the latter work this statement is not found in subsequent editions.

[79] Schneider, *Buechergesetze*, p. 146; Hollweck, *Buecherverbot*, p. 44; Lehmkuhl, *Theologia Moralis*, II, 765; Genicot, *Addita*, p. 67; Hurley, *Commentary*, p. 212; Harty, "Binding force of the Rules of the Index, Necessity of an Imprimatur, Prohibition of Books not having the necessary Imprimatur," *Irish Ecclesiastical Record* (Dublin, 1864—), fourth series, Vol. XX (1906), 548 (hereafter cited as *IER*).

[80] Litt. encycl. "*Pascendi*," 8 sept. 1907, §44, IV—*Fontes*, n. 689.

[81] Gagnon, *La Censure*, p. 216. Ferreres (*Compendium*, I, 408, n. 3) alone held that it remained in force after the Code. Some authors erred in holding that this subsequent censorship supplanted the precensorship of periodicals and articles written for periodicals, e.g., Laurentius, *Institutiones*, p. 432, n. 2; Wernz-Vidal, *Ius Canonicum*, IV, pars 2, 135–136; Ferreres, *Institutiones*, II, 127. The subsequent censorship that he ordered was an additional measure.

[82] Claeys Bouuaert-Simenon, *Manuale*, III, 133; Blat, *Commentarium*, III, partes 2–6, 332; Beste, *Introductio*, pp. 697–698; Cance, *Le Code*, III, 156, n. 5; Boudinhon, *Nouv. Législ.*, p. 277; Augustine, *Commentary*, VI, 437; Davis, *Theology*, II, 412; Marc-Gestermann-Raus, *Institutiones*, I, 853–854.

[83] Gagnon, *La Censure*, pp. 215–217. When speaking of the branches of knowledge, the following expressly include periodicals: De Meester, *Compendium*, III, pars 1, 258; Pruemmer, *Manuale*, p. 485; Sipos, *Enchiridion*, p. 712, n. 8; Woywod, *HPR*, XXVIII (1928), 861–862; Seraphinus a Loiano, *Institutiones*, II, 633; Berutti, *Institutiones*, IV, 421, 422.

interpretation of "books" in this canon mention nothing about periodicals devoted to any of the religious or moral branches[84] though some admit that periodicals are subject to the law if they reach the size of books.[85]

The writer holds that periodicals are included under the term "books" in canon 1385, §1, 2°, for the following reasons:

(1) The general rule, stated in canon 1384, §2, holds in this canon. Since periodicals are expressly mentioned in canon 1384, §2, they are also included in canon 1385, §1, 2°, because the term must be understood in its technical meaning. Sufficient evidence is lacking to warrant the strict interpretation.

(2) A further argument is drawn from canon 1392, §2, which states that excerpts taken from periodicals and published separately are not considered new editions, and hence do not need a *new* approbation. The obvious implication is that certain periodicals and certain articles require precensorship when they are first published. The only canon in which periodicals could be included is canon 1385, §1, 2°.[86]

(3) A decision of the Sacred Congregation of the Council confirms the view that periodicals are subject to precensorship. Bishops and religious superiors were exhorted to insist on the observance of canon 1385 in regard to the publication of certain papers (*ephemerides*).[87] The view becomes cer-

---

When speaking of works which foster piety, the following expressly mention periodicals: Wernz-Vidal, *Ius Canonicum*, IV, pars 2, 135; Vermeersch-Creusen, *Epitome*, II, 504; Ubach, *Theol. Moral.*, I, 557; Cocchi, *Commentarium*, VI, 150; Cance, *Le Code*, III, 151; Jombart, *DDC*, III, 160; De Meester, *Compendium*, III, pars 1, 258. As far as could be determined, no author opposes the inclusion of periodicals in this group.

When speaking of works in which there is something of special interest to religion or morals, the following expressly mention periodicals: De Meester, *Compendium*, III, pars 1, 259; Ferreres, *Institutiones*, II, 150; Blat, *Commentarium*, III, partes 2–6, 333; Santamaria, *Comentarios*, IV, 288; Coronata, *Institutiones*, II, 317, n. 1.

[84] E.g., Raus, *Institutiones*, p. 544; Cocchi, *Commentarium*, VI, 150; Noldin-Schmitt, *Summa*, II, 639; Claeys Bouuaert, *Capita*, p. 97.

[85] Vermeersch-Creusen, *Epitome*, II, 504; Wernz-Vidal, *Ius Canonicum*, IV, pars 2, 135.

[86] Goodwine, *The Jurist*, X (1950), 165–166 (16–17).

[87] Decr. 7 iun. 1932—*AAS*, XXIV (1932), 241. When consulting this decree one is bound to notice that the reference in the decree is to canon 1386 (which prescinds from the question of precensorship) and not to canon 1385. Bouscaren (*Canon Law Digest*, I, 596) has the same citation in his translation of this decree. However, the citation of canon 1386 was a typographical error, as was noted in a subsequent issue of the *AAS*, XXIV (1932), 461, as follows: "Quaedam corrigenda in Vol. XXIV (1932), . . . Pag. 241, lin. 18 et 41, a calce, loco eius quod est, *1386*, legendum *1385* s." The correction does not indicate the precise paragraph of canon 1385, but the only possible reference is §1, 2°. Maroto ("Animadversiones in S. Congregationis Concilii decretum de gratiarum et oblationum in piis ephemeridibus evulgatione,"—*Apollinaris* [Romae, 1928—], V [1932], 274–276) suspected the presence of a typographical error; but neither he nor any other writer has adverted to the official "*Quaedam corrigenda*" inserted in the last issue of volume XXIV of the *AAS*.

tain from two recent documents emanating from the Sacred Congregation of the Holy Office. In a letter to the Archbishop of Boston, Aug. 8, 1949, the Sacred Congregation declared that

> it is no wise to be tolerated that certain Catholics shall claim for themselves the right to publish a periodical, for the purpose of spreading theological doctrines, without the permission of competent Church Authority, called the "imprimatur," which is prescribed by the sacred canons.[87a]

On June 30, 1952, the Holy Office issued an instruction on sacred art; it ordered the bishops and religious superiors to refuse the permission to publish books, papers or periodicals ("*folia vel libellos periodicos*") in which are printed any pictures ("*imagines*") opposed to the mind and decress of the Church.[87b]

(4) An *a pari* formulated argument may be drawn from canon 1394, §1, and 1388, §1. In canon 1394, §1, the term "book" is found, together with folio and image. Yet, no one holds that the term "book" must be interpreted strictly here, simply because of the presence of the other two items. All admit that the *Imprimatur* must be printed in all published works without exception. Similarly, in canon 1388, §1, the term "book" is found together with summary, booklet, folio, etc. Here, too, the term must be interpreted in an extended sense. The mere presence of other terms in the same canon does not demand the strict interpretation of "book" in canons 1394, §1, and 1388, §1; neither does it in canon 1385, §1, 2°.

Even though periodicals are included under the provisions of canon 1385, §1, 2°, it would be false to conclude that all periodicals must be submitted for precensorship. All secular periodicals, e.g., those which are primarily literary, scientific, political, philosophical, educational, recreational, journalistic, etc., in character would not require precensorship. Thus, many diocesan papers would not be subject to precensorship, though certain articles found therein might need it, either because of their subject matter, or because of their special interest to religion or morals.

In regard to the numerous religious periodicals, there is a practical difficulty if all were to be submitted for precensorship. For those which appear at longer intervals a precensorship might readily prove feasible, but for most weekly periodicals it would be a moral impossibility to carry out this policy. A practical solution might be, as Goodwine indicates, that the editor or

---

[87a] The Latin text and the official English translation of this letter may be found in *AER*, CXXVII (1952), 307–315. The passage quoted is given on p. 315.

[87b] S. C. S. Officii, Instructio ad Locorum Ordinarios "*De arte sacra*," 30 junii 1952, *De arte figurativa*, n. 6—*AAS*, XLIV (1952), 545. In the official footnote to the passage cited, reference is made to canons 1385 and 1399, 12°. See below, footnote 97.

one of the nearby priests be designated as censor, and one could even be authorized to grant the *Imprimatur*.[88] If it be entirely impossible to observe the practice of a precensorship, then possibly that of a subsequent censorship, as outlined by Pope Pius X, might be employed as a substitute.[89]

Article III. Holy Pictures (Canon 1385, §1, 3°)

Over and above the ordinary works which must be submitted for precensorship, the Code makes one noteworthy addition. It mentions that holy pictures are also included in the law. The text reads:

> Nisi censura ecclesiastica praecesserit, ne edantur . . . 3°. Imagines sacrae quovis modo imprimendae, sive preces adiunctis habeant sive sine illis edantur.

The commentary on this canon will be divided into: A. The nature of holy pictures; B. The process of printing; C. The presence or absence of prayers; C. Various things not included in the canon.

A. The Nature of Holy Pictures[90]

Since pictures are visible surface representations of persons, objects or scenes, holy pictures are those whose exemplar is holy or sacred. In the

[88] Goodwine, *The Jurist*, X (1950), 167–168 (18–19); Gagnon, *La Censure*, p. 216.

[89] After the appearance of the "*Officiorum ac munerum*" in 1897, some European periodicals began to print the *Imprimatur* in each issue, e.g., *Ephemerides Liturgicae*, *Analecta Ecclesiastica*, *Nouvelle Revue Théologique*, *Le Canoniste Contemporain*, while others, according to *L'Ami du Clergé* (XXIV [1902], 811–812), were published without an *Imprimatur*. In more recent times many European periodicals bear the *Imprimatur*, e.g., *Antonianum*, *Gregorianum*, *Angelicum*, *Biblica*, *Verbum Domini*, *Commentarium pro Religiosis*, *Jus Pontificium*, *Periodica*, *Apollinaris*, *Ephemerides Liturgicae*, *Ephemerides Theologicae Lovanienses*, *Divus Thomas*, *Collectanea Franciscana*, *Nouvelle Revue Théologique*, *Sanctificatio Nostra*, *The Irish Ecclesiastical Record*, *The Irish Theological Quarterly*, *L'Ami du Clergé*, *Unitas*, *Revue des Communautes Religieuses*. In Canada the *Imprimatur* is found in *L'Echo de Saint Francois* and *Mediaeval Studies*.

Several European periodicals carry "*cum licentia superiorum*" or a similar phrase, e.g., *Perfice Munus*, *Il Massaia*, *L'Italia Francescana*, *Studi Francescani*, *La France Franciscaine*, *Etudes Franciscaines*, *Civilta Cattolicà*, *Revue des Sciences Philosophiques et Theologiques*, *The Clergy Review*, *Zeitschrift fuer katholische Theologie*. In Canada the same is found in *The Franciscan Review* and *St. Anthony's Record*. Still other European periodicals are published without any indication of approval or even permission.

In the United States there is a usage to the effect that no one submits periodicals for precensorship. As far as is known, not a single periodical bears the *Imprimatur*. Some carry the "*Cum licentia superiorum*" or a similar phrase, which may indicate that canon 1386, §1, has been observed, e.g., *The American Ecclesiastical Review*, *The Homiletic and Pastoral Review*, *Franciscan Studies*, *The Thomist*, *Theological Studies*, *Review for Religious*, *Orate Fratres*, *The Catholic Biblical Quarterly*, *The Jurist*, *The Catholic Mission Digest*, *The Catholic Art Quarterly*, etc. Most periodicals make no mention of any permission whatever. When the II Plenary Council of Baltimore (1866) spoke of Catholic diocesan newspapers (nn. 505–510), it did not mention the need of precensorship.

[90] Since the Code is here speaking of printed sacred images, the term "*imagines sacrae*" may be translated simply as "holy pictures."

strict sense holy pictures are those which represent sacred persons who are the object of public or private religious worship, e.g. The Divine Persons, Jesus Christ Incarnate, the Blessed Virgin Mary, the angels, the Saints and Blessed, the Servants of God. It is immaterial whether the picture be a natural resemblance or a symbolical representation. In a broad sense the term "holy pictures" also includes those which represent religious mysteries, sacred scenes or biblical events.

Sacred images serve a very useful purpose in the Church. They are an effective means of instruction in the truths and facts of the Catholic religion. They also provide an incentive to Christian piety and devotion. Sacred images may become the object of worship, either private or public, if they represent a sacred person. It must always be understood that such worship is not absolute, but relative, i.e., it terminates in the exemplar, not in the picture or image itself. On the other hand, sacred images may at times fail in their purpose and even produce the opposite effect. A faulty image may directly or indirectly teach a false doctrine or give occasion to error in the minds of the simple faithful. A sacred image offends against Christian morals, if it begets irreverence or derision, provokes disgust, arouses sensual pleasure, or stirs up heated controversy, etc. For these reasons the Church exercises control over the exposition of sacred images and the publication of holy pictures.[91]

To be subject to precensorship the pictures need not be holy pictures in the strict sense, that is, representations of sacred persons. It suffices that they be holy pictures in the broad sense. The term "*imagines sacrae*" includes representations of the mysteries of our religion, sacred scenes from the Bible, and the like.[92] Though the texts of canons 1385, §1, 3°, and 1399, 12° were taken from n. 15 of the Constitution "*Officiorum ac munerum*,"[93] there is evidence that the Code extended the law when it substituted the term "*imagines sacrae*" for the word "*novae*" in the sentence requiring the precensorship of holy pictures. In its decree "on the invocation, veneration, and relics of saints, and on sacred images" the Council of Trent employed the term in its

[91] Cf. canons 1279 and 1399, 12°. Conc. Trident., sess. XXV, *De invocatione, veneratione et reliquiis sanctorum, et sacris imaginibus;* Grumel, "Images (culte des)," *DTC*, VII, 766–844, esp. 787–794; Gfoellner, "Kirchliche Bildervorschriften," *ThPrQs*, LVIII (1905), 99–120, esp. 101–103; Hurley, *Commentary*, pp. 127–128.

[92] Augustine, *Commentary*, VI, 438; Blat, *Commentarium*, III, partes 2–6, 333; Coronata, *Institutiones*, II, 317–318; Cance, *Le Code*, III, 158; *L'Ami*, XLIV (1927), 365; Beste, *Introductio*, p. 697; Gagnon, *La Censure*, p. 108. Berutti (*Institutiones*, IV, 422) and Wernz-Vidal (*Ius Canonicum*, IV, pars 2, 136) hold that the term means pictures of sacred persons, e.g., of God, Christ, the angels, the saints, etc.

[93] "Imagines quomodocumque impressae Domini Nostri Iesu Christi, Beatae Mariae Virginis, Angelorum atque Sanctorum, vel aliorum Servorum Dei ab Ecclesiae sensu et decretis difformes, omnino vetantur. Novae vero, sive preces habeant adnexas, sive absque illis edantur, sine Ecclesiasticae potestatis licentia non publicentur."—*Fontes*, n. 632.

broad signification.[94] In canon 1385, §1, 3°, the Code adopted the same term and it makes no specific reference to images of Our Lord Jesus Christ, the Blessed Virgin Mary, the angels, etc., as it does in canon 1399, 12°. The broad interpretation also harmonizes better with the general scope of precensorship as it is set forth in canon 1385, §1, 2°.

The sacredness of a picture depends solely upon the exemplar it represents.[95] A widely held opinion, however, requires a second element. Images representing a religious exemplar are not regarded as sacred unless they are intended by the author or the publisher to serve a pious or sacred use. If the pictures are reproduced only for secular purposes, e.g., for the spread or cultivation of art, for illustrations in papers or periodicals, they may be published without ecclesiastical approval.[96] The Code, however, does not distinguish between the religious or secular purposes for which the holy pictures are published. Neither does the Sacred Congregation of the Holy Office in a recent instruction on sacred art. The instruction contains a paragraph on the precensorship of pictures printed in books, leaflets and periodicals.[97] Pictures representing an object of religion are capable of a religious or a secular use regardless of the purpose intended by the author or the publisher. The Church is interested in the conformity of these pictures with ecclesiastical standards because of their potentially religious use. The application of the law of precensorship to holy pictures must depend upon the objective character of the pictures, not upon the subjective intentions of the author or publisher to provide pictures for secular or religious purposes. Otherwise the law can be evaded too easily.

The Code raises no question whether the pictures are of ancient or of modern design, whether they are traditional or new.[98] All sacred images

---

[94] Conc. Trident., sess. XXV, *De invocatione, veneratione et reliquiis sanctorum, et sacris imaginibus.*

[95] Augustine, *Commentary,* VI, 438; Blat, *Commentarium,* III, partes 2–6, 333; Cance, *Le Code,* III, 158; *L'Ami,* XLIV (1927), 365.

[96] Claeys Bouuaert-Simenon, *Manuale,* III, 134; De Meester, *Compendium,* III, pars 1, 259; Noldin-Schmitt, *Summa,* II, 639; Seraphinus a Loiano, *Institutiones,* II, 630; Ubach, *Theol. Moral.,* I, 558; Vermeersch-Creusen, *Epitome,* II, 505; Vermeersch, "De prohibitione imaginum," *Periodica,* XIV (1926), p. (96); Sipos, *Enchiridion,* p. 712, n. 9; Ayrinhac, *Admin. Legisl.,* pp. 279–280; Coronata, *Institutiones,* II, 317–318; Berutti, *Institutiones,* IV, 422; Wernz-Vidal, *Ius Canonicum,* IV, pars 2, 136; Gagnon, *La Censure,* pp. 108–109.

[97] S.C.S.Off., Instructio ad Locorum Ordinarios "*De Arte Sacra,*" 30 iunii, 1952, *De arte figurativa,* 6: "Episcopi et Superiores religiosi denegent licentiam edendi libros, folia vel libellos periodicos, in quibus imagines impressae sint, ab Ecclesiae sensu et decretis alienae (cfr. can. 1385 et 1399, 12°)."—*AAS, XLIV* (1952), 545.

[98] Article 15 of "*Officiorum ac munerum*" spoke of *new* images or pictures. Canonists had several ways of interpreting the meaning of those *new* pictures, but since the word was dropped when canon 1385, §1, 3°, was formed, those former interpretations are no longer apropos to the law of precensorship.

and holy pictures that are to be published must be submitted for precensorship, even new editions of older pictures according to the provisions of canon 1392.[99] Norms for the censor are given with the commentary on canon 1393, §2.

B. The Process of Printing

The only time when holy pictures are to be precensored is when they are to be published. Publishing must be taken in its ordinary sense, i.e., as making a thing available for all indiscriminately, either by sale or free distribution, or at least by offering the pictures for sale or distribution. Hence if the sacred picture is not to be published, it does not need precensorship. This is the basic reason why small remembrance cards, e.g., such as are distributed to select groups at first masses, jubilees, funerals, etc., are not governed by the law on precensorship. Theirs is not a true publication. The publisher, however, who produces such cards and makes them available to all indiscriminately, would be bound by the law of precensorship.

The Code mentions explicitly that the method of reproduction is immaterial. Hence it makes no difference whether these pictures are multiplied by any of the modern or more ancient processes, e.g., by engraving, etching, photography, photogravure, photolithography, photochromography, printing, etc. The law applies to all holy pictures, whether they are printed on paper, cloth, leather, etc., provided they are really published.[100]

Holy pictures need precensorship not only when they are published separately as picture cards or leaflets but also when they are printed in a book or a periodical publication. The Code makes no distinction, and the Sacred Congregation of the Holy Office, in its recent instruction of June 30, 1952 on sacred art, evidently regards all of them as subject to the law.[101]

---

[99] Augustine, *Commentary*, VI, 438; Ayrinhac, *Admin. Legisl.*, p. 279; Beste, *Introductio*, p. 698; Berutti, *Institutiones*, IV, 422; Claeys Bouuaert-Simenon, *Manuale*, III, 134; Cance, *Le Code*, III, 158; De Meester, *Compendium*, III, pars 1, 259; Nevin, *Australasian Catholic Record*, II (1925), 53; Sipos, *Enchiridion*, p. 712, n. 9; Vermeersch-Creusen, *Epitome*, II, 505; Vermeersch, *Periodica*, XIV (1926), p. (94); Wernz-Vidal, *Ius Canonicum*, IV, pars 2, 136, n. (20); Woywod, *Commentary*, II, 141; Coronata, *Institutiones*, II, 317; Cocchi, *Commentarium*, VI, 150; Genicot-Salsmans, *Institutiones*, I, 386; Bouscaren-Ellis, *Canon Law*, p. 707; Gagnon, *La Censure*, p. 109. Coronata (*loc. cit.*), Cocchi (*loc. cit.*) and Genicot-Salsmans (*loc. cit.*) hold that a new approbation is unnecessary when a holy picture already approved is reprinted unchanged by the same publisher.

[100] Blat, *Commentarium*, III, partes 2–6, 333; Beste, *Introductio*, p. 698; Claeys Bouuaert-Simenon, *Manuale*, III. 134; Vermeersch-Creusen, *Epitome*, II, 505; Augustine, *Commentary*, VI, 438; Ayrinhac, *Admin. Legisl.*, p. 279; De Meester, *Compendium*, III, pars 1, 259–260; Piat, *NRT*, XXXI (1899), 16; Gagnon, *La Censure*, p. 109; Goodwine, *The Jurist*, X (1950), 164 (15).

[101] Cf. *supra*, footnote n. 97 in this Chapter.

C. The Presence or Absence of Prayers

In order to obviate the impression that holy pictures might be subject to the law of precensorship only because they contained prayers, the law states explicitly that holy pictures themselves are subject, whether they contain or completely lack accompanying prayers.[102]

D. Things not Included in This Canon

Medals are not included in this canon, even though they receive the impression of a sacred image, and are multiplied and distributed widely. They are not printed, but struck; they are not called images ("*imagines*") but medals ("*numismata*").[103]

Statues are not printed or published, and are not included in the law, either explicitly or implicitly. Paintings and drawings, etc., are not subject to the law of precensorship when they are done by hand. However, if the paintings and drawings are printed and really published, they do fall under the tenor of the law.[104]

Slides and films are not included under the general law of the Church.[105]

---

[102] Boudinhon (*Nouv. Législ.*, p. 148) observes that private persons who compose prayers are not always the most accurate theologians, and at times are given to prayers which betray bad taste, or are affected, or even offensive.

[103] Some few authors hold that medals are included by the law, e.g., Ubach, *Theol. Moral.*, I, 558; Pruemmer, *Manuale*, p. 497; Wernz-Vidal, *Ius Canonicum*, IV, pars 2, 136, n. (20). The great majority, however, agrees that medals are not meant, e.g., Pennacchi, *ASS*, XXX (1897–1898), 310; *Theol. Mechlin.*, p. 213; Van Coillie, *Commentarius*, p. 56; Moureau, *Nouv. Législ.*, p. 110; Piat, *NRT*, XXXI (1899), 17; Augustine, *Commentary*, VI, 438; Ayrinhac, *Admin. Legisl.*, p. 279; Blat, *Commentarium*, III, partes 2–6, 333; Beste, *Introductio*, p. 698; Coronata, *Institutiones*, II, 318; Claeys Bouuaert-Simenon, *Manuale*, III, 134; De Meester, *Compendium*, III, pars 1, 260; Seraphinus a Loiano, *Institutiones*, II, 630; Vermeersch-Creusen, *Epitome*, II, 505; Vermeersch, *De Prohibitione*, p. 92. It would be difficult to imprint the *Imprimatur* on a medal, as prescribed by canon 1394, §1, were these subject to the law.—Berutti, *Institutiones*, IV, 422.

[104] Pennacchi, *ASS*, XXX (1897–1898), 309–310; Piat, *NRT*, XXXI (1899), 16; Vermeersch, *De Prohibitione*, p. 93; Augustine, *Commentary*, VI, 438; Beste, *Introductio*, p. 698; Claeys Bouuaert-Simenon, *Manuale*, III, 134.

[105] A particular decree has been promulgated for his diocese by the local ordinary of the diocese of Osnabrueck, in virtue of which "glass or celluloid slides showing single pictures, composite slides, often made of film, showing a number of still pictures, and motion picture films" are subject to the rules of precensorship. The entire decree and a discussion of it is given by Creyghton, "Vicarius Generalis Dioecesis Osnabrugensis Decretum: Annotationes," *Periodica*, XXVI (1937), 543–550. The translation quoted above is taken from Bouscaren, *The Canon Law Digest*, II, 435–436. Another pertinent article is that of Lopez, "Prelum catholicum et cinematographum," *Periodica*, XXIV (1935), 52*–54*. Goodwine advances the opinion that films and slides are subject to the law of precensorship in virtue of canon 20.—*The Jurist*, X (1950), 168–169 (19–20). Gagnon (*La Censure*, pp. 219–220) maintains the contrary view.

Article IV. Summary of Canon 1385, §1

(1) Canon 1385, §1, 1°, prescribes that all books of the Bible, as well as all annotations and commentaries on the Bible, may not be published unless they have been precensored. This rule holds, no matter how much or how little of the Bible is reproduced or annotated or commented on. It is immaterial whether the Bible be published in an original, ancient or modern language. The Vulgate edition is still the official and authentic text, but other Latin editions may be published under the usual conditions.

Annotations and commentaries on the Bible, i.e., all glosses, scholia and explanations of the text of the Bible, whether scientific or popular, may not be published unless they have been precensored. Again, this rule holds for works on the whole Bible or any part thereof.

Any of the above listed works which are published without the *Imprimatur* of a competent authority are, by that very fact, forbidden books, according to the tenor of canon 1399, 1° and 5°. Publishers and authors who print such works automatically incur an excommunication not reserved to anyone, according to the tenor of canon 2318, §2.

(2) Canon 1385, §1, 2°, prescribes that all works which pertain to religion and morals must be submitted for precensorship. This includes:

(a) Books pertaining to Sacred Scripture, sacred theology, ecclesiastical history, canon law, natural theology, ethics, and other religious or moral branches of knowledge.

(b) Books and booklets which pertain more directly to the practice of religion, that is, prayerbooks, books and booklets of devotion, of religious, moral, ascetical and mystical doctrine and instruction, and other similar works must be precensored, even though they seem to foster piety.

(c) All writings which contain something of special interest to religion or morals are to be submitted for precensorship.

It is the opinion of the writer that the term "books" must be interpreted in its extended sense in this canon, according to the norm established in canon 1384, §2. It is also the opinion of the writer that periodicals are included in this canon, in so far as they fall under one of the above mentioned categories.

Any of the above named works which are published without the *Imprimatur* are not, by that very fact, forbidden books, except those books and booklets which relate new apparitions, revelations, visions, prophecies or miracles, as well as those which introduce new devotions, even though such are introduced privately. This is mentioned in canon 1399, 5°, which makes explicit reference to canon 1385, §1, 2°.

(3) Canon 1385, §1, 3°, prescribes that all holy pictures must be submitted for precensorship when they are to be published. Medals, statues, hand

paintings, slides, films, etc., are not included under the present law. Pictures of Our Lord Jesus Christ, of the Blessed Virgin Mary, of the Angels and the Saints, or of other servants of God, which are foreign to the mind and decrees of the Church are automatically forbidden, no matter how they are printed, according to the tenor of canon 1399, 12°.

CHAPTER VII

THE AUTHORITY COMPETENT TO GRANT PERMISSIONS (CANONS 1385, §§2-3; 1386, §§1-2)

The Code determines not only the matter which is to be submitted for precensorship but also the authorities who are competent to grant the necessary permissions. Some of these permissions are to be given by ecclesiastical authorities; others by religious authorities. Each will be treated in turn, and the chapter will close with a summary.

SECTION I. PERMISSIONS GRANTED BY ECCLESIASTICAL AUTHORITIES

There are four distinct ecclesiastical permissions mentioned in the Code: (1) The permission which authorizes the publication of a work after precensorship has been performed; (2) the permission which authorizes the publication of a work for which precensorship is not required; (3) the permission which authorizes a person to write for or to manage periodicals; (4) the judgment concerning contributions to forbidden periodicals.[1] Each of these four functions will be treated in succession.

ARTICLE I. THE PERMISSION WHICH AUTHORIZES THE PUBLICATION OF A WORK AFTER PRECENSORSHIP HAS BEEN PERFORMED (CANON 1385, §2)

The first type of permission is that which attends the *Nihil Obstat*, and is given only after precensorship has been performed. This permission is given by a local ordinary, or, in the case of certain special works mentioned in law, by a higher authority, to whom the granting of such permission is reserved (canons 1387-1391). Since these special works are not treated in this dissertation, the rules governing them will be mentioned summarily prior to the treatment of the permission given by the local ordinary.

A. The Authority Competent to Grant Permission for Special Works

(1) The Roman Pontiff, in virtue of the supreme jurisdiction vested in him (canon 218, §1), may give such permission to any subject for any work, according as he sees fit. The Holy Father rarely uses this prerogative. He also enjoys the right to reserve to himself the granting of certain permissions, e.g., in the case of publications of extreme importance. However, he has not done so.[2]

---

[1] This last-mentioned function is not the granting of a permission, but, because of the similarity, it is treated with the permissions.

[2] Gagnon, *La Censure*, p. 178.

(2) The Roman Congregations and Offices, in virtue of the power vested in them, enjoy competence to grant permissions for the publication of certain works.

(a) The Holy Office supervises the output of the press in all its forms.[3] At the present time, it has not reserved to itself the granting of permissions to publish writings. When approached in particular instances, it usually remands the censorship to the local ordinary, or to other qualified censors, adding pertinent instructions if necessary. The Holy Office is the proper authority to which recourse is had against an allegedly unjustified refusal of a local ordinary to grant permission to publish.

Although the Holy Office took an active part in precensorship in former times,[4] at the present time it usually restricts its work to the subsequent censorship of works, which it may or may not prohibit, depending upon the verdict of its censors. The Holy Office also issues decrees of precensorship.[5]

(b) The Sacred Congregation of Rites enjoys competence to grant permission for the publication of the acts of the causes of beatification and canonization.[6] It also enjoys competence to grant permission for the publication of liturgical books, according to the tenor of the decree of 1946.[7]

(c) The Sacred Penitentiary enjoys competence to grant permission for the publication of certain works containing lists of indulgences.[8]

(d) Each Roman Congregation enjoys competence to grant permission for the publication of a collection of its own decrees.[9]

(e) The Congregation for the Propagation of the Faith enjoys competence to grant permissions to its subjects according to the norms found in the Code, with the proviso that all applications to the various Congregations be channelled through this same Congregation.[10]

---

[3] Canon 247, §4.

[4] The Holy Office, then the Sacred Inquisition, exercised the function of precensorship by appointing inquisitors whose office it was to precensor works simultaneously with, but independently of, the local ordinary. Local inquisitors were appointed by Leo X, const. "*Inter Sollicitudines*," 4 maii 1515, §2—*Fontes*, n. 68. Further regulations were established by Pius IV in the *Regulae Indicis Sacrosanctae Synodi Tridentini Iussu Editae, Regula X*—*Fontes*, n. 426; by Clement VIII, instr., 17 oct. 1595, §§I–VI—*Fontes*, n. 426. When the practice of appointing local inquisitors fell into desuetude, their functions also ceased. The office was abolished by Leo XIII, const. "*Officiorum ac munerum*," 27 ian. 1897—*Fontes*, n. 632.

[5] E.g., decr., 20 mart. 1941—*AAS*, XXXIII (1941), 121; decr., 17 apr. 1942—*AAS*, XXXIV (1942), 149.

[6] Canon 1387.

[7] S.R.C., decr., 10 aug. 1946—*AAS*, XXXVIII (1946), 371–372.

[8] Canon 1388, §2.

[9] Canon 1389.

[10] It is only since the Code was published that mission territories were placed on an equal footing with other territories in this regard. Previously, stringent regulations demanded that

(f) The Congregation for the Oriental Church enjoys competence over Orientals, if and when the laws of precensorship apply to them.

(g) Other Roman Congregations deal with precensorship only incidentally, in connection with the field in which they enjoy competence, e.g., the Congregation of the Council recently corrected certain abuses at shrines, among which was an item concerning precensorship of periodicals connected with those shrines.[11]

B. The Authority Competent to Grant Permission for Ordinary Works

Canon 1385, §2, establishes the general rule that works for which precensorship is required (i.e., those mentioned in §1 of the same canon) may not be published until a local ordinary has given permission to do so. The text of the law reads:

> Licentiam edendi libros et imagines de quibus in §1, dare potest vel loci Ordinarius proprius auctoris, vel Ordinarius loci in quo libri vel imagines publici iuris fiant, vel Ordinarius loci in quo imprimantur ita tamen ut, si quis ex iis Ordinariis licentiam denegaverit, eam ab alio Ordinario petere auctor nequeat, nisi eumdem certiorem fecerit de denegata ab alio licentia.

For the explanation of this part of the canon, the commentary will be divided as follows: (1) the meaning of "local ordinary"; (2) the competent local ordinary in a given instance; (3) the nature of the power exercised; (4) the persons bound by this law; (5) the obligation of accepting a work that is submitted for precensorship; (6) the granting of a permission after a previous refusal; (7) the unauthorized granting of permission.

(1) The Meaning of "Local Ordinary"

The term local ordinary means not only the Roman Pontiff, but also, for their respective territories: (a) residential bishops, not however a titular bishop, nor an auxiliary bishop, unless he is also a vicar general; (b) an abbot or prelate *nullius* (canons 319, 323); (c) a vicar general (canon 366);[12]

---

almost every writing had to be submitted to Rome for precensorship and permission. Cf. S.C. de Prop.Fide, decr., 6 dec. 1655—*Collectanea S. Congregationis de Propaganda Fide* (2 vols., Romae, 1907), n. 124 (hereafter cited as *Collectanea*). This law was mitigated somewhat by a later decree, 28 dec. 1770—*Collectanea*, n. 482 (*Fontes*, n. 4552). The Code, however, places the ecclesiastical superiors of missionary territories on the same level as other local ordinaries in regard to precensorship. A recent instruction, however, points out the necessity of exercising prudence in publishing works on the missions. Cf. S.C. de Prop. Fide, instr., 9 iun. 1939—*AAS*, XXXI (1939), 269, and in Bouscaren, *The Canon Law Digest*, II, 420–421.

[11] S.C.C., decr., 7 iun. 1932—*AAS*, XXIV (1932), 340–341.

[12] Canon 368, §1, states that a vicar general has the same powers as the bishop; he needs no mandate for the granting of permissions, unless the bishop has reserved to himself the granting of permissions for certain works. Cf. Berutti, *Institutiones*, IV, 424, n. 5; Gagnon,

(d) an apostolic administrator (canons 312, 313, 315); (e) a vicar apostolic (canon 293) and a perfect apostolic (canon 293);[13] (f) those who, in default of any of the above, temporarily succeed to the government, according to the norms of law.[14] Other ordinaries, e.g., religious ordinaries, are not local ordinaries.[15]

(2) The Competent Local Ordinary in a Given Instance

Although every local ordinary enjoys competence to grant permission to publish by law, yet, not every one is competent to grant that permission in a given instance. The Code mentions three local ordinaries—the proper local ordinary of the author, the local ordinary of the place of publication, and the local ordinary of the place of printing. Each will be treated in turn.

(a) The proper local ordinary of the author

The proper local ordinary of the author is the local ordinary of the place where the author has his domicile or his quasi-domicile, or of the place where the author happens to be staying, if he has no fixed abode.[16]

In the case of the diocesan clergy, the proper local ordinary of the author is the local ordinary of the diocese in which the cleric is incardinated, and also the local ordinary of any other place where the cleric legitimately has a domicile or a quasi-domicile, even though he might not be incardinated in that diocese.[17]

La Censure, p. 179. Coronata (*Institutiones*, II, 318) claims that the vicar general is not included under the term "*episcopus*" in canon 1391, but others hold that the vicar general is meant in this case also, e.g., Seraphinus a Loiano, *Institutiones*, II, 632; Claeys Bouuaert-Simenon, *Manuale*, III, 185; Ayrinhac, *Admin. Legisl.*, p. 284.

[13] In former times the authority of the vicar and the prefect apostolic in this regard was very limited, according to the tenor of the decrees of the S. Congregation for the Propagation of the Faith, dated 6 dec. 1655, 28 dec. 1770, and 2 aug. 1871—*Collectanea*, nn. 124, 482, and 1373 respectively. The Code, however grants them an authority that is equal to that of other local ordinaries in the matter of precensorship.

[14] Thus, pro-vicars and pro-prefects apostolic, vicars capitular, etc. The summary of local ordinaries is taken from Bouscaren-Ellis, *Canon Law*, p. 135.

[15] Canon 198, §2. A chancellor is not an ordinary, and hence possesses no authority in this matter, unless it has been given him by the bishop or the vicar general. Cf. Berutti, *Institutiones*, IV, 424, n. 5.

[16] Canon 94.

[17] Toso, *Ad Codicem Juris Canonici Commentaria Minora* (5 vols., Taurini-Romae, 1921–1927), II, pars 1, p. 66 (hereafter cited as *Commentaria*); Wernz-Vidal, *Ius Canonicum*, II, 66–67; Vindex, "Domicilium et Quasi-Domicilium," *Jus Pontificium* VI (1926), 47–48; Michiels, *Principia Generalia de Personis in Ecclesia* (Lublin: Universitas Catholica, 1932), pp. 142–143 (hereafter cited as *Principia*); McBride, *Incardination and Excardination of Seculars*, The Catholic University of America Canon Law Studies, N. 145 (Washington, D. C.: The Catholic University of America Press, 1941), pp. 320, 357–358; Gillet, *Jus Pontificium*, XI (1931), 58; Berutti, *Institutiones*, IV, 424; Gagnon, *La Censure*, p. 182; Claeys Bouuaert-Simenon, *Manuale*, III, 135.

In the case of religious, both exempt and non-exempt, the proper local ordinary of the author is the local ordinary of the territory in which is situated the religious house to which the religious is assigned,[18] or also, if the religious is legitimately residing elsewhere, the local ordinary of the diocese in which he has a domicile or a quasi-domicile.[19]

If any one of these persons (lay, cleric or religious) has several domiciles or quasi-domiciles, the local ordinary of each and every residence would be a proper local ordinary. It is quite immaterial whether these residences be established in consequence of an act of personal selection (voluntary) or as the result of a disposition made by the law (legal).[20] The term author is not to be understood in its strict sense, but in a broader meaning, so as to include not merely the author properly-so-called, but also the writer, compiler, editor, translator, etc.[21]

(b) The local ordinary of the place of publication

The Code speaks of the local ordinary of the place of publication, rather

---

[18] This norm is applied to exempt religious by De Meester, *Compendium*, III, pars 1, 260; Claeys Bouuaert-Simenon, *Manuale*, III, 135; Beste, *Introductio*, p. 698; Vermeersch-Creusen, *Epitome*, II, 506; Ubach, *Theol. Moral.*, I, 559; Bouscaren-Ellis, *Canon Law*, p. 707; Raus, *Institutiones*, p. 352.

This same norm is applied to all religious by Ayrinhac, *Admin. Legisl.*, p. 280; Coronata, *Institutiones*, II, 318; Berutti, *Institutiones*, IV, 424; Gagnon, *La Censure*, p. 182; Woywod, *HPR*, XXVIII (1928), 863.

Schaefer (+1948) confused the proper ordinary for precensorship with the proper ordinary for ordination, and hence became hopelessly involved. In his third edition (1940) he held that the proper local ordinary of religious is either the local ordinary of the place of origin or of his domicile or quasi-domicile; but, after perpetual profession, only the local ordinary of the place where is situated the religious house to which he is assigned. In his fourth edition (1947) he held that after perpetual profession the only proper local ordinary of a religious is the local ordinary of the place of origin. In practice, this would involve many absurdities. The reference may be found in *De Religiosis*, nn. 487 and 1417 respectively. Pejska holds Schaefer's earlier view.—*Ius Canonicum Religiosorum* (3. ed., Friburgi im Breisgau, 1927), p. 170.

[19] Gagnon, *La Censure*, p. 182. No conclusive argument seems to exist which proves religious to be legally incapable of acquiring a domicile or at least a quasi-domicile according to the provisions of canon 92. The dictum that religious, by their profession, possess no "*velle et nolle*" of their own has been overworked by some canonists.—Goyeneche, *Principia*, I, 125–126.

[20] Michiels, *Principia*, pp. 164–168, 172; Coronata, *Institutiones*, I, 127; Boudinhon, *Nouv. Legisl.*, p. 249; Gagnon, *La Censure*, p. 181.

[21] Vermeersch, De *Prohibitione*, p. 147; Sleutjes, *De Prohibitione et Censura Librorum* (Galopiae, 1903), p. 54; Piat, *NRT*, XXXII (1900), 567; Blat, *Commentarium*, V, 206; Ciprotti, *De Consummatione Delictorum attento eorum elemento obiectivo in iure canonico* (Romae: Apud Custodiam Librariam Pont. Instituti Utriusque Iuris, 1936), p. 27; Cerato, *Censurae*, p. 70; Coronata, *Institutiones*, IV, 310; Regatillo, *Institutiones*, II, 399. Boudinhon (*Nouv. Législ.*, p. 285) claimed that a translator cannot be considered an author.

than the local ordinary of the publisher.[22] The mere fact that a work is to be published in that territory is sufficient; it is not required that the publisher be the subject of that local ordinary.[23]

That local ordinary is the local ordinary of the place of publication who has territorial jurisdiction over the place where the publishing firm maintains its office and makes the work available to the public. If a publishing firm has several offices, there seems to be no reason why the term should not apply to each and every place, provided the work is really published in each place. Thus, Sheed and Ward may publish a work simultaneously in New York and London. Very often, however, the work is published at the main office, and the branch offices merely serve as centers of distribution where a work that is already published is distributed. Thus, Benziger Brothers maintain branch-offices in several cities throughout the United States, but the firm does not publish works at all of those addresses. In this case the branch offices are the equivalent of book-stores.[24]

It is not required that the printing be done at the place of publication. A publisher often sub-lets a printing contract to printeries, and it is possible that a publisher never do any of his own printing.

Some Catholic firms inform the author of a manuscript they have contracted to publish that they will take care of submitting the manuscript for precensorship and obtaining the required permission. Such a procedure is perfectly in accord with the law.

[22] The following translate the text of the law to read "the local ordinary of the publisher": Cance, *Le Code*, III, 158; Boudinhon, *Nouv. Législ.*, p. 248; Cance-Arquer, *El Código de Derecho Canónico* (2 vols., Barcelona: Editorial Liturgica Española, S.A., 1934), I, 840 (hereafter cited as *El Código*); Creusen-Garesché, *Religious Men and Women in Church Law* (Milwaukee: Bruce Publ. Co., 1931), p. 221. A publisher may live in a diocese different from that in which he maintains his business.

[23] In spite of the fact that according to former law the permission should have been obtained from the local ordinary of the place of printing, a custom arose according to which the *Imprimatur* was obtained from the local ordinary of the place of publication. Cf. Boudinhon, *Nouv. Législ.*, p. 247; Desjardins, *Etudes*, LXXI (1897), 364. In the United States this practice received official sanction in the I Plenary Council of Baltimore (1852), when it was decreed that the permission ought to be sought *only* from the local ordinary of the place of publication. Cf. *Concilium Plenarium*, 1852, p. 46, n. VIII; and also *Conc. Plen. Balt. II* (1866), p. 255, n. 503. Finally Leo XIII made this the general rule for the entire Church in his const. "*Officiorum ac munerum*," 27 ian. 1897, n. 35—*Fontes*, n. 632. In Germany, however, it had been customary to obtain the *Imprimatur* from the local ordinary of the place of printing or of the place of publication. Some held that either could still be approached, despite the fact that Leo XIII had mentioned only the local ordinary of the place of publication, e.g., Hollweck, *Strafgesetze*, p. 176, §108, n. 2; [Heiner], *AKKR*, LXXVIII (1898), 187. The Code finally granted an option of three local ordinaries.

[24] Berutti, *Institutiones*, IV, 424; Boudinhon, *Nouv. Législ.*, p. 248; Ferreres, *Institutiones*, II, 151; Vermeersch, *De Prohibitione*, p. 135; Piat, *NRT*, XXXII (1900), 19; Ubach, *Theol. Moral.*, I, 559.

(c) The local ordinary of the place of printing

The Code does not speak of the local ordinary of the printer,[25] but of the local ordinary of the place of printing. The mere fact that a work is printed in a certain territory is sufficient; it is not required that the author or the printer be a subject of that local ordinary. The place of printing is that where the work is actually multiplied. If a work is multiplied in one place and bound in another (diocese), the place of multiplication is the one specified in the law, i.e., the place of printing.[26]

(3) The Nature of the Power Exercised

When a local ordinary grants permission to publish, he is exercising the power of jurisdiction. Since this is an ordinary power, it may be delegated, either for individual cases, or even for habitual use.[27] The act of precensoring a work (i.e., the examination and formation of the judgment whether the work conforms or fails to conform to ecclesiastical standards) is not an act of jurisdiction, but merely a preparatory step upon which the authority bases his decision to grant the permission, or to refuse it.

(4) The Persons Bound by This Law

Although no persons are mentioned explicitly in §2 of canon 1385, the opening sentence of §1, which §2 cites, mentions the laity explicitly. The use of the phrase "*etiam a laicis*" implies that the clergy and the religious are also bound.

The Code makes no exceptions to the rule of precensorship, as it does in favor of cardinals and all bishops in regard to the laws concerning the prohibition of books in canon 1401. Hence, it must be maintained that all the clergy are bound by the law of canon 1385, §2. However, if a local ordinary authors a work, he may exercise this voluntary jurisdiction in his own

---

[25] The following translate the canon to read "the local ordinary of the printer": Boudinhon, *Nouv. Législ.*, p. 248; Cance, *Le Code*, p. 158; Regatillo, *Institutiones*, II, 112–113. A printer, like a publisher, may live in a diocese other than that in which the firm is situated.

[26] In former times the place of printing was of greater importance, because it invariably happened that it was also the place of publication. Boudinhon (*Nouv. Législ.*, p. 246) stated that publishers as distinct from printers were unknown at that time. Until the time of Leo XIII, the law demanded that the permission be obtained from the local ordinary of the place of printing, though, as has been seen, the custom gradually arose that the permission be obtained from the local ordinary of the place of publication. Today, the Code gives an option of three local ordinaries, and there is no legal title why one should be preferred to another. Wernz-Vidal (*Ius Canonicum*, IV, pars 2, 141, n. [27]) state that the main reason for giving this option was to lighten the burden of the local ordinary of the place of publication.

[27] Canon 199, §1; Gagnon, *La Censure*, p. 180.

favor.[28] He does not need the permission of any other local ordinary, even though he print or publish the work outside his own diocese.[29]

Religious are bound to the observance of this law. The long history of the various opinions which held for the privilege of exemption in this matter is no longer pertinent. The simple fact is that all religious, also exempt religious, even religious who are ordinaries, are bound by the law of precensorship enacted in canon 1385, §2.[30]

(5) The Obligation of Accepting a Work that is Submitted for Precensorship

The Code does not expressly mention that the local ordinary has an obligation to accept a work that is submitted for precensorship. However, this obligation is implicitly contained in the subject's duty to submit his work, and in the necessity of appointing censors.[31] A local ordinary is not free to refuse precensorship merely because other local ordinaries whom the person might also approach are equally competent. For a reasonable cause, however, he may decline.[32] A local ordinary might suggest that precensorship be sought elsewhere, e.g., if his own censors are so overburdened with work that they cannot perform the task within a reasonable time. If no other local ordinary is competent, e.g., if the place of printing and publication happen to be in the same diocese where the author has his one and only place of residence, then the competent local ordinary must provide.

A local ordinary may appoint clerics other than the official censors for individual cases. It may happen that a local ordinary desire the services of a qualified expert for a specialized work, and, if none can be found in his own diocese, he may request the service elsewhere, and grant the permission according to the verdict of that censor. It is quite evident that he cannot impose such a task upon a cleric who is not his own subject.

---

[28] Coronata, *Institutiones*, II, 318–319; Augustine, *Commentary*, VI, 439; Beste, *Introductio*, p. 698; Goyeneche, "De censura librorum quando Ordinarius est editor, de Ordinario religioso editore, de superiore religioso concedente licentia," *Commentarium pro Religiosis* (Romae, 1920—), VII (1926), 99 (hereafter cited as *CpR*).

[29] The correct view is found in Berutti, *Institutiones*, IV, 425, n. 1; Augustine, *Commentary*, VI, 439; Gagnon, *La Censure*, p. 182, n. 21. The following are unduly attached to the pre-Code law, for they hold that a local ordinary who publishes his own work must obtain permission from the local ordinary of the place of printing or publication, e.g., Sipos, *Enchiridion*, p. 712; Eichmann, *Lehrbuch*, p. 465; Haring, *Grundzuege*, II, 372.

[30] S.C.Relig., 15 iun, 1911—*AAS*, III (1911), 270–271. Cf. also Vermeersch, *De Prohibitione*, p. 53; Desjardins, *Etudes*, LXXI (1897), 365; Gagnon, *La Censure*, pp. 179–180.

[31] Formerly the law was explicit on this point, and obliged him to do so without delay. Serious failure in this regard was penalized with an excommunication. Cf. Leo X const. (in Conc. Lateranen. V) "*Inter sollicitudines*," 4 maii, 1515—*Fontes*, n. 68. The present law does not mention any penalty.

[32] Seraphinus a Loiano, *Institutiones*, II, 631; Bouix, *De Curia Romana*, pp. 565–566.

In case a local ordinary refuses to accept a work for precensorship, the author may approach another local ordinary who is competent, or, if there be none, he may have recourse, *in devolutivo*, to the Holy Office.

The nature of the permission, and its actual granting, will be treated fully under canon 1394, §1.

(6) The Granting of Permission After a Previous Refusal

The text of canon 1385, §2, reads:

> . . . ita tamen ut, si quis ex iis Ordinariis licentiam denegaverit, eam ab alio Ordinario petere auctor nequeat, nisi eumdem certiorem fecerit, de denegata ab alio licentia.

The supposition is that there is another competent local ordinary in that instance.[33] The reason for the law seems to be the avoidance of disagreement between members of the hierarchy. A second local ordinary could judge a work suitable for publication, whereas a prior local ordinary may have rendered a contrary judgment, in line with local circumstances, or possibly in consequence of personal considerations.[34]

The following points will be investigated: (a) The "other" local ordinary; (b) the obligation to mention the fact of a previous refusal; (c) the authority of the other local ordinary; (d) the meaning of "author"; (e) the status of a permission given without mention of the refusal.

(a) The "other" local ordinary is any one whom the author may be entitled to ask, according to the option granted in canon 1385, §2. The fact that the author has already approached one local ordinary does not affect the competence of the local ordinaries who had not been approached. There is no legal objection to asking the same local ordinary at a later time,[35] or to approaching his successor in office. The vicar general, in this instance, will have to act according to the norm of canon 44, §2.

(b) The obligation to mention the fact of a previous refusal rests upon the petitioner. The local ordinary is not obliged to ask whether or not there has been a previous refusal. This obligation, however, must be understood as of a refusal to permit publication. If a local ordinary declines to accept a work for precensorship, he does not act at all, and this cannot be regarded as the refusal mentioned in the law. In this case the petitioner is free to approach a second competent local ordinary without mentioning the fact that another local ordinary was approached first. If the local ordinary

[33] In the case wherein no other local ordinary is competent, e.g., when the place of publication and the place of printing are in the same diocese wherein the author has his one and only place of residence, the only alternative is to have recourse to the Holy Office against the allegedly unjust refusal.

[34] Blat, *Commentarium*, III, partes 2-6, 334; *L'Ami*, XLIII (1926), 400.

[35] Berutti, *Institutiones*, IV, 425, n. 2.

knows from reliable sources that a work which will be presented is unfit for publication, he should shoulder the responsibility of refusing the permission.[36]

(c) The authority of the other local ordinary remains unimpaired, even though the petitioner was refused by a previous local ordinary. It is proper that he first seek the reason for the refusal from the first local ordinary.[37] Prudence demands that the exchange of letters be done through the respective curias, and not through the intermediation of the interested party. After receiving the pertinent information, the "other" local ordinary is juridically free to act according to his own judgment.[38] He is not obliged to concur in the decision of the previous local ordinary, but may act upon his own responsibility and authority.

(d) The law states that the "author" may not ask the permission without mentioning the fact of the first refusal. The word author is to be taken in its extended sense, so as to include any other person who seeks that permission for the work in question, e.g., the publisher.[39] It should be needless to remark that it means clerics and religious, as well as lay persons.[40]

---

[36] Canon 1385, §2, imposes the obligation of mentioning the refusal of any local ordinary, regardless of whether that was the proper local ordinary or any other. Canon 44, §1, speaks only of approaching another ordinary after being refused by one's proper ordinary. Hence, canon 1385, §2, is an extension of the general norm of canon 44, §1. Cf. Berutti, *Institutiones*, IV, 425, n. 3; Van Hove, *De Rescriptis*, Commentarium Lovaniense in Codicem Iuris Canonici,. Vol. I, tom. IV (Mechliniae: H. Dessain, 1936), p. 162; Wernz-Vidal, *Ius Canonicum*, I, 406, n. (49). Gillet (*Jus Pontificium*, XI [1931], 58) holds that if an author have several proper local ordinaries, e.g., by reason of a plurality of domiciles or quasi-domiciles, he could lawfully approach a second proper local ordinary, after having been refused by a first, without being obliged to mention the fact of the refusal. It is true that canon 44, §1, does not exclude such an interpretation, but canon 1385, §2, does.

[37] Augustine, *Commentary*, VI, 439. Canon 44, §1, imposes upon an ordinary the obligation of inquiring from the proper ordinary the reason for his refusal. It says nothing about such an obligation when the petitioner has proceded to a proper local ordinary after being refused by another; or when neither of the two local ordinaries are proper local ordinaries. Woywod (*HPR*, XXVIII [1928], 862) stated that it is a matter of courtesy to do so. Others state that there is no obligation to request the reason, e.g., Gillet, *Jus Pontificium*, XI (1931), 58; Berutti, *Institutiones*, IV, 425; Blat, *Commentarium*, III, partes 2–6, 334; Gagnon, *La Censure*, p. 184; Seraphinus a Loiano, *Institutiones*, II, 633; *L'Ami*, XLIII (1926), 400. The purpose of the law of 1385, §2, seems strongly to recommend such a procedure in all instances.

[38] *L'Ami*, XLIII (1926), 400; Michiels, *Normae*, II, 182; Vromant, *Introductio*, p. 18.

[39] Blat, *Commentarium*, III, partes 2–6, 334; Coronata, *Institutiones*, II, 318; Woywod, *HPR*, XXVIII (1928), 862; De Meester, *Compendium*, III, pars 1, 260; Vermeersch-Creusen, *Epitome*, II, 506; Augustine, *Commentary*, VI, 439. In their commentaries on canons 43 and 44 some authors demand the identity of person, but this is not demanded in canon 1385, §2, because of the nature of precensorship, upon which the permission is founded.

[40] *L'Ami*, XLIII (1926), 400.

(e) If the permission of the other local ordinary was secured fraudulently, i.e., without mention of the previous refusal, the permission is valid, though illicitly obtained.[41-42]

(7) The Unauthorized Granting of Permission

If a manuscript is submitted to a local ordinary other than those mentioned in the law, that local ordinary is not authorized to grant the permission.[43] This might easily happen when an author submits a manuscript to a local ordinary where he expects to have the work published, and, after securing the permission, fails to engage the services of the publisher, or freely chooses another. In strict compliance with the law the author would be obliged to submit the work for a new precensorship and a new approbation.[44] The second local ordinary, however, could have a new precensorship

---

[41-42] Beste, *Introductio*, p. 698; Cappello, *Summa*, II, 421; Coronata, *Institutiones*, II, 318; Boudinhon, *Nouv. Législ.*, p. 248; De Meester, *Compendium*, III, pars 1, 260; Ciprotti, *De Consummatione Delictorum*, I, 28, n. (47); Blat, *Commentarium*, III, partes 2–6, 334; Gillet, *Jus Pontificium*, XI (1931), 58; Cerato, *Censurae Vigentes*, p. 71; Jombart, *DDC*, III, 161; Berutti, *Institutiones*, IV, 425; Gagnon, *La Censure*, p. 184.

The following hold that such a permission would be invalid: Ubach, *Theol. Moral.*, I, 559; Cance-Arquer, *El Código*, I, 840; Ramstein, *A Manual of Canon Law* (Hoboken: Terminal Printing and Publishing Co., 1947), p. 545. Claeys Bouuaert-Simenon (*Manuale*, III, 134) held for invalidity in their third edition, but pointed simply to illicitness in the fourth edition.

The term "*nequeat*" is not always used as connoting an invalidating law in the Code.

[43] Some authors overlook the point of competence entirely in their definition, e.g., Blat, *Commentarium*, III, partes 2–6, 326; Ayrinhac, *Admin. Legisl.*, p. 278; Raus, *Institutiones*, p. 555; Aertnys-Damen, *Theol. Moral.*, I, 750; Wernz-Vidal, *Ius Canonicum*, IV, pars 2, 131; Vermeersch-Creusen, *Epitome*, II, 503; Seraphinus a Loiano, *Institutiones*, II, 626.

Others make express mention of competence in their definition, e.g., Pruemmer, *Manuale*, p. 484; Sipos, *Enchiridion*, p. 712; Cance, *Le Code*, III, 156; De Meester, *Compendium*, III, pars 1, 247; Cappello, *Summa*, II, 420.

[44] It is not clear whether the permission given by an unauthorized local ordinary is only illicit or also invalid. Since he is not empowered by the Code to give the permission, he cannot, it seems, validly grant what he lacks the power to give. Ciprotti (*De Consummatione Delictorum*, I, 28) apparently inclines toward this view. On the other hand, a number of authors hold that the permission given by any local ordinary, even if he be not one of those who are mentioned in canon 1385, §2, is valid though illicit, and sufficient to enable the author and publisher to escape the penalty laid down by canon 2318, §2, e.g., Heylen, *De Censuris* (4. ed., Mechliniae: H. Dessain, 1945), p. 164; Pellé, *Le Droit Pénal de l'Eglise* (Paris: P. Lethielleux, 1939), p. 369; Cappello, *De Censuris*, p. 346; De Meester, *Compendium*, III, pars 1, 316; Van der Velden, *Principia*, II, 861. Perhaps they base their view on the fact that the canon does not contain any invalidating clause and that there exists a sufficient assurance that the work may be published without harm to faith or morals or ecclesiastical discipline even when the work was precensored and approved by an unauthorized local ordinary. Pennacchi (*ASS*, XXX [1897–1898], 492) added that the work had thus received approval by ecclesiastical authority, whereby the author had also shown himself submissive to the authority of the Church.

performed if he so desired, though he would also be justified in accepting the verdict of the authentic *Nihil Obstat* from another diocese, and then grant his own permission on the strength of the original *Nihil Obstat*.[45]

ARTICLE II. THE PERMISSION AUTHORIZING THE PUBLICATION OF A WORK THAT DOES NOT REQUIRE PRECENSORSHIP (CANON 1386, §1)

Over and above the permission which attends a *Nihil Obstat*, the local ordinary also enjoys the power to grant permission to publish certain works for which precensorship is not required by law. The text of the law reads:

> Vetantur clerici saeculares sine consensu suorum Ordinariorum, religiosi vero sine licentia sui Superioris maioris et Ordinarii loci, libros quoque, qui de rebus profanis tractent, edere . . .

The explanation of this part of the canon will be treated under the following headings: (1) the meaning of "local ordinary"; (2) the nature of the power exercised; (3) the matter included under the term "books"; (4) the meaning of "*quoque*"; (5) the nature of the permission; (6) the persons bound by this law.

(1) The Meaning of "Local Ordinary"

When the Code demands that the diocesan clergy obtain this permission, it speaks of obtaining it from "their" local ordinaries, and when speaking of religious, it merely mentions the ordinary of the place. In the case of the diocesan clergy, the phrase "their local ordinaries" certainly means the proper local ordinary of the author—the local ordinary of the diocese of incardination as well as the local ordinary of the place where the cleric may have acquired a domicile or a quasi-domicile, even though he is not incardinated in that diocese. The local ordinary of the place of printing and the local ordinary of the place of publication are excluded.[46] The reason for this limitation is the necessity of judging the feasibility of the cleric's en-

[45] S. C. Indicis, dubium, 9 maii 1912—*AAS*, IV (1912), 370. At the time the decision was rendered, the proper local ordinary of the author was not authorized, by law, to grant this permission. Hence, the origin of the doubt, and the solution.

[46] The following mention only the local ordinary of the diocese of incardination: Claeys Bouuaert-Simenon, *Manuale*, III, 135; De Meester, *Compendium*, III, pars 1, 261; Beste, *Introductio*, p. 698; Gillet, *Jus Pontificium*, XI (1931), 59; Sipos, *Enchiridion*, p. 712; Augustine, *Commentary*, VI, 441.

The following mention also the local ordinary of the place of domicile or quasi-domicile: Vermeersch-Creusen, *Epitome*, II, 509; Gagnon, *La Censure*, p. 126; Coronata, *Institutiones*, II, 319; Brys, "De prohibitione librorum," *Collationes Brugenses* (Brugis, 1896—), XXVIII (1928), 37 (hereafter cited as *CB*); Nevin, *ACR*, II (1925), 54; M[ahoney], "Imprimatur," *Clergy Review* (London, 1931—), VII (1934), 252 (hereafter cited as *CR*). Brys altered his view later in *CB*, XXXIII (1933), 411.

gaging in that type of activity, the expediency of publishing a work on certain profane topics and the duty of obedience to proper authorities.[47]

In the case of religious the proper local ordinary is the local ordinary of the territory in which is situated the religious house to which the religious is assigned, or also the local ordinary of the place of domicile or quasi-domicile if the religious is legitimately residing elsewhere.[48]

(2) The Nature of the Power Exercised

The power which the local ordinary exercises, in this instance, is the power of jurisdiction. No rules govern the granting or refusing of the permission in the present law, but the pre-Code law had stated several, e.g., the safeguarding of ecclesiastical discipline, or of religious discipline, as well as the preservation of the respect due to the clerical state. If an ordinary refuses permission, he should give his reasons.[49] If an author feels that he is aggrieved, he may have recourse, *in devolutivo*, to the Holy See.

(3) The Matter Included under the Term "Books"

According to the norm established in canon 1384, §2, the term book is to be understood in its extended meaning unless the contrary is evident. There appears to be no reason why the term should be restricted in this canon, save the one fact that small works are not as important as books. One could

---

[47] Pennacchi, *ASS*, XXX (1897–1898), 506; Hurley, *Commentary*, p. 226; De Meester, *Compendium*, III, pars 1, 261; Schneider, *Buechergesetze*, p. 150; Jombart, "Quelque notions sur l'Index," *Revue des Communautés Religieuses* (Louvain, 1925—), I (1925), 111 (hereafter cited as *RCR*); *L'Ami*, XXXIX (1922), 117–118; XLII (1925), 140; Woywod, *HPR*, XXVIII (1928), 864; Fanfani, *De Iure Religiosorum* (2. ed., Taurini, 1925), p. 316; Beste, *Introductio*, p. 698; Vermeersch-Creusen, *Epitome*, II, 509–510.

[48] The following limit the meaning of the "local ordinary" for religious to the local ordinary of the place in which the religious house is situated: Claeys Bouuaert-Simenon, *Manuale*, III, 135; De Meester, *Compendium*, III, pars 1, 261; Sipos, *Enchiridion*, p. 712; Coronata, *Institutiones*, II, 319; Woywod, *HPR*, XXVIII (1928), 866; Augustine, *Commentary*, VI, 441, n. 12; Davis, *Theology*, II, 413; Gillet, *Jus Pontificium*, XI (1931), 59; Nevin, *ACR*, II (1925), 54.

The following commentators hold that a religious shows his obedience to his own religious superiors, and hence may obtain the permission from any of the three local ordinaries mentioned in canon 1385, §2, e.g., Vermeersch-Creusen, *Epitome*, II, 510; Blat, *Commentarium*, III, partes 2–6, 335; Fanfani, *De Iure Religiosorum*, p. 316; Schaefer, *De Religiosis*, n. 1419; Cappello, *Summa*, II, 424; Ubach, *Theol. Moral.*, I, 560; Seraphinus a Loiano, *Institutiones*, II, 633; Wernz-Vidal, *Ius Canonicum*, IV, pars 2, 145; Tummolo-Iorio, *De Censuris*, p. 810; Beste, *Introductio*, p. 698; Ayrinhac, *Admin. Legisl.*, p. 281. To the writer, however, it seems that the same reasons hold for religious as for the diocesan clergy, and the only local ordinary in a position to judge is the one where the religious resides. Cf. also Gagnon, *La Censure*, p. 127.

[49] Coronata, *Institutiones*, II, 320; Augustine, *Commentary*, VI, 443. Augustine's statement that the author may seek another printer or publisher is no way out of the difficulty.

readily grant the merit of the old axiom in this case, "de minimis non curat praetor".[50]

(4) The Meaning of "*quoque*"

The term "*quoque*" has given rise to considerable discussion among canonists. Some hold that by its presence the law includes works on religious and profane topics, while others claim that profane topics alone are meant. The second interpretation is the one preferred by the writer.[51]

---

[50] The following adhere to the restricted meaning of books in this canon: Blat, *Commentarium*, III, partes 2–6, 335; Seraphinus a Loiano, *Institutiones*, II, 634; Santamaria, *Comentarios*, IV, 240. The following hold that the term is to be taken in the extended meaning: Coronata, *Institutiones*, II, 319; Brys, *CB*, XXVIII (1928), 37; De Meester, *Compendium*, III, pars 1, 261; Bouscaren-Ellis, *Canon Law*, p. 707.

[51] The first group points out that "*quoque*" means an obligation which is additional to that of canon 1385, §1; hence, not merely works on religious topics, but *also* those on profane topics. They claim that if permission were required only for works on profane topics, then "*quoque*" should not be in the law; that if permission is required for works on profane topics, then *a fortiori* for works on religious topics; that the pre-Code law favored this view; and that it is the mind of the legislator that both be included. The following adhere to this view: Ayrinhac, *Admin. Legisl.*, p. 281; De Meester, *Compendium*, III, pars 1, 261; Fanfani, *De Iure Religiosorum*, p. 316; Pruemmer, *Manuale*, p. 485, n. 2; Haring, "Druckerlaubnis und Publikationserlaubnis," *ThPrQs*, LXXXV (1932), 822–823; Brys, *CB*, XXVIII (1928), 37; Coronata, *Institutiones*, II, 318–319; Vermeersch-Creusen, *Epitome*, II, 509; Vermeersch, "De librorum conscriptione," *Periodica*, XI (1923), pp. (15)–(17); Creusen-Garesché, *Religious Men and Women in Church Law*, p. 220; Boudinhon, *Nouv. Législ.*, p. 279; Goyeneche, *CpR*, VII (1926), 101; Cance, *Le Code*, III, 161; *L'Ami*, XXIXX (1922), 117; Sabetti-Barrett, *Compendium Theologiae Moralis*, (34. ed., Neo-Eboraci-Cincinnati: F. Pustet, 1939), p. 336.

The second group points out that "*quoque*" points to the previous canon, but to the fact that the laity, the clergy and the religious are obliged to that canon, while only the clergy and the religious are bound by canon 1386, §1; that other examples abound in the Code where a similar use of "*quoque*" is found; that the "*libros quoque*" is an addition to the previous canon, which mentions only works on religious and moral topics; that unless this view is correct, canon 1385, §3, is entirely superfluous; that in practice the opposite view would impose too heavy a burden, which all its adherents try to mitigate. The following support this second view: Cappello, *Summa*, II, 423; Woywod, *HPR*, XXVIII (1928), 864; Pellé, *Le Droit*, p. 369; Gagnon, *La Censure*, p. 128–130; Berutti, *Institutiones*, IV, 427; Regatillo, *Institutiones*, II, 113; Gillet, *Jus Pontificium*, XI (1931), 59–60; Tummulo-Iorio, *De Censuris*, p. 813; Augustine, *Commentary*, VI, 441; M[ahoney], *CR*, VII (1934), 252–253; Nevin, *ACR*, II (1925), 54; Aertnys-Damen, *Theol. Moral.*, I, 751; Davis, *Theology*, II, 413.

A third group avoids the issue by speaking in terms so ambiguous that either interpretation might be gathered from their text, e.g., Wernz-Vidal, *Ius Canonicum*, IV, pars 2, 144–145; Claeys Bouuaert-Simenon, *Manuale*, III, 135; Blat, *Commentarium*, III, partes 2–6, 335; Sipos, *Enchiridion*, pp. 712–713; Beste, *Introductio*, p. 698; Pejska, *Ius Canonicum Religiosorum*, p. 170; Seraphinus a Loiano, *Institutiones*, II, 633; Genicot-Salsmans, *Institutiones*, I, 387; Ubach, *Theol. Moral.*, I, 560; Marc-Gestermann-Raus, *Institutiones*, I, 854; Noldin-Schmitt, *Summa*, II, 710; Bargilliat, *Praelectiones*, I, 443; Cocchi, *Commentarium*, VI, 153; Bouscaren-Ellis, *Canon Law*, p. 707; Piscetta-Gennaro, *Elementa Theologiae Moralis ad Codicem Iuris Canonici Exacta* (5. ed., 7 vols., Torino: Societa Editrice Internazionale, 1938–1943), II, 89–90 (hereafter cited as *Elementa*).

(5) The Nature of the Permission

The permission allows the publication of works on profane topics. It is personal, and given directly to the writer. No precensorship is required.[52] Hence, a general permission may suffice, and this may be granted expressly, either explicitly or implicitly, or tacitly, and may be presumed when the conditions so warrant.[53] This permission may also be given under a time limit. There is no obligation to print the notice of the granting of this permission in the book.[54]

(6) The Persons Bound by This Law

The law states expressly that it obliges clerics and religious. Lay persons are not bound by this law. By clerics are meant all those who have received first tonsure. By religious are meant all those who have taken public vows in a religious institute. Exempt religious are included, but novices and postulants are not to be identified with religious in the present context.[55]

Article III. The Permission Authorizing the Writing for and Managing of Periodicals (Canon 1386, §1)

There is still another permission, mentioned in the same canon, by which the local ordinary authorizes a person to write for or to manage periodicals. The text of the law reads:

> Vetantur clerici saeculares sine consensu suorum Ordinariorum, religiosi vero sine licentia sui Superioris maioris et Ordinarii loci, libros quoque, qui de rebus profanis tractent, edere, et in diariis, foliis, vel libellis periodicis scribere vel eadem moderari.

---

[52] Gagnon, *La Censure*, p. 74; Wernz-Vidal, *Ius Canonicum*, IV, pars 2, 144; Berutti, *Institutiones*, IV, 419, n. 141; De Meester, *Compendium*, III, pars 1, 256; Boudinhon, *Nouv. Législ.*, p. 279; Seraphinus a Loiano, *Institutiones*, II, 633; Regatillo, *Institutiones*, II, 112; Nevin, *ACR*, II (1925), 54; Gillet, *Jus Pontificium*, XI (1931), 58. Some try to read into the term "*consensu*" the meaning that this is a permission which does not require precensorship. They fail to observe that the term "*licentia*" is also used in the same canon.

[53] De Meester, *Compendium*, III, pars 1, 257; Jombart, *RCR*, I (1925), 112; Coronata, *Institutiones*, II, 315, 320; Beste, *Introductio*, p. 698; Pruemmer, *Manuale*, p. 485; Wernz-Vidal, *Ius Canonicum*, IV, pars 2, 145, n. (34); Ayrinhac, *Admin. Legisl.*, p. 281; Vermeersch, *Periodica*, XI (1923), (17).

[54] Ubach, *Theol. Moral.*, I, 560; Boudinhon, *Nouv. Législ.*, p. 279; Gillet, *Jus Pontificium*, XI (1931), 58; Nevin, *ACR*, II (1925), 54; Jombart, *RCR*, I, (1925), 112; Beste, *Introductio*, p. 698, who says that the notice of the granting of this permission is ordinarily printed in a book.

[55] Beste, *Introductio*, p. 698; Wernz-Vidal, *Ius Canonicum*, IV, pars 2, 145; Vermeersch-Creusen, *Epitome*, II, 509–510; Berutti, *Institutiones*, IV, 427; Schaefer, *De Religiosis*, n. 1419; Boudinhon, *Nouv. Législ.*, p. 279; Augustine, *Commentary*, VI, 442. O'Brien (*The Exemption of Religious in Church Law* [Milwaukee: The Bruce Publishing Co., (1943)], p. 279) still holds out for the exemption of Regulars.

The explanation of this text will be divided as follows: (1) the meaning of "local ordinary"; (2) the nature of the power exercised; (3) the matter included under the term "periodicals"; (4) the functions of writing and managing; (5) the nature of the permission; (6) the persons bound by this law; (7) the purpose of the law.

(1) The Meaning of "Local Ordinary"

The local ordinary, in this case, is the local ordinary as described above, in connection with the treatment of the writing of books on profane topics. It is the identical canon.

(2) The Nature of the Power Exercised

The nature of the power exercised is that of jurisdiction, as explained above.

(3) The Matter Included under the Term "Periodicals"

The Code uses the terms "*diariis, foliis, vel libellis periodicis.*" This evidently means all periodicals, including newspapers, whether religious or secular. No distinction is made.[56]

(4) The Functions of Writing and Managing

The Code uses the word "*scribere,*" which means "to write for," i.e., to compose and send in for publication. Since no distinction is made, there apparently is included all writing, not merely habitual and frequent writing, but also each and every contribution, even though infrequent. Historically, however, the law was particularly interested in, and legislated for, those clerics who acted as correspondents and collaborators of newspapers or periodicals, and hence were habitual contributors.[57] It is not easy to determine just how much writing constitutes habitual writing, though it is quite immaterial whether the writing be done for one or more periodicals. It is probable, not only because of the history of the law and because of its context, but also because of the absurd consequences of a literal interpretation, that only habitual or frequent writing is still meant.[58]

[56] Pennacchi, *ASS*, XXX (1897–1898), 344, 508; Van Coillie, *Commentarius*, p. 64; Cappello, *De Curia Romana* (2 vols., Romae, 1911–1912), I, 286; Vermeersch, *De Prohibitione*, p. 107; De Meester, *Compendium*, III, pars 1, 261; Blat, *Commentarium*, III, partes 2–6, 335; Beste, *Introductio*, p. 699; Augustine, *Commentary*, VI, 441; *L'Ami*, XLI (1924), 14; Wernz-Vidal, *Ius Canonicum*, IV, pars 2, 144–145; Tummulo-Iorio, *De Censuris*, 816–817; Boudinhon, *Nouv. Législ.*, p. 173; Ayrinhac, *Admin. Legisl.*, p. 281; Schneider, *Buechergesetze*, p. 152; Moureau, *Nouv. Législ.*, p. 95; Desjardins, *Etudes*, LXXI (1897), 369; Brys, *CB*, XXXIII (1933), 410; Coronata, *Institutiones*, II, 320; Seraphinus a Loiano, *Institutiones*, II, 633.

[57] Leo XIII, const. "*Officiorum ac munerum,*" 27 ian. 1897, art. 42—*Fontes*, n. 632; Pius X, encycl. "*Pascendi,*" 8 sept. 1907, §44, IV—*Fontes*, n. 689.

[58] Ayrinhac, *Admin. Legisl.*, p. 281; Nevin, *ACR*, II (1925), 55; Van Hove, *De Legibus*, p. 263; Brys, *CB*, XXXIII (1933), 410–411; Coronata, *Institutiones*, II, 319–320; Genicot-Salsmans, *Institutiones*, I, 387; Beste, *Introductio*, p. 699; Haring, *Grundzuege*, I, 175, n. 5;

The Code also uses the term "*moderari*," which means to manage, direct, supervise, superintend. This indeed one may do alone, or together with others, e.g., as a member of a board, firm, or corporation. Often the business management is separated from the editorial management. The editorial management (*directio*, *rédaction*, *comité de direction*, *Schriftleitung*) determines the policies of the periodical as well as the contents of each issue; it solicits and prepares the material for publication. When its organization is more complex, there may be an editor-in-chief, carrying the principal responsibility, and several assistants who are placed in charge of various departments as literary editors, book review editors, etc., or who by their own writings furnish much of the material for publication and are known as contributing editors or the like. They compose the editorial board or staff. The business management (*administratio*) is responsible for the circulation of the periodical by sale or subscriptions, for the printing of each issue on its own press or by a distinct printing establishment, for the distribution or delivery of the printed copies; it also handles the finances connected with the publication. The person in charge is usually called the business manager, who may be assisted by a treasurer, a circulation manager, an advertising manager, etc. Sometimes the business management is in the hands of a distinct publishing firm. In this canon, the term "to manage" connotes the editorial direction,[59] at least the person or persons who have the primary moral responsibility for the periodical, such as the editor or editor-in-chief.[60] However, in a reply to the Bishop of Metz, dated November 3, 1928, Cardinal Peter Gasparri, acting as president of the Pontifical Commission for Interpreting the Code, stated that the words "*scribere*" and "*moderari*" in canon 1386, §1, also evidently forbid the clergy to be members of the editorial board ("*comité de rédaction*") or of the board of inspectors ("*conseil de surveillance*") of a policital newspaper or journal.[60a]

Boudinhon, *Nouv. Législ.*, p. 281; Augustine, *Commentary*, VI, 442; M[ahoney], "'Scribere' in Canon 1386, §1," *CR*, XIX (1940), 353; Woywod, *HPR*, XXVIII (1928), 864; Cappello, *Summa*, II, 424; Ferreres, *Institutiones*, II, 151; Jombart, *DDC*, III, 168; Gagnon, *La Censure*, p. 132.

The following would also include a single notable or important contribution: Davis, *Theology*, II, 413; Boudinhon, *Nouv. Législ.*, p. 281; M[ahoney], *CR*, XIX (1940), 353; Augustine, *Commentary*, VI, 442; Beste, *Introductio*, p. 699; Genicot-Salsmans, *Institutiones*, I, 460; Ayrinhac, *Admin. Legisl.*, p. 281; Wernz-Vidal, *Ius Canonicum*, IV, pars 2, 145, n. (34).

The following specify that even habitual minor contributions are included: Van Hove, *De Legibus*, p. 263; Brys, *CB*, XXVIII (1928), 38; Vermeersch-Creusen, *Epitome*, II, 510; Sipos, *Enchiridion*, p. 712; M[ahoney], *CR*, XIX (1940), 353–354.

[59] Hurley, *Commentary*, p. 228; Ayrinhac, *Admin. Legisl.*, p. 281; Augustine, *Commentary*, VI, 440, 442; Davis, *Theology*, II, 413; Woywod, *HPR*, XXVIII (1928), 863.

[60] Cappello, *Summa*, II, 424; Boudinhon, *Nouv. Législ.*, p. 281.

[60a] The text of this document may be found in *CpR*, X (1929), 24, and in Schaefer, *De Religiosis*, n. 1419, p. 844.

(5) The Nature of the Permission

The permission allows the writing for, or the managing of, periodicals. Less reason is needed to write for than to manage a periodical. It is a personal permission, which does not attach to the periodical, but to the individual.[61] Hence, when an editor lapses from office, each new editor needs a new permission. For this reason, the permission prescinds entirely from the question whether or not the articles in that periodical need precensorship. That matter is determined completely by canon 1385, §1. If the matter fall under that canon, precensorship is required; otherwise, not.[62]

(6) The Persons Bound by This Law

All clerics and religious, as mentioned above, are bound by this law. The Constitution "*Officiorum ac munerum*" had legislated only for secular clerics, but Pius X extended that law to include religious. The Code is most explicit. All writers agree that a cleric or a religious who engages a layman to do this type of work for him, even though he allow the layman to use his own [the layman's name], is really writing or managing. The law applies to such a cleric because he is acting through an agent.[63]

(7) The Purpose of the Law

It is the purpose of this law to prevent the neglect of spiritual duties, and also to preclude the writing of articles that might lessen the regard for the clerical or the religious state.[64] Harm might occur if a cleric or a religious engaged in writing on secular topics without being properly qualified to do so, or to engage in secular pursuits which are less fitting for the clergy or religious. The Church does not forbid clerics or religious to do these things, but

---

[61] Hence, a general permission to write for a certain periodical, or for all Catholic periodicals, could readily be granted to individuals or to groups. Some restrictions may be imposed concerning the matter to be treated. Cf. Brys, *CB*, XXXIII (1933), 412. The authors cited above, when treating of the nature of the permission to write profane works, hold the same views in this place.

[62] Brys, "De licentia scribendi in diariis et periodicis," *Collationes Brugenses*, XXXIII (1933), 413; Vermeersch-Creusen, *Epitome*, II, 510; De Meester, *Compendium*, III, pars 1, 262; Nevin, "Censorship of Books," *Australasian Catholic Record*, II (1925), 55.

[63] Wernz, *Ius Decretalium*, III, 132, n. (111); Pennacchi, *ASS*, XXX (1897–1898), 511; Vermeersch, *De Prohibitione*, p. 146; Desjardins, *Etudes*, LXXI (1897), Boudinhon, *Nouv. Législ.*, p. 281; Hurley, *Commentary*, p. 228; De Meester, *Compendium*, III, pars 1, 262; Beste, *Introductio*, p. 699; Brys, *CB*, XXVIII (1928), 38. O'Brien claims that Regulars enjoy exemption in this regard. Cf. *The Exemption of Religious in Church Law*, p. 279.

[64] Jombart, "Censure des Livres," *Dictionnaire de Droit Canonique* (Paris, 1924—), III, 168 (hereafter cited as *DDC*); Gagnon, *La Censure*, p. 132.

wishes to safeguard its subjects while doing them, in such a way that they enhance the clerical and religious state, and promote the regard for the clerical and religious profession.[65]

Article IV. The Judgment Concerning Contributions to Forbidden Periodicals (Canon 1386, §2)

A special point mentioned in the law concerns written contributions made to forbidden periodicals. Ordinarily the making of such contributions is forbidden, but in view of special circumstances a sufficient reason may exist to warrant such a procedure. The local ordinary is to judge the sufficiency of the reason. This is not a grant of permission, but, because of the similarity to that function, it is treated in conjunction with it. The text of the law reads:

> In diariis vero, foliis, vel libellis qui religionem catholicam aut bonos mores impetere solent, nec laici catholici quidpiam conscribant, nisi iusta ac rationabili causa suadente, ab Ordinario loci probata.

The explanation of this law will be divided as follows: (1) the meaning of "local ordinary"; (2) the prohibition of the natural law; (3) the prohibition of the ecclesiastical law; (4) the cessation of this prohibition; (5) the nature of the judgment; (6) the persons bound by the law.

(1) The Meaning of "Local Ordinary"

Canon 1386, §2, mentions that the cause for writing in a forbidden periodical must be judged by the "local ordinary," but it does not specify that term any further. The law also prescinds from the problem of precensorship as such. Hence, it seems that the local ordinary would have to be understood in the same sense as the proper local ordinary mentioned above.[66] The very same arguments hold in this case, as in the preceding cases, where the local ordinary judges the fitness of writing books on profane topics, or of writing for or managing periodicals.

(2) The Prohibition of the Natural Law

The natural law forbids the co-operation of a person in the sin of another, and also forbids the giving of scandal. Both are implied to a lesser or greater extent in a Catholic's act of writing for forbidden periodicals. Co-operation is given by editors, writers, publishers, vendors, subscribers, advertisers, etc.

---

[65] Brys, *CB*, XXXIII (1933), 409; Schneider, *Buechergesetze*, p. 151; Pennacchi, *ASS*, XXX (1897–1898), 512; Boudinhon, *Nouv. Législ.*, pp. 281–282; Jombart, *DDC*, III, 168.

[66] Canon 1386, §1. Blat, *Commentarium*, III, partes 2–6, 337; Woywod, *HPR*, XXVIII (1927–1928), 865. Berutti (*Institutiones* IV, 420) includes the ordinary of the place where the writing is published. Seraphinus a Loiano (*Institutiones*, II, 634) holds that "local ordinray" here means one of the three mentioned in canon 1385, §1 [§2?].

The positive law mentions only the writers. Strictly regarded, a contributor need not hold the views, nor subscribe to the policies of a magazine to which he contributes. However, every co-operation is at least a material co-operation. Formal co-operation is intrinsically evil, and never permissible. Merely material co-operation is not intrinsically evil, and may be permitted when there is sufficient reason for it and when the danger of scandal is removed or greatly lessened. Greater reason is required for habitual or frequent contributions than for a contribution in an isolated instance.[67]

(3) The Prohibition of the Ecclesiastical Law

The object of the prohibition of ecclesiastical law is mentioned explicitly in the law, namely, all periodicals which frequently or habitually attack the Catholic religion,[68] or good morals.[69] The Code uses the word "*solent*," which means that the anti-Catholic character of the periodical must be evident from repeated attacks, not merely in one or the other issue, but such as bespeak a general tendency or practice.[70]

The Code postulates that these periodicals *attack* the Catholic religion or good morals. Authors usually give equivalents of that term in their commentaries, all of which indicate one or the other of the following activities: to attempt to overthrow, to assault the truth, to deride openly, to fight for false ideals and to attempt to disseminate them, to teach and defend the opposite of what the Catholic Church holds, to propagate heresy or schism, etc. Some examples are: to defend divorce, to justify immoral practices, e.g., birth-control, to propose a false system and to support it with arguments and reasoning, to advocate pornographic magazines, etc.[71]

---

[67] Noldin-Schmitt, *Summa*, II, 126; Aertnys-Damen, *Theol. Moral.*, I, 335–336; Arndt, *Commentarii*, p. 237; Hurley, *Commentary*, p. 168; Genicot-Salsmans, *Institutiones*, I, 188; Jombart, *DDC*, III, 161–162; Marc-Gestermann-Raus, *Institutiones*, I, 335.

[68] The term "Catholic religion" is a further determination of the law of "*Officiorum ac munerum*" (art, 21–22), which merely stated that periodicals which attacked religion were the object of the law. Hence, the present law is more specific. However, the term "Catholic religion" must be understood to mean not only the Catholic religion as it appears today, but all attacks against the true religion, e.g., against natural religion which is the rational foundation for revealed religion; against one or the other dogma, even though it does not attack all dogmas, or against any precept of the divine or ecclesiastical law. Cf. Pennacchi, *ASS*, XXX (1897–1898), 344–345; Hurley, *Commentary*, pp. 150, 167; Tummulo-Iorio, *De Censuris*, p. 806; Beste, *Introductio*, p. 699; Coronata, *Institutiones*, II, 319; Ubach, *Theol. Moral.*, I, 567; Jombart, *DDC*, III, 168–169.

[69] By good morals is meant all that pertains to ethics, or moral theology. This means the system as a whole, or any part of it, e.g., against one or the other particular precept, e.g., birth control, onanism, etc. Cf. Augustine, *Commentary*, VI, 469; Hurley, *Commentary*, p. 167; Pernicone, *Prohibition*, p. 133; Vermeersch, *De Prohibitione*, p. 111; Seraphinus a Loiano, *Institutiones*, II, 648; Genicot-Salsmans, *Institutiones*, I, 375.

[70] Hurley, *Commentary*, pp. 164–167.

[71] Tummulo-Iorio, *De Censuris*, p. 806; Vermeersch-Creusen, *Epitome*, II, 509; Seraphinus a Loiano, *Institutiones*, II, 648; Marc-Gestermann-Raus, *Institutiones*, I, 860; Blat, *Commen-*

These attacks on the Catholic religion need not be direct attacks, for it suffices also that they be indirect attacks. They may be intentional or unintentional. The pre-Code law contained the words "*data opera*," which are not found in the present law.

Authors dispute about the problem of advertising in such periodicals. The Code uses the words "*quidpiam conscribere*," which could seem to include all types of writing. However, authors contend that those things which are not written, e.g., ads, announcements, notices of rent, notices of sale of property, etc., are not really composed, or, if composed, they would not fall under the term "*conscribere*." This view seems probable even today, in view of the extrinsic authority of those who allow it.[72]

(4) The Cessation of the Prohibition

When there is a just and reasonable cause to permit material co-operation in the [material or formal] sin of another, and when there is reason to believe that scandal will be averted, the prohibition of the natural law ceases. In such instances, the local ordinary is permitted to allow the publication of a writing in a forbidden periodical. Lest anyone be deluded in judging the sufficiency of the reason, or become guilty of imprudent action, the decision is placed in the hands of the local ordinary.[73]

At times, greater scandal would be occasioned by the appearance of an article written by a cleric or a religious than by a lay person; though, conversely, an article by a cleric might receive greater respect. Sufficient reasons for writing in such magazines are the utility of answering a false accusation, the necessity of refuting attacks on religion or morals, the obligation of defending the rights of the Church, etc. An inadequate defense may do more

---

tarium, III, partes 2–6, 337; Beste, *Introductio*, p. 699; Genicot-Salsmans, *Institutiones*, I, 374–375; De Meester, *Compendium*, III, pars 1, 284; Claeys Bouuaert-Simenon, *Manuale*, III, 141–142.

[72] The following hold that such contributions imply co-operation and are forbidden both by the natural and by the ecclesiastical law: Blat, *Commentarium*, III, partes 2–6, 336; Marc-Gestermann-Raus, *Institutiones*, I, 855; Ayrinhac, *Admin. Legisl.*, p. 281; Beste, *Introductio*, p. 699.

The following deny the prohibition by the ecclesiastical law, but admit the prohibition by the natural law: Coronata, *Institutiones*, II, 321; De Meester, *Compendium*, III, pars 1, 262; Cance, *Le Code*, III, 161, n. 2; Vermeersch-Creusen, *Epitome*, II, 509; Claeys Bouuaert-Simenon, *Manuale*, III, 135; Aertnys-Damen, *Theol. Moral.*, I, 751; Jombart, *DDC*, III, 168; Gagnon, *La Censure*, p. 133.

[73] Arndt, *Commentarii*, p. 237; Hollweck, *Strafgesetze*, p. 45, n. 1; Claeys Bouuaert-Simenon, *Manuale*, III, 135; Coronata, *Institutiones*, II, 321; Hurley, *Commentary*, p. 168; Jombart, *DDC*, III, 168; Ayrinhac, *Admin. Legisl.*, p. 282; Blat, *Commentarium*, III, partes 2–6, 337; Wernz-Vidal, *Ius Canonicum*, IV, pars 2, 146; Woywod, *HPR*, XXVIII (1928), 865; Seraphinus a Loiano, *Institutiones*, II, 634; Vermeersch, *Theologia Moralis*, III, 895.

harm than good, simply because the article fails to meet the issue properly, and then such an article might confirm people in their false opinions and errors.[74]

(5) The Nature of the Judgment

The local ordinary is empowered to judge the sufficiency of the reason and the presence or the absence of scandal. If he deems that the occasion warrants it, he will declare that the reason is sufficient. Nothing is mentioned about the granting of permission, or about precensorship. The supposition is that if the matter falls under the material mentioned in canon 1385, §1, it is already subject to the law of precensorship. The Code does not exempt the writer from this obligation in canon 1386, §2. The local ordinary may even prescribe the precensorship of an article on a profane topic, but unless that were specifically mentioned, such an article would not require precensorship.[75]

If the reason for writing in a forbidden periodical endures, the local ordinary may readily judge that the writing may be done over a considerable period of time. This is similar to a habitual permission.

(6) The Persons Bound by This Law

The Code uses the words "*nec laici catholici*" and does not mention the clergy and religious explicitly. However, the context of the law makes it apparent that the obligation rests on the clergy and on religious, exempt and non-exempt, as well as on the laity.[76]

Section II. Permissions Granted by Religious Superiors (Canons 1385, §3; 1386, §1)

In view of the fact that they are subject to the superiors of their institute in all things, religious must also obtain the permission of their superiors for the writing and publication of works mentioned in law. The law specifies three different occasions when the religious superior is to exercise that authority: (1) the permission which is required for the publication of works on religious or moral topics (canon 1385, §3); (2) the permission which is required for the publication of works on profane topics (canon 1386, §1), and (3) the permission which is required for writing for or managing peri-

[74] Desjardins, *Etudes*, LXXI (1897), 216; Cappello, *De Curia Romana*, I, 288; Marc-Gestermann-Raus, *Institutiones*, I, 855; Blat, *Commentarium*, III, partes 2–6, 336; Ayrinhac, *Admin. Legisl.*, p. 281; Cance, *Le Code*, III, 161, n. 1; Jombart, *DDC*, III, 168; Pennacchi, *ASS*, XXX (1897–1898), 348–349; Hurley, *Commentary*, p. 168; Gagnon, *La Censure*, p. 133.

[75] Berutti *Institutiones*, IV, 420.

[76] Wernz-Vidal, *Ius Canonicum*, IV, pars 2, 146; Vermeersch-Creusen, *Epitome*, II, 509–510; Aertnys-Damen, *Theol. Moral.*, I, 751; Blat, *Commentarium*, III, partes 2–6, 336; Seraphinus a Loiano, *Institutiones*, II, 634; Ayrinhac, *Admin. Legisl.*, p. 281; Coronata, *Institutiones*, II, 320.

odicals (canon 1386, §1). All three may be taken simulataneously, for there is little that differentiates one from the other. The texts of the law read:

> Canon 1385, §3. Religiosi vero licentiam quoque sui Superioris maioris antea consequi debent.
>
> Canon 1386, §1. Vetantur . . . religiosi vero sine licentia sui Superioris maioris et Ordinarii loci, libros quoque, qui de rebus profanis tractent, edere, et in diariis, foliis, vel libellis periodicis scribere vel eadem moderari.

The explanation of the law will be divided as follows: (1) the meaning of the term "major superior"; (2) the nature of the power exercised; (3) the meaning of the term "religious"; (4) the permission required by canon 1385, §3; (5) the permission demanded by canon 1386, §1; (6) the nature of the permission granted.

(1) The Meaning of the Term "Major Superior"

The following superiors are known as major superiors: the abbot primate, the abbot superior of a monastic congregation, the abbot of an independent monastery, even though it belong to a monastic congregation, the superior-general of an entire institute, the provincial superior, the vicars of all the afore-mentioned, and likewise all others having powers equivalent to those of provincials.[77] Those who are local superiors are not major superiors.[78] Although nothing is mentioned in the Code, particular law may reserve certain permissions to the highest religious superior.[79]

(2) The Nature of the Power Exercised

Since the Code makes no distinction between exempt and non-exempt religious but speaks of all together, even those of lay institutes, it is reasonable to conclude that the power which the superior exercises when giving this permission is not jurisdiction, but dominative power. The purpose of the law is that subjects show proper subjection to their superiors, and there is no call for using jurisdiction if the superior possess it. Hence, it is admitted that the power used is dominative power.[80] Religious are assigned to specific duties and offices, and certain types of writing might not be con-

[77] Canon 488, 8°. The translation is taken from Bouscaren-Ellis, *Canon Law*, p. 232.

[78] Schaefer, *De Religiosis*, nn. 425–429; Gagnon, *La Censure*, p. 127.

[79] Gagnon, *La Censure*, p. 185. Berutti (*Institutiones*, IV, 425, n. 4) writes: "S.C.S.Off. d. 5 maii 1924 supremis Religionum Moderatoribus iniunxit ut ad se avocent facultatem concedendi propriis subditis religiosis licentiam edendi libros et quaelibet alia scripta *ad rem biblicam spectantia*. Nunquam autem huiusmodi licentiam concedant nisi praevia scripti recognitione in Curia Generalitia diligentissime peracta per revisores ad rem designandos," and he cites *Analecta Ordinis Praedicatorum*, XVI, 459, as his source. The *Constitutiones Ordinis Fratrum Minorum Cappuccinorum* (Romae, 1927) contain such legislation in article 215. Similar legislation is cited in an article by Goyeneche, *CpR*, VII (1926), 101.

[80] Schaefer, *De Religiosis*, n. 450, K), n. 14.

sidered compatible with those duties or offices. Furthermore, there is the question of the disposition of the manuscript, and also the expenses connected with the printing and publishing arrangements—all of which have a bearing on the vow of poverty.[81] Finally, the good name of the institute may be at stake, and may be enhanced or seriously impaired by the writings of certain religious.[82]

When it is a question of giving permission for private printings within the institute, superiors may grant such permissions without submitting the manuscript to the local ordinary for precensorship, or without asking his permission. These are purely internal affairs, fully within the competence of the religious superiors.[83]

(3) The Meaning of the Term "Religious"

By religious are meant all those who take public vows in a religious institute approved by the Church. This does not include novices or postulants, nor those members of institutes which do not have public vows. If a major superior publishes a book, he does not need the permission of a higher superior, unless that be demanded by common or particular law.[84]

(4) The Permission Required by Canon 1385, §3

Canon 1385, §3, imposes on religious the duty of obtaining a twofold permission: the obligation of submitting the work to the local ordinary for precensorship and for obtaining his permission to publish it, and the duty of first securing the permission of the religious superior to publish the work. Some canonists hold that there must be a precensorship by religious authorities as well as by ecclesiastical authorities.[85] Particular law may, and often

---

[81] Turner, *The Vow of Poverty*, The Catholic University of America Canon Law Studies, No. 54 (Washington, D. C.: The Catholic University of America, 1929), pp. 93–106.

[82] Jombart, *DDC*, III, 168.

[83] Gagnon, *La Censure*, p. 185.

[84] Goyeneche, *CpR*, VII (1926), 101.

[85] De Meester, *Compendium*, III, pars 1, 260; Berutti, *Institutiones*, IV, 425; Seraphinus a Loiano, *Institutiones*, II, 627. Augustine (*Commentary*, VI, 439) says: "Superiors ought to subject every book that is to be published to an examination by competent scholars." Berutti restricts canon 1385, §3, to clerical religious, by stating that lay religious need the consent of their superiors, according to their constitutions, but that they do not need the permission required by canon 1385, §3, since these superiors are considered incompetent to pass judgment in the Church on matters pertaining to faith and morals.

A *monitum* of the S.C.S.Off., 29 mart. 1941—*AAS*, XXXIII (1941), 121—seems to imply that religious superiors are charged with the obligation of appointing expert censors. A similar opinion may be gathered from a decree of the S.C.C., 7 iun. 1932—*AAS*, XXIV (1932), 240. Pre-Code law also required precensorship by the religious superiors: cf. Conc. Trident., sess. IV, *de editione et usu sacrorum librorum;* Leo XIII, const. "*Officiorum ac munerum,*" 25 ian. 1897, n. 36—*Fontes*, n. 632; S.C.de Rel., 15 iun. 1911—*AAS*, III (1911), 270–271.

does, require such precensorship within the religious institute,[86] but the general law of the Code does not impose it.[87] The canon does not distinguish; it includes all religious. It would be incongruous were it obligatory for superiors of lay institutes, especially of women, to pass judgment on matters which are not properly their field of activity.

The term "*antea*" means that the religious is to observe a definite order in seeking and obtaining permission. He is to approach his religious superior before going to the ecclesiastical superior, and also before making arrangements for printing, publishing and distribution.

(5) The Permission Demanded by Canon 1386, §1

Canon 1386, §1, requires the religious to obtain the permission of their major superiors, besides that of the local ordinary, for the publishing of profane works and for the writing for or managing of periodicals. Common law does not prescribe that the religious superiors subject writings on profane matters to previous examination, though particular law may demand it.[88] This permission need not precede that of the local ordinary. In fact, the local ordinary may give a general permission to the members of a certain religious house, or at least to those members who have received or who will receive the permission of their major superiors.[89]

(6) The Nature of the Permission Granted

The permission of the religious superior is personal, and may be a general permission. Particular law may require individual permission. The permission granted by the religious superior need not be shown to the local ordinary, nor need notice of its granting be printed in the book, unless that be prescribed by particular law.[90]

If superiors refuse to grant this permission, recourse may be had to higher superiors, or, if there be no higher superiors, to the Sacred Congregation for Religious. Such recourse would be *in devolutivo*.

With proper permission a religious may donate a manuscript to others. If the other then proceeds to publication, that is his own affair.[91] However,

[86] Gagnon, *La Censure*, p. 185. The major superiors of clerical exempt religious institutes possess the power of jurisdiction in the external forum; being ordinaries, they seem to be competent to perform precensorship in the proper sense in regard to the religious works of their subjects and to grant them an *Imprimatur*. Gagnon, *loc. cit.*

[87] Nevins, *ACR*, II (1925), 50; Vermeersch-Creusen, *Epitome*, II, 503, 509–510; Ubach, *Theol. Moral.*, I, 561; Pejska, *Ius Canonicum Religiosorum*, p. 171; Wernz-Vidal, *Ius Canonicum*, IV, pars 2, 144–145.

[88] Berutti, *Institutiones*, IV, 425.

[89] Jombart, *DDC*, III, 167–168.

[90] Berutti, *Institutiones*, IV, 426; Blat, *Commentarium*, III, partes 2–6, 335; Vermeersch-Creusen, *Epitome*, II, 503.

[91] Vermeersch, "Annotationes," *Periodica*, VI (1912), 68; VII (1914), 165.

a religious is not allowed to hand his manuscript to others with the stipulation that it be printed anonymously, or under another name, so as to escape the necessity of obtaining the permission, and thus circumvent the law.[92]

Section III. Summary

The Church prescribes that certain permissions be obtained in connection with the publication of books. This permission is always to be sought from the ecclesiastical superiors, though religious have the additional obligation of obtaining similar permissions from their religious superiors.

Every local ordinary is empowered to grant all permissions save those which by law are reserved to higher superiors. However, only designated local ordinaries are competent to grant permission in a given instance—the proper local ordinary of the author, the local ordinary of the place of publication, and the local ordinary of the place of printing.

For lay people, the proper local ordinary of the author is the local ordinary of the place of the author's domicile or quasi-domicile; or, if he have neither, of the place where he happens to be. For the diocesan clergy, the proper local ordinary is the local ordinary of the diocese of incardination, as well as the local ordinary of the place where the cleric has a domicile or a quasi-domicile. For religious, the proper local ordinary is the local ordinary of the place where is situated the religious house to which he is assigned, or also the local ordinary of the place of domicile or quasi-domicile if the religious is legitimately residing elsewhere.

The law specifies that the permission may also be obtained from the local ordinary of the place of publication or of printing, i.e., the place where these firms are situated. If a firm prints or publishes at two or more different addresses, the local ordinary of each of these places is competent. However, a branch office which does not print or publish, but merely distributes works that are printed and published elsewhere, is not the place of printing or publication, but a book-agency.

Permission to publish works on religious or moral topics must be sought by all, lay people, clerics and religious. This permission may be given only after precensorship has been performed. Clerics and religious are obliged to obtain permission to publish works on profane topics, but for these precensorship is not required by law. Clerics and religious must also obtain permission to write for or to manage periodicals. This last permission is a personal permission, and prescinds from precensorship, which may or may not be required, depending on the nature of the periodical or the articles published in it.

---

[92] S.C. de Religiosis, Dubia, 15 iun. 1911—*AAS*, III (1911), 270.

The local ordinary is also the judge of the sufficiency of the reason for the publishing of articles in forbidden periodicals. This holds for all, lay people, clerics and religious. It is reserved to the local ordinary to decide if and when material co-operation may be permitted. Formal co-operation is never allowed. The local ordinary is also the judge of the scandal which may arise, and how it is to be lessened or removed.

A second competent local ordinary may grant permission for the publication of a work on religious or moral topics, even though a first local ordinary has refused such permission, provided he has sufficient grounds for making such a decision.

All the above mentioned permissions must be obtained by religious, who, in addition, are to seek similar permissions from their own major superiors. Common law does not demand precensorship in these cases of additional permissions, though particular law may, and often does. Permission sought from religious superiors should precede that sought from the local ordinary. Notice of its granting need not, however, be printed in the book.

CHAPTER VIII

TRANSLATIONS AND NEW EDITIONS (CANON 1392)

Over and above the fact that a work may originally have received ecclesiastical approval, the Code, in canon 1392, demands that translations and new editions of that work be submitted for new precensorship and approval. The text of the law reads:

> §1. Approbatio textus originalis alicuius operis, neque eiusdem in aliam linguam translationibus neque aliis editionibus suffragatur; quare et translationes et novae editiones operis approbati nova approbatione communiri debent.
>
> §2. Excerpta e periodicis capita seorsim edita novae editiones non censentur nec proinde nova approbatione indigent.

Since the law speaks of a "new" approbation, it is evident that it treats only of those works which stand in need of precensorship in their original or first edition.[1] The commentary on this canon will be divided as follows: (1) the matter included by this canon; (2) the authorities competent to grant the approval; (3) the nature of the approval; (4) the persons bound to seek such approval; (5) the purpose of the law; (6) a summary.

(1) The Matter Included by This Canon

The canon speaks of translations and new editions. A *translation* is the equivalent of a work, obtained by rendering it into a language other than the original. Sometimes the process of turning a work from one language to another is precise and accurate, in which case the new version is called a literal translation. At other times the process is less rigid, in which case the new version is called a free translation. There are varying degrees of freedom possible in translation, some of which render the original more reliably than others, and some of which depart quite radically from the original and assume the character of adapted versions.

Ecclesiastical law does not prescribe the character of translations, save in the case of indulgences, certain official decrees and documents, etc., where exact and precise fidelity is demanded. The law does not concern itself with the person of the translator, whether he be the original author or someone else. Neither does the law concern itself about the language from which or into which the work is being turned. The only point at issue is that the work in its new form is considered a new work, and hence must follow the prescribed rule for precensorship.[2]

---

[1] Pennacchi, *ASS*, XXX (1897–1898), 519; Schneider, *Buecbergesetze*, p. 155; Piat, *NRT*, XXXII (1900), 569; Woywod, *HPR*, XXVIII (1928), 970.

[2] *Theol. Mechlin.*, p. 229; Pennacchi, *ASS*, XXX (1897–1898), 520.

A *new edition* is a later publication of a work that had already been published. *New impressions*, i.e., new printings from the original plates or standing type, may be considered as a continuation of the earlier edition of the work, at least if they are produced within a short time after the previous issues and provided that no important alterations or additions are made in the text; incidental changes, e.g., corrections of spelling mistakes, an adjusting of misplaced lines, an emendation of citations, etc., do not make the new impression a new edition.[3] This might happen easily, e.g., when a work runs through a half dozen impressions within a year. Similarly, some European publishers print several "editions" at one impression and announce the publication of two or more "editions" on the same day or after brief intervals of time.[4] In the canonical sense there is but one edition, and one approval suffices.[5]

On the other hand, it is obvious that enlarged or revised editions are new editions and required a new approval.[6] It is immaterial whether the altered or enlarged edition be issued by the same or by another publisher. It is a new edition not only if it is produced from new type or plates, but also if the revisions are incorporated in the original type or plates. If a previously published work is reprinted in condensed form, it is an altered edition and needs a new approbation.[7]

In like manner, *reprints*, i.e., new printings, without important alteration in content, from new or original type or plates, and facsimile reproductions, i.e., made by a mechanical or a photomechanical process, are to be regarded as new editions.[8] The law does not distinguish between revised and unre-

[3] Augustine, *Commentary*, VI, 450; Woywod, *Commentary*, II, 126; Woywod-Smith, *Commentary*, II, 146; Jombart, "Censura praevia pro nova editione," *Periodica*, XXIV (1935), 36*–37*; Coronata, *Institutiones*, II, 327; Wernz-Vidal, *Ius Canonicum*, IV, pars 2, 140. Berutti (*Institutiones*, IV, 430) states that, if the work is reissued unchanged within a very short time, for instance within a year, it is not a new edition. Jombart (*DDC*, III, 162) holds that it suffices to get a new *Imprimatur* annually.

[4] In their terminology an "edition" means a certain number of copies; thus, one, two or three thousand copies constitute one edition. Several German works bear a note on the title page, "Dritte bis fuenfte Auflage." Piscetta-Gennaro's *Elementa*, Vol. V, bears the note "4 & 5 ed."

[5] Jombart, *Periodica*, XXIV (1935), 37*; Jombart, *DDC*, III, 162; Cance, *Le Code*, III, 160, n. 3.

[6] Pennacchi, *ASS*, XXX (1897–1898), 519; Ayrinhac, *Admin. Legisl.*, p. 285.

[7] Thus, many articles reprinted in the *Catholic Digest* are really new editions of larger writings published elsewhere.

[8] The following hold that all new editions, even those which do not contain any important alterations, are contemplated by the law: Arndt, *Commentarii*, pp. 298–299; Pennacchi, *ASS*, XXX (1897–1898), 519; Cappello, *De Curia Romana*, I, 299; Blat, *Commentarium*, III, partes 2–6, 345; De Meester, *Compendium*, III, pars 1, 267; Vermeersch, *De Prohibitione*, p. 148; Claeys Bouuaert-Simenon, *Manuale*, III, 137; Vermeersch-Creusen, *Epitome*, II, 508; Ayrinhac, *Admin. Legisl.*, pp. 284–285; Seraphinus a Loiano, *Institutiones*, II, 629; Nevin, *ACR*, II

vised editions. Reprint editions produced by another publisher, or even by the same publisher,[9] represent a new issue of the work to the general public, a republication of the same work.[10]

Offprints, i.e., impressions of an article, chapter, or other portion of a larger work, printed from the type or plates of the original and separately issued,[11] are not new editions and do not need a new approval if the original issue was precensored.[12] This is the meaning of the phrase "*vulgo tirages à part*" as used by the S.C.Indicis in the reply dated May 23, 1898.[13] Therefore, if the excerpts are printed from new type, they are reprint editions or new editions in the sense of the Code.[14] It is disputed whether successive chapters, taken from periodicals, could be separately issued in book form without the need of a new approval.[15]

Holy pictures and other sacred images are subject to the same norm. If the new printing is from the original plates and is issued within a reasonably short time after the previous edition, no new approval is required. Otherwise it must be classed as a new edition.[16]

(1925), 54; Gagnon, *La Censure*, p. 122. The following, however, seem to deny that reprint editions are new editions in the sense of the Code: Augustine, *Commentary*, VI, 450; Coronata, *Institutiones*, II, 327; Wernz-Vidal, *Ius Canonicum*, IV, pars 2, 140.

[9] For instance, after the work has been out-of-print for some time.

[10] Even new impressions, produced from the original plates or standing type and substantially unaltered, are regarded by Jombart (*DDC*, III, 162) and Berutti (*Institutiones*, IV, 430) as new editions in the sense of the Code if more than a year has elapsed since the previous approbation.

[11] *A.L.A. Glossary of Library Terms*, prepared by Elisabeth H. Thompson, (Chicago: American Library Association, 1943), p. 93.

[12] Canon 1392, §2.

[13] *ASS*, XXX (1897–1898), 698, and *Fontes*, n. 5152; Pennacchi, "Ad Commentarium in const. '*Officiorum ac munerum*' additiones," *ASS*, XXXIII (1900–1901), 314; Boudinhon, *Nouv. Législ.*, p. 287. This reply is the original source of canon 1392, §2.

[14] The writer disagrees with Goodwine (*The Jurist*, X [1950], 167 [18]), who holds that "The *Catholic Digest* and *The Catholic Mind*—as well as similar publications—may claim exemption from the rule of censorship, since they carry reprints of articles that have appeared elsewhere in Catholic publications."

[15] The following hold that a new approbation is not necessary: Ayrinhac, *Admin. Legisl.*, p. 285; Blat, *Commentarium*, III, partes 2–6, 345; Coronata, *Institutiones*, II, 327; Regatillo *Institutiones*, II, 114; Jombart, *DDC*, III, 162, who adds the condition that no important changes be made. The following require a new approval for such a book: Moureau, *Nouv. Législ.*, p. 93; Vermeersch, *De Prohibitione*, p. 148; Boudinhon, *Nouv. Législ.*, p. 278; De Meester, *Compendium*, III, pars 1, 267; Augustine, *Commentary*, VI, 450; Woywod, *Commentary*, II, 126; Gagnon, *La Censure*, p. 123; Berutti, *Institutiones*, IV, 431. The writer subscribes to the first opinion in regard to offprints of articles already submitted to precensorship and approved, but he agrees with the second opinion if the excerpts have not yet been approved or if they are not true offprints but rather reprints produced from new type or plates.

[16] De Meester, *Compendium*, III, pars 1, 259. "*Officiorum ac munerum*" (art. 15) spoke of "*novae imagines*," which some understood to mean new designs, i.e., original designs, while others understood the law to mean new impressions or editions. The Code fails to use the

(2) The Authorities Competent to Grant This Approval

The ordinary rules of precensorship apply in connection with the seeking of the needed approval for a new edition. Thus, if a work is reserved, the approval must be sought from the authority to whom the granting of the needed permission is reserved. Otherwise, any of the three local ordinaries mentioned in canon 1385, §2, may be approached.

(3) The Nature of the Approval

As indicated in the chapter on terminology, the term "approval" was used in the pre-Code law, and is still used in canon 1392. It means that the work must be submitted for precensorship, after which the authority grants the *Imprimatur*, provided the *Nihil Obstat* was obtained as a result of the examination. The canon does not speak of the renewal of the permission demanded by canon 1385, §3, or that demanded by canon 1386, §§1-2. These latter permissions are personal, and could easily endure for subsequent editions. The wording of the original grant would have to be consulted in these instances. It might have occurred that the permission was granted for one edition only.

(4) The Persons Bound by This Law

The law does not mention explicitly which persons are bound by it, but from the context it is evident that the law binds not merely the authors, but also the publishers. As before, this obligation is an obligation *in solidum*, which allows that, if any one of the interested parties obtains the permission, all the rest are free to use it.[17]

(5) The Purpose of the Law

Translations and new editions are to be submitted for a new precensorship because the original may be altered considerably in the translation or new edition. Similarly, a work which is adjudged suitable in one language or locality, may be less suitable or even harmful in another language or locality.[18] Furthermore, the changes inserted into new editions may contradict faith or morals; or, opinions that were formerly tolerated may now be proscribed or condemned; or, later decisions and decrees may have rendered

---

term "*novae*," and hence all pictures are meant. Nevertheless, the following authors maintain, even after the Code, that reprints of holy pictures already approved do not need a new approbation: Jombart, *DDC*, III, 161; Cocchi, *Commentarium*, VI, 150; Coronata, *Institutiones*, II, 317.

[17] Schneider, *Buechergesetze*, p. 156.

[18] Pennacchi, *ASS*, XXX (1897–1898), 520; Boudinhon, *Nouv. Législ.*, p. 287; Noldin-Schmitt, *Summa*, II, 641; *Theol. Mechlin.*, p. 229; Schneider, *Buechergesetze*, p. 155; Blat, *Commentarium*, III, partes 2–6, 345; Claeys Bouuaert-Simenon, *Manuale*, III, 137; Sipos, *Enchiridion*, p. 714; Beste, *Introductio*, p. 701; Dilgskron, *Anal. Eccl.*, IV (1896), 474.

former positions untenable.[19] Were these matters to appear under an *Imprimatur*, the faithful would easily be misled to believe that they are not contrary to faith or morals, or that there is nothing objectionable about them. It would give the appearance that the ecclesiastical authority approved those things which should be disapproved. In a certain sense, the publisher would be guilty of misrepresentation.

(6) Summary

The fact that a work originally obtained ecclesiastical approval does no-imply that all translations and new editions of that work are likewise approved. On the contrary, the general rule is that translations and new editions require a new approval. Offprints of articles in periodicals, and new printings of books from standing type or the original plates, if they are reprinted within a reasonably short time after the previous impression, are merely new impressions, and are not classed as new editions. The same rule holds for the reprinting of holy pictures.

The competent authority to grant the new approval is any of the three local ordinaries mentioned in canon 1385, §2, unless the granting of the permission for special works is reserved to higher authorities. The new approval is not a positive approval, but a negative approval which is contained in the permission that attends the *Nihil Obstat*. All persons are bound by this law, though it is not a strictly personal obligation resting on the author. Printers and publishers may also obtain this approval.

The purpose of the law is to safeguard the faithful from the possibility of serious misrepresentation. Publishers might reproduce older works, or revised works under the *Imprimatur* which the original work bore. A work reproduced with alterations, or also the same work when reproduced unchanged at a notably later time, must be submitted for a new precensorship.

[19] De Brabandere, *Compendium*, II, 516; Arndt, *Commentarii*, p. 298; Vermeersch, *De Prohibitione*, p. 148; Berutti, *Institutiones*, IV, 430; Ayrinhac, *Admin. Legisl.*, p. 285; Vermeersch-Creusen, *Epitome*, II, 508; Nevin, *ACR*, II (1925), 54; Jombart, *Periodica*, XXIV (1935), 37*.

CHAPTER IX

PRECENSORS (CANON 1393)

The law on precensorship cannot attain its objective unless the canons of the Code are carried into effect by competent officials. Incompetent officials administer the law more or less arbitrarily, either with undue rigor or with superficiality. Undue severity hinders progress, abbreviates legitimate freedom of discussion, obstructs the clearing of religious and moral issues, chokes a healthy independence of thought and renders the publication of many useful books most difficult, if not impossible. Defective precensorship tends to degenerate into a meaningless formality which fails to prevent evil at its source, while it would still be relatively easy to do so. Canon 1393 is designed to regulate the choice of the precensor and to guide him in the performance of his duties. The text of the law reads:

> §1. In universis Curiis episcopalibus censores ex officio adsint, qui edenda cognoscant.
>
> §2. Examinatores in suo obeundo officio, omni personarum acceptione deposita, tantummodo prae oculis habeant Ecclesiae dogmata et communem catholicorum doctrinam quae Conciliorum generalium decretis aut Sedis Apostolicae constitutionibus seu praescriptionibus atque probatorum doctorum consensu continetur.
>
> §3. Censores ex utroque clero eligantur aetate, eruditione, prudentia commendati, qui in doctrinis probandis improbandisque medio tutoque itinere eant.
>
> §4. Censor sententiam scripto dare debet. Quae si faverit, Ordinarius potestatem edendi faciat, cui tamen praeponatur censoris iudicium, inscripto eius nomine. Extraordinariis tantum in adiunctis ac perquam raro, prudenti Ordinarii arbitrio, censoris mentio omitti poterit.
>
> §5. Auctoribus censoris nomen pateat nunquam, antequam hic faventem sententiam ediderit.

The commentary on this canon will be divided as follows: (1) The nature of the office of precensor; (2) the persons empowered to constitute precensors; (3) the persons who are appointed precensors; (4) the appointment; (5) the assignment of a particular work; (6) the functions of precensors; (7) the report to the ecclesiastical authority; (8) the remuneration of precensors; (9) a summary.

Article I. The Nature of the Office of Precensor

A precensor is an official appointed in the capacity of an extrajudicial expert, whose function is to give a balanced judgment on intended publications according to the principles and rules of his art.[1] It is the task of the precensor to establish facts and determine the true nature of intended publications. The sum total of his duties constitutes the office of precensor. This is not an ecclesiastical office in the strict sense, for it does not entail a participation in the power of orders or of jurisdiction.[2] However, it is an ecclesiastical office in the broad sense, for it entails the performance of legitimate functions demanded by the spiritual aim of the Church.[3] Intrinsically a layman could be appointed to this office, but because of §3, which limits the holding of this office to clerics, this is no longer allowed.[4] Although canon 363, §2, does not explicitly list the precensor among the members of the diocesan curia, he belongs to that family.[5]

Article II. The Persons Empowered to Constitute Precensors

It is the general law of the Church that each bishop is to appoint precensors *ex officio* for his own diocese.[6] It is not sufficient that the bishop appoint precensors for individual cases as they arise.[7] A vicar general may make such appointments without a special mandate, because this is not a question of appointing to an ecclesiastical office in the strict sense.[8] The vicar capitular enjoys the same right.[9]

In religious institutes, major superiors may constitute precensors for works that fall within their competence. This is not demanded by the law of the Code, but it is often required by some particular law of the institute.[10]

---

[1] His role is somewhat analagous to that of experts in judicial trials, canons 1792–1805.

[2] Canon 145, §1: "Officium ecclesiasticum . . . stricto autem sensu est munus ordinatione sive divina sive ecclesiastica stabiliter constitutum, ad normam sacrorum canonum conferendum, aliquam saltem secumferens participationem ecclesiasticae potestatis, sive ordinis sive iurisdictionis." Cf. Gagnon, *La Censure*, p. 195.

[3] Canon 145, §1: "Officium ecclesiasticum lato sensu est quodlibet munus quod in spiritualem finem legitime exercetur . . . "

[4] Boudinhon (*Nouv. Législ.*, p. 286) held that laymen are excluded only from holding the office of precensor *ex officio*, and hence they could still be deputed to precensor individual works. Gagnon, however (*La Censure*, p. 187), states that it must always be a cleric.

[5] Blat, *Commentarium*, III, partes 2–6, 345; Gagnon, *La Censure*, p. 195.

[6] Canon 1393, §1. Berutti (*Institutiones*, IV, 431) suggests that in small dioceses where clerics are few and little is published the vicar general and another official of the curia could be appointed.

[7] Gagnon, *La Censure*, p. 195. The practice in the United States may be learned through a consulting of the Catholic Directory. Goodwine has tabulated the results of such an investigation in *The Jurist*, X (1950), 170–171 (21–22). He stresses the fact that the appointment is obligatory in all dioceses.

[8] Gagnon, *La Censure*, p. 196.

[9] Cappello, *Summa*, II, 423.

[10] Some hold that major superiors, at least those in clerical exempt institutes, are bound to the same obligation as local ordinaries in this regard, e.g., Pruemmer, *Manuale*, p. 498; De Meester, *Compendium*, III, pars 1, 267, n. 9; Cocchi, *Commentarium*, VI, 154. The Code

ARTICLE III. PERSONS WHO ARE APPOINTED TO THE OFFICE OF PRECENSOR

If he wish, the local ordinary may personally perform the task of precensor,[11] though it is the common experience of local ordinaries that they cannot do so because of the multitude of their duties, or also because it sometimes requires a specialized knowledge which they are not expected to have. For these reasons the law obliges them to appoint precensors *ex officio*. However, even after precensors *ex officio* have been constituted, the local ordinary may still reserve to himself any work he wishes to precensor. In any case, the local ordinary needs no special appointment.

Precensors may be of two types: precensors *ex officio* and deputed precensors ("*censor deputatus*"). Both are official appointments, however.[12]

Precensors *ex officio* are those who are vested with a general appointment to examine intended publications. The position entails some degree of stability.

Deputed precensors are those who, while not among the precensors *ex officio*, are chosen in particular instances for one or the other work. It sometimes becomes advisable, or even necessary, to make such special appointments. The precensors *ex officio* may be impeded; the work itself may be so specialized that none of the precensors *ex officio* is properly qualified; or, a regularly qualified precensor might suffer harm were he to review this particular work. In all these and similar cases, there is sufficient reason to depute a special precensor for a given work.[13] The precensor is not chosen by the author of the work, or even selected or designated at the suggestion of the author. In every case, the precensor should have the qualifications demanded in law.

The Code specifies that there should be more than one precensor *ex officio* in each diocese, though it does not specify how many there should be. The appointment of only one precensor makes it quite impossible to observe

---

does not demand it. However, a decree of the Holy Office, dated March 29, 1941 (*AAS*, XXXIII [1941], 121) also includes religious superiors when prescribing that precensors be chosen very carefully. Gagnon (*La Censure*, p. 185, n. 32) mentions that the decree probably is dealing with those precensors who are demanded by particular law. Cf. also Mothon, *Institutions Canoniques* (3 vols., Paris, 1922–1924), I, 282 (hereafter cited as *Institutions*); Berutti, *Institutiones*, IV, 431.

[11] What he does through others, he may do himself. Cf. Berutti, *Institutiones*, IV, 431; De Meester, *Compendium*, III, pars 1, 269, n. 3; Coronata, *Institutiones*, II, 328; Gagnon, *La Censure*, p. 186; Vermeersch, *Periodica*, IV (1909), 56–57.

[12] Both Augustine (*Commentary*, VI, 451) and Ayrinhac (*Admin. Legisl.*, p. 285) translate the phrase "*censores ex officio*" as "officially appointed censors." It seems to imply that deputed precensors are not appointed officially. Augustine himself adds that the censor should be a regular censor, not merely one appointed for an emergency.

[13] Wernz-Vidal, *Ius Canonicum*, IV, pars 2, 142; Hollweck, *Buecherverbot*, pp. 56–57; Vermeersch, *De Prohibitione*, pp. 135–136; Vermeersch, *Periodica*, VI (1912), 221; Gagnon, *La Censure*, pp. 200–201.

canon 1393, §5, which demands that the name of the precensor be not known by the author until a favorable judgment has been given. Hence, a minimum of two precensors is demanded by law.[14]

The requisite qualifications of precensors are mentioned in canon 1393, §3, and have been stressed several times by the Holy See in recent years.[15]

The first requirement is that the precensor be a cleric, either secular or religious. It is not required that he be a priest. Still, because of the knowledge that is required, it will rarely happen today that a precensor be anyone other than a priest.[16] It would be contrary to law, however, to restrict the appointment of precensors to religious or to diocesan priests exclusively, though circumstances may warrant that the incumbents be of one or the other class at a given time.[17] When it is a question of precensoring matters that pertain to the religious life, religious will usually be better qualified and acquainted with its history, institutions, spirit, etc.

A second requirement is maturity of age, though the Code does not establish a minimum age requirement. Maturity often gives that balance which is lacking in impetuous youth, who often tend toward indiscreet zeal or laxity.[18]

Mere accumulation of years, however, is not sufficient. The Code also demands learning in the precensor. He should be an expert, not merely in one thing, but in a wide field of knowledge. Since it is quite impossible to have a single man learned in all fields, it is advisable to employ experts in the various fields, e.g., a scripture scholar, a theologian, a canonist, a historian, a religious, etc.[19]

---

[14] When Pius X first prescribed that there be a plurality of precensors, the chief concern was that there be sufficient officials to carry on the work. This is evident from the text of the law itself; cf. litt. encycl. "*Pascendi,*" 8 sept. 1907—*Fontes,* n. 680. Some authors mention explicitly that it is required now that there be two or more precensors, e.g., Augustine, *Commentary,* VI, 452; Coronata, *Institutiones,* II, 327, n. 5; Gagnon, *La Censure,* p. 197; Goodwine, *The Jurist,* X (1950), 171–172 (22–23); *L'Ami,* XXXIX (1922), 196. Berutti (*Institutiones,* IV, 431) adds that there should be enough to handle all work without delay. Périès (*L'Index,* p. 188) proposed that there should be a board of precensors, i.e., a permanent commission, which he felt was obligatory in virtue of articles 38 and 39 of "*Officiorum ac munerum.*" This is not obligatory. Cf. Piat, *NRT,* XXXII (1900), 343, n. 2; Boudinhon, *CC,* XXI (1898), 242; Gagnon, *La Censure,* pp. 199–200.

[15] S.C.S.Off., monitum, 29 mart. 1941—*AAS,* XXXIII (1941), 121; decr., 17 apr. 1942—*AAS,* XXXIV (1942), 149. Cf. also *The Jurist,* II (1942), 394–395.

[16] Gagnon, *La Censure,* pp. 186–187.

[17] *L'Ami* XXXIX (1922), 194; Gagnon, *La Censure,* p. 197: Goodwine, *The Jurist,* X (1950), 170-172 (21-23).

[18] Augustine, *Commentary,* VI, 452; Ayrinhac, *Admin. Legisl.,* p. 285; Woywod, *Commentary,* II, 125–126; Blat, *Commentarium,* III, partes 2–6, 346; *L'Ami,* XXXIX (1922), 193. Gagnon (*La Censure,* pp. 187–188) suggests a minimum age of thirty years.

[19] The long history of exhortations, decrees, monitories, and constitutions of the Popes shows how concerned the Pontiffs are about this problem. The *monitum* of 1941 (S.C.S.Off.,

The final quality demanded by the Code is prudence, by means of which the precensor is enabled to steer a safe middle course in forming his judgment. He may not be moved by rigor or leniency; by human affection or prejudice; by haste. He must be pious, conscientious, trustworthy, and able to act according to his principles, even when that is unpleasant.[20]

Pope Alexander VIII (1689-1691) had forbidden the appointment of a relative or a friend of the author as precensor, but this restriction is no longer found in the present law. The same Pope ruled that a religious could not act as precensor for a work written by a member of the same institute, but that law has also been abrogated.

Article IV. The Appointment of the Precensor

The act of appointment of a precensor is a commission, by mandate, to perform certain services for the ecclesiastical superior.[21] It is not a delegation of authority. The precensor is to contribute an expert opinion, which is not a juridically authoritative pronouncement. This latter is given by the local ordinary when he grants permission or refuses permission to publish the work in question.

The appointment may confer the position of precensor *ex officio*, or it may be a deputation for a certain designated work (works). Even if the appointment is that of precensor *ex officio*, it may be limited in time, e.g., for a period of five years, or to certain types of works, e.g., biblical works, etc. If no time limit is specified, and there are no other restrictions made in the appointment, then the appointment lasts until it is revoked.[22] The appointment should be made in writing. The local ordinary may impose this task on his own subjects, and, in the case of religious, may request that certain designated (or to be designated) religious function in that capacity in his curia. The local religious superior, it seems, may give that permission.[23]

---

29 mart. 1941—*AAS*, XXXIII [1941], 121), for example, stresses the fact that the precensor have expert knowledge precisely in the matter wherein he examines. Cf. Goodwine, *The Jurist*, X (1950), 172–173 (23–24); Gagnon, *La Censure*, pp. 188–190.

[20] Cf., for example, the instruction of Clement VIII: "Curent Episcopi . . . quorum muneris erit facultatem libros imprimendi concedere, ut eis examinandis spectatae pietatis, et doctrinae viros adhibeant, de quorum fide, et integritate sibi polliceri queant, nihil eos gratiae daturos, nihil odio, sed omni humano affectu posthabito, Dei dumtaxat gloriam spectaturos, et fidelis populi utilitatem."—*Fontes*, n. 426. Cf. also Vermeersch-Creusen, *Epitome*, II, 508–509; Jombart, *DDC*, III, 164–165; Gagnon, *La Censure*, pp. 190–193.

[21] *L'Ami*, XXXIX (1922), 196; Gagnon, *La Censure*, pp. 193–194.

[22] Cappello, *Summa*, II, 423; Berutti, *Institutiones*, IV, 431; Augustine, *Commentary*, VI, 451, who urges that the diocesan precensors be listed in the *Catholic Directory;* likewise, Gagnon, *La Censure*, p. 195. Goodwine tabulates the listings as he found them in 1949, in *The Jurist*, X (1950), 170–171 (21–22).

[23] Pius X prescribed that the provincial superior had to be approached. Cf. litt. encycl. "*Pascendi*," 8 sept. 1907, §44, ad IV—*Fontes*, n. 680. De Meester (*Compendium*, III, pars 1,

A profession of faith is required before the precensor assumes office, according to the norm of canon 1406, §1.[24] Since canon 1406, §1, speaks only of the more permanent offices, and refers back to canon 1393, §1, which speaks only of the precensor *ex officio*, it seems that the law does not prescribe the profession of faith for deputed precensors, though the same reasons would hold for their making it. The oath against modernism is not prescribed in either case.[25] By making the profession of faith the precensor agrees to keep inviolate the purity of faith and morals in all the works he examines, taking care to uphold ecclesiastical discipline, public order, and other ecclesiastical standards. It is his function to prevent harm to souls by stopping the publication of those things which would harm the life of the Church, either in doctrine or in practice.

A precensor may be removed from office for any reasonable cause. He is constituted *ad nutum episcopi*.[26]

Article V. The Assignment of a Particular Work to a Precensor

A particular work is assigned to an individual precensor by the local ordinary. The latter may also commission the chancellor or one of the precensors *ex officio* to assign the task.[27] The precensor is not selected by the author, nor is he designated at the latter's suggestion.[28]

The chancellor is the normal intermediary between the author and the precensors and the local ordinary. The author should send his manuscript directly not to the precensor, but to the chancery, so that the designation of the precensor may be made in accordance with the law, in secret. The chancellor forwards the work to the precensor designated by the local ordinary or his delegate. The chancellor receives the report of the precensor and relays it to the local ordinary. He also transmits the local ordinary's decision to the author. If the precensor has need of communicating with the author, this should be done through the chancery. The data and the documents pertinent to the precensorship of the book should be kept in the archives.[29]

268) holds that this regulation is still in force. Coronata (*Institutiones*, II, 327, n. 5) admits that this regulation was imposed, but thinks that it no longer holds, and allows the local superior to grant this permission; Gagnon, *La Censure*, p. 187. Berutti (*Institutiones*, IV, 432) speaks of the permission of the proper superior of the religious, and then repeats the pre-Code law.

[24] This profession of faith the precensor is to make before assuming the office, i.e., before beginning to exercise this function. Cf. Haring, *Grundzuege*, II, 374; Mothon, *Institutions*, I, 91.

[25] Coronata, *Institutiones*, II, 327, n. 6; Haring, *Grundzuege*, II, 374, n. 2.

[26] Cappello, *Summa*, II, 423; Wernz-Vidal, *Ius Canonicum*, IV, pars 2, 142; Berutti, *Institutiones*, IV, 431; Goodwine, *The Jurist*, X (1950), 172 (23).

[27] Gagnon, *La Censure*, p. 205.

[28] Seraphinus a Loiano, *Institutiones*, II, 635.

[29] Gagnon, *La Censure*, pp. 205–206.

It is no longer necessary to submit the manuscript itself, as it was formerly. A typewritten copy is preferable to one written out in long hand. It is entirely permissible to submit the galley or page proofs.[30] The law does not demand that the work be submitted before printing, but simply before publication.[31] However, in every case the author must be prepared to accept the verdict of the precensor, either with regard to incidental alterations, or substantial corrections, or even to the disallowance of the entire work.[32] Hence, there is the financial risk of printing a work before precensorship has occurred. It is no longer required to submit two copies for precensorship.[33]

If a precensor declare himself unqualified to review a certain work, another precensor should be assigned. This might happen in regard to a highly specialized work. If necessary, a special precensor should be deputed.[34] If a qualified precensor is not available within the diocese, the local ordinary may request the services of a precensor outside the diocese, and then issue the *Imprimatur* in accordance with the verdict of that precensor.[35] In certain works on controversial issues, it might be in place to submit the work to two or more precensors, who may be required to submit their verdict independently, or by way of a collegiate decision, as of a board.[36]

The identity of the precensor assigned to the work must be kept secret until a favorable verdict has been reached.[37] If the verdict is unfavorable, the precensor's name should never be revealed.[38] The purpose of this ruling is to protect the precensor's freedom in the exercise of his function when he examines the work and passes judgment upon it. Otherwise, pressure might

---

[30] Thaler, "Die Bitte des kirchlichen Zensors," *AKKR*, XCII (1912), 361; Seraphinus a Loiano, *Institutiones*, II, 627; Boudinhon, *Nouv. Législ.*, p. 263; Genicot-Salsmans, *Institutiones*, I, 458; Cocchi, *Commentarium*, VI, 149; Gagnon, *La Censure*, p. 204; Jombart, *DDC*, III, 159. Most precensors prefer this, for obvious reasons.

[31] According to canons 1391 and 2318, §2, however, the books of Sacred Scripture and their annotations or commentaries may not be printed for publication without the requisite permission having first been obtained. The meaning of the word "printed" will be explained below in Chapter XII, (3).

[32] Hollweck, *Buecherverbot*, p. 58; Schneider, *Buechergesetze*, p. 142; Wernz, *Ius Decretalium*, III, 131, n. (108); Vermeersch, *De Prohibitione*, p. 131; Ojetti, *Synopsis*, I, 718; Boudinhon, *Nouv. Législ.*, p. 263; Cocchi, *Commentarium*, VI, 149; Ubach, *Theol. Moral.*, I, 556; Seraphinus a Loiano, *Institutiones*, II, 627; Piscetta-Gennaro, *Elementa*, II, 84; Cance, *Le Code*, III, 156; Cance-Arquer, *El Código*, I, 842, n. 4; Berutti, *Institutiones*, IV, 433; Wernz-Vidal, *Ius Canonicum*, IV, pars 2, 143, n. (30); Gagnon, *La Censure*, p. 204.

[33] Gagnon, *La Censure*, pp. 205, 211.

[34] Schneider, *Buechergesetze*, p. 133.

[35] Vermeersch, "Adnotatio," *Periodica*, VI (1912), 221; Gagnon, *La Censure*, p. 199.

[36] The law demands only one precensor for each work, but there is no prohibition to use more. Cf. Tummolo-Iorio, *De Censuris*, p. 812, n. 1; Hollweck, *Buecherverbot*, pp. 56–57; Boudinhon, *Nouv. Législ.*, pp. 256, 263.

[37] Canon 1393, §5.

[38] Ayrinhac, *Admin. Legisl.*, p. 286; Wernz-Vidal, *Ius Canonicum*, IV, pars 2, 142.

be put on him by the author or his friends while the work is being examined. Fear of molestation and retaliation in case of an unfavorable verdict might cause a precensor to be unfaithful to his duty.[39] Secrecy should, therefore, be observed by the local ordinary, by the chancery office, and especially by the precensor himself. The ruling of canon 1393, §5, can hardly be observed if the diocese has only one precensor *ex officio*. It is not permissible to allow the author to select or suggest the precensor. Neither may the local ordinary tell the author to "send your manuscript to Father N., who will be your censor." The precensor himself should be conscientiously and prudently reticent.[40] If need should arise for consultation between the precensor and the author, this should be done anonymously through the chancery office.[41]

Article VI. The Functions of the Precensor

After the precensor obtains the copy of the manuscript from the local ordinary or his delegate, he begins the actual work of examining the contents of that work. He should be well aware of the obligations of his office, the duties incumbent upon him, and the limitations of his task. Historically, the norms for precensors are contained in the ten Tridentine Rules, the Instruction of Clement VIII, the constitution "*Sollicita ac provida*" of Benedict XIV, the constitution "*Officiorum ac munerum*" of Leo XIII, the encyclical letter "*Pascendi*" of Pius X, and, since the promulgation of the Code of Canon Law, the most recent decrees of the Holy See. By means of these invaluable guides, a precensor is enabled to judge whether or not a given work contains anything contrary to ecclesiastical standards.

Ecclesiastical standards are four: (1) doctrinal norms; (2) textual norms; (3) disciplinary norms; (4) norms for sacred images.[42]

(1) Doctrinal norms include not only those truths which have been declared dogmas by the infallible authority of the Church, but also the common teaching of the Church, known from the general councils, the constitutions and prescriptions of the Holy See, and the consent of approved authors. Therefore, a precensor may not judge according to personal views, but must

---

[39] Pius X, litt. encycl. "*Pascendi,*" 8 sept. 1907, §44, IV—*Fontes*, n. 680; Blat, *Commentarium*, III, partes 2–6, 347; Cocchi, *Commentarium*, VI, 155; Coronata, *Institutiones*, II, 328; Eichmann, *Lehrbuch*, p. 466; Pruemmer, *Manuale*, p. 499; Seraphinus a Loiano, *Institutiones*, II, 635; Wernz-Vidal, *Ius Canonicum*, IV, pars 2, 142; *L'Ami*, XXXIX (1922), 196–197; Gagnon, *La Censure*, pp. 192, 206.

[40] Examples of imprudence in this regard are mentioned by Gagnon (*La Censure*, p. 206) and *L'Ami* (XXXIX [1922], 196–197).

[41] Gagnon, *La Censure*, p. 206. The opinion once held by Pennacchi (*ASS*, XXX [1897–1898], 499) and Schneider (*Buechergesetze*, p. 133) that the precensor could deal directly with the author is no longer tenable.

[42] Gagnon, *La Censure*, pp. 135–169.

allow a probable opinion whenever that is admissible.[43] The original source of canon 1393, §2, reads:

> De variis opinionibus atque sententiis in unoquoque libro contentis, animo a praeiudiciis omnibus vacuo, iudicandum sibi esse sciant. Itaque nationis, familiae, scholae, instituti affectum excutiant; studia partium seponant; Ecclesiae sanctae dogmata, et communem catholicorum doctrinam, quae conciliorum generalium decretis, Romanorum Pontificum constitutionibus, et orthodoxorum patrum atque doctorum consensu continetur, unice prae oculis habeant; hoc de cetero cogitantes, non paucas esse opiniones, quae uni scholae, instituto, aut nationi certo certiores videntur, et nihilominus, sine ullo fidei aut religionis detrimento, ab aliis catholicis viris reiiciuntur atque impugnantur, oppositaeque defenduntur, sciente ac permittente Apostolica Sede, quae unamquamque opinionem huiusmodi in suo probabilitatis gradu relinquit.[44]

As is evident, the tenets understood here are religious tenets of the Catholic faith, and not literary, artistic, political, scientific, etc., except in so far as any of these might be connected with dogmatic or doctrinal matters.[45]

(2) Textual norms are few. In general, certain works may not be printed unless their text conform to the text of typical editions, or to original documents. In these cases the original has already passed precensorship, which, often enough, was reserved to higher authorities. The republication of these works is permitted on the condition that the secondary edition conform to the primary edition. Hence, the precensorship is concerned only with the literal conformity of the one text to the other. This is demanded in canon 1388, which treats of republishing grants of indulgences; in canon 1389, which treats of republishing decrees of the Roman Congregations; in canon 1390, which treats of republishing litanies and liturgical works, etc.[46]

(3) Disciplinary norms are those which, over and above the norms of faith and morals. pertain more to circumstances of time, place, person, etc. The works in themselves may be correct theologically, may contain no doctrinal errors, but would have an untoward effect upon Catholic people, cause scandal, give offense, disturb public order, or disrupt ecclesiastical discipline. For example, the publication of biographies, historical works, or of the processes of canonization of a recent saint might compromise the position of people still living, especially ecclesiastical authorities. Similarly, the publi-

[43] The Code uses the words "*recognoverit*" (canon 1384, §1), "*examinare*" (canon 1393, §2), "*examinatores*" (canon 1393, §2), "*cognoscere*" (canon 1393, §1). Perhaps the best English term is the simple "review."

[44] Benedictus XIV, const. "*Sollicita ac provida*," 9 iul. 1753, §17—*Fontes*, n. 426.

[45] Berutti, *Institutiones*, IV, 415; Gagnon, *La Censure*, pp. 136–149.

[46] Blat, *Commentarium*, III, partes 2–6, 326; Boudinhon, *Nouv. Législ.*, p. 75; De Meester, *Compendium*, III, pars 1, 256; Schneider, *Buechergesetze*, p. 139; Aertnys-Damen, *Theol. Moral.*, I, 752; Jombart, *DDC*, III, 165; Gagnon, *La Censure*, pp. 150–161.

cation of certain revelations or visions, which might be good or authentic in themselves, could cause public disturbances among the people, particularly in certain countries or localities.[47] The disciplinary norm may be expressed most succinctly in the simple statement of whether or not it be *opportune* to publish this work here and now, under the present circumstances.[48]

(4) Norms for sacred images or holy pictures entail the following rules, based on canon 1399, 12°, which forbids sacred images that are opposed to the mind and decrees of the Church, namely:[49]

(a) Those which convey false dogmatic notions, or lead the ignorant into danger of error, even though they be correct in themselves;[50]

---

[47] Goodwine makes a good point in stressing the recent decree of the Holy Office (17 apr. 1942—*AAS*, XXXIV [1942], 149) in *The Jurist*, X (1950), 176 (27).

[48] Most authors state that the precensor's competence is limited to a judgment on the doctrinal content of the work, the orthodoxy of its doctrine; that he may not refuse the *Nihil obstat* if he regard the publication of the work as inopportune, but that he may call the local ordinary's attention to this fact, e.g., Vermeersch-Creusen, *Epitome*, II, 508; Coronata, *Institutiones*, II, 315, 328; Seraphinus a Loiano, *Institutiones*, II, 626; Beste, *Introductio*, p. 701; De Meester, *Compendium*, III, pars 1, 268; Claeys Bouuaert-Simenon, *Manuale*, III, 138; Regatillo, *Institutiones*, II, 114; Jombart, *DDC*, III, 165; Gagnon, *La Censure*, pp. 145–146; Goodwine, *The Jurist*, X (1950), 174–175 (25–26). This opinion seems to have arisen from a false interpretation of the words "*tantummodo prae oculis habeant Ecclesiae dogmata et communem catholicorum doctrinam* . . . " in canon 1393, §2. The text states the norm to be followed when judging the doctrinal content of the work; it does not say, however, that the precensor's review must confine itself to this. Other authors are less rigid, for they speak of the precensor's attempt to discover whether the work contains anything of danger to faith or morals, e.g., Cance, *Le Code*, III, 156; Sipos, *Enchiridion*, p. 712; Pruemmer, *Manuale*, p. 483; Cocchi, *Commentarium*, VI, 148; Augustine, *Commentary*, VI, 433. Even that is still too narrow. Cappello (*Summa*, II, 420) best expresses the object of precensorship when he writes: "Superior nempe ecclesiasticus videt et auctoritative decernit, utrum liber quidquam contineat contra fidem vel mores aut disciplinam; utrum, perpensis omnibus circumstantiis, noxius sit fidelibus necne; utrum ex lectione aliquod damnum spirituale seu religiosum obvenire queat necne."

[49] Cf., Gagnon, *La Censure*, pp., 163–167.; S.C.S. Officii, Instructio ad Locorum Ordinarios "De arte sacra," 30 junii 1952, *De arte figurativa*, n.6: "Episcopi et Superiores religiosi denegent licentiam edendi libros, folia vel libellos periodicos, in quibus imagines impressae sint, ab Ecclesiae sensu et decretis alienae. [In nota:] Cfr. can. 1385 et 1399, 12°."—*AAS*, XLIV (1952), 545.

[50] Fundamentally these rules stem from the Council of Trent, sess. XXV, *De invocatione, veneratione et reliquiis sanctorum, et sacris imaginibus*. More proximately, canon 1279, §3, reads: "Nunquam sinat Ordinarius in ecclesiis aliisve locis sacris exhiberi falsi dogmatis imagines vel quae . . . aut rudibus periculosi erroris occasionem praebeant." Cf. also S.C.S.Off. decr., 8 apr. 1916—*AAS*, VIII (1916), 146; S.C.S.Off., decr., 16 mart. 1928—*AAS*, XX (1928), 103; Gfoellner, *ThPrQs*, LVIII (1905), 106–107.

(b) those which lack decency or propriety, inasmuch as they are obscene, abhorrent, gruesome, hideous, irreverent, ludicrous, etc.;[51]

(c) those which depart from the approved usages of the Church.[52]

A special point derives from the requirement that the beatified are to be portrayed with rays, and the canonized with the nimbus.[53]

In creating new sacred images, artists ought to preserve the special attributes or characteristics which tradition assigns to saints and by which sacred persons are often distinguished, e.g., the instrument of their martyrdom, the miracles wrought during their lives, the special favors obtained through their intercession, pertinent scriptural references, etc.

These, then, are the norms with which precensors are enabled to examine works and to form their judgment accordingly. After the completion of his examination, the precensor draws his conclusion in the form of a syllogism:

The Church has no objection to the publication of works that conform to ecclesiastical standards.

This work conforms (does not conform) to ecclesiastical standards.

Therefore, the Church has no (an) objection to the publication of this work.

The Latin formula has given the name to the favorable result of this judgment, namely, "*Nihil obstat (aliquid obstat) ex parte Ecclesiae quominus imprimatur et publicetur.*" The unfavorable verdict will be absolute if the work as a whole is erroneous or dangerous and is hardly capable of revision. If the objectionable passages can be amended, the unfavorable verdict will be temporary "*donec opus corrigatur,*" until the corrections indicated by the pre-

---

[51] "Nunquam sinat Ordinarius . . . exhiberi . . . imagines vel quae debitam decentiam et honestatem non praeseferant."—Canon 1279, §3. Cf. also Urbanus VIII, const. "*Sacrosancta,*" 15 mart. 1642—*Fontes*, n. 223; Benedictus XIV, ep. "*Sollicitudines,*" 1 oct. 1745, §§26, 28—*Fontes*, n. 362; S.C.S.Off., decr., 30 mart. 1921—*AAS*, XIII (1921), 197; Maréchal, "Un décret récent du Saint-Office en matière d'iconographie," *NRT*, XLVIII (1921), 337.

[52] Urbanus VIII, const. "*Sacrosancta,*" 15 mart. 1642, §1—*Fontes*, n. 223; Benedictus XIV, ep. "*Sollicitudines,*" 1 oct. 1745, §§11–36—*Fontes*, n. 362; S.C.S.Off., 28 febr. 1875, 3 apr. 1895, 16 mart. 1928—*AAS*, XX (1928), 103; S.R.C., *Platien.*, 29 nov. 1878—*Decreta Authentica Congregationis Sacrorum Rituum ex actis eiusdem collecta eiusque auctoritate promulgata sub auspiciis SS. Domini nostri Leonis Papae XIII* (5 vols. & 2 Appendices, Romae, 1898–1927), n. 3470 (hereafter cited as *Decr. Auth.*); S.R.C., *Tridentini*, 23 febr. 1894, ad II—*Decr. Auth.*, n. 3818; S.R.C., decr., 28 mart. 1914—*AAS*, VI (1914), 147; S.R.C., decr., 15 iul. 1914—*AAS*, VI (1914), 382–383; S.R.C., decr., 9 nov. 1921—*AAS*, XIII (1921), 545. Cf. also Boudinhon, *Nouv. Législ.*, p. 153; Vermeersch-Creusen, *Epitome*, II, 508.

[53] Urbanus VIII, const. "*Coelestis Hierusalem,*" 5 iul. 1634, §1—*Fontes*, n. 213; Benedictus XIV, *De Servorum Dei Beatificatione, et Beatorum Canonizatione*—*Opera Omnia* (17 vols., Prati, 1839–1846), Lib. I, cap. 41; Lib. II, cap. 11, 14; Lib. IV, cap. 10, 21; S.C.S.Off., decr., 13 mart. 1625—*Fontes*, n. 719; S.R.C., decr., 14 et 27 aug. 1894—*Decr. Auth.*, n. 3835. Cf. also Boudinhon, *Nouv. Législ.*, pp. 148–149, 152, 154; Seraphinus a Loiano, *Institutiones*, II, 654; Sipos, *Enchiridion*, p. 720; Pernicone, *Prohibition*, pp. 184–186; Pennacchi, *ASS*, XXX (1897–1898), 312–316; Coronata, *Institutiones*, II, 344; Claeys Bouuaert-Simenon, *Manuale*, III, 145; Beste, *Introductio*, p. 698; Augustine, *Commentary*, VI, 475; De Meester, *Compendium*,

censor have been made.[54] As mentioned above, the precensor's judgment is not the exercise of judicial authority, as in a trial, but an expert opinion, which, when joined with the decision of the local ordinary, becomes a summary and administrative judgment.[55]

Article VII. The Report to the Ecclesiastical Authority

After the precensor has finished his examination of the work in the light of ecclesiastical standards and formed his judgment, he then presents that judgment, in the form of a written report, to the ecclesiastical superior. He does not relay this judgment to the author or any other interested party. If the local ordinary of another diocese requested this function, it is proper that the message be sent through the chancery of the precensor's diocese.

The written report is not required for the validity of the verdict nor for that of the *Imprimatur* following it, but for the sake of record, and it should be kept in the diocesan archives.[56] If the judgment is favorable, it may be expressed with the simple formula: *Nihil obstat*. The precensor should sign his name to the report. The addition of the date is advisable.

The report of the precensor possesses simply the value of an expert, private opinion. The title of precensor confers no weight or canonical value upon his private opinions. Nor does his "*Nihil obstat*" contribute any authority to the views expressed by the author in his book.[57] The precensor's report does, however, furnish the information needed by the ecclesiastical supesior before the latter can prudently perform his duty, whether it be to allow or to disallow the publication of the work. Fundamentally a favorable judgment demands that the local ordinary permit the publication of the work. Similarly, an unfavorable judgment demands that the local ordinary disallow the publication of the work.[58]

The precensor should indicate his reasons, if he renders an unfavorable judgment, for the simple reason that the local ordinary is obliged to state such reasons if he is asked to do so. If it is possible to correct the work, the

---

III, pars 1, 276; and the excellent, critical work on sacred images, *De Historia SS. Imaginum et Picturarum, pro vero earum usu contra abusus, Libri quattuor*, auctore Joanne Molano: Joannes Natalis Paquot recensuit, illustravit, supplevit (Lovanii, 1771), which work is found in Migne, *MPL*, Vol. XXVII.

[54] Gagnon, *La Censure*, pp. 206–207.

[55] *L'Ami*, XXXIX (1922), 197.

[56] Cappello, *Summa*, II, 422; Gagnon, *La Censure*, p. 207; Berutti, *Institutiones*, IV, 433. It is not necessary, as Boudinhon (*Nouv. Législ.*, p. 263) claimed, to affix the "*nihil obstat*" to each page of the author's manuscript or printed proof-sheets.

[57] Pius X, litt. encycl. "*Pascendi*," 8 sept. 1907, §44, IV—*Fontes*, n. 680; Augustine, *Commentary*, VI, 452.

[58] Blat, *Commentarium*, III, partes 2–6, 326; Boudinhon, *Nouv. Législ.*, p. 75; De Meester. *Compendium*, III, pars 1, 256; Schneider, *Buechergesetze*, p. 139; Aertnys-Damen, *Theol, Moral.*, I, 753; Gagnon, *La Censure*, pp. 169–170; Jombart, *DDC*, III, 165.

places of correction should be indicated.[59] For weighty reasons a local ordinary may set aside the judgment of a precensor. This might happen if he discovered that the choice of the precensor was unfortunate, either because the person proved unequal to his task, or because of bias, etc.[60] In such a case the work may be given to another precensor. This may also be done at any time, e.g., when the first precensor doubts the merit of the work.

Article VIII. The Remuneration of the Precensor

In the pre-Code law a precensor was not allowed to accept anything for his services, but was obliged to render them gratis. This law has been abrogated. In places where the office of precensor is a full-time occupation, the sustenance of the precensor should be met out of the funds devoted to the diocesan curia. He belongs to the family of the curia. Even when the office of precensor is considered an adjunct to another office, it is fitting that the precensor be recompensed for services rendered.[61] The method of payment, however, should not give rise to occasions for favoritism, or even the suspicion thereof. If the local ordinary sees fit to establish a tax for the performance of the arduous duty of precensorship, he can accomplish his aim by having the fee paid to the chancery when the manuscript is submitted to the chancery, and to the precensor upon the completion of his task.[62]

Article IX. A Summary

The office of precensor is not an ecclesiastical office in the strict sense, for it does not entail the exercise of jurisdiction; it is an office in the wide sense. Each bishop is to appoint precensors for his diocese, who are to exercise their function *ex officio*, though others may also be deputed to precensor individual works, if necessary. He may impose this task on his subjects, and request it of religious and others not his subjects. Major religious

---

[59] Goodwine, *The Jurist*, X (1950), 176 (27).

[60] Vermeersch, *De Prohibitione*, p. 139–140; Ojetti, *Synopsis*, I, 725; Bouscaren-Ellis, *Canon Law*, p. 711; Cappello, *Summa*, II, 425; Coronata, *Institutiones*, II, 328; Wernz-Vidal, *Ius Canonicum*, IV, pars 2, 142; Woywod, *HPR*, XXVIII (1928), 971–972; Gagnon, *La Censure*. p. 170.

[61] Boudinhon, *Nouv. Législ.*, p. 266; De Meester, *Compendium*, III, pars 1, 269; Coronata, *Institutiones*, II, 329, n. 1; Pennacchi, *ASS*, XXX (1897–1898), 500–501; Périès, *L'Index*, p. 205; Gagnon, *La Censure*, p. 213; Schneider, *Buechergesetze*, p. 14; Blat, *Commentarium*, III, partes 2–6, 347. Some of these authors suggest that a fee be paid by the author or publisher on the occasion of precensorship and the granting of permission. Wernz (*Ius Decretalium*, III, 130, n. 107) and Wernz-Vidal (*Ius Canonicum*, IV, pars 2, 143) held that it was not permissible to demand a fee from the author or publisher. Evidently, canon 1507 would have to be observed, were that to be done.

[62] Schneider, *Buechergesetze*, p. 141; Boudinhon, *Nouv. Législ.*, p. 266; Van Coillie, *Commentarius*, p. 85; Pennacchi, *ASS*, XXX (1897–1898), 501; Gagnon, *La Censure*, p. 212.

superiors may constitute precensors for those works which fall within their competence.

Precensors are to be chosen from the ranks of the secular and the religious clergy. They must be clerics, of mature age, learned and prudent. They are to make the profession of faith before beginning to exercise their office. They may be removed from office for any reasonable cause, since their appointment is constituted *ad nutum episcopi*.

The task of precensors is to examine the submitted works according to the doctrinal, textual, disciplinary and pictorial standards of the Church. The judgment of the precensor is to be given to the local ordinary and not to the interested party. This report has scientific value only, but the local ordinary is fundamentally obliged to allow or to disallow the publication of a work according to the verdict of the precensor. For weighty reasons, he may overrule the decision of the precensor.

Several precensors should be appointed. The author is to submit his work to the chancery, and is not to know the identity of the precensor until a favorable verdict has been reached. If necessary, a second or a third precensor may be appointed for any given work.

A precensor has a title to remuneration for services rendered. However, the remuneration should be implemented in a way that does not give rise to scandal or furnish occasion for any abuse of office.

CHAPTER X

THE GRANT OR REFUSAL OF PERMISSION TO PUBLISH (CANONS 1393, §4, AND 1394, §§1-2)

After precensorship has occurred, the verdict is submitted to the local ordinary in the form of a "*Nihil Obstat*" or "*Aliquid Obstat.*" It is the local ordinary who then renders the decision to allow or to disallow the publication of the work in question. The decision is followed by the actual grant or refusal of permission to publish. The text of the law reads:

> 1393, §4. Censor sententiam scripto dare debet. Quae si faverit, Ordinarius potestatem edendi faciat, cui tamen praeponatur censoris iudicium, inscripto eius nomine. Extraordinariis tantum in adiunctis ac perquam raro, prudenti Ordinarii arbitrio, censoris mentio omitti potest.
>
> 1394, §1. Licentia, qua Ordinarius potestatem edendi facit, in scriptis concedatur, in principio. . . .
>
> 1394, §2. Si vero licentia deneganda videatur, roganti auctori, nisi gravis causa aliud exigat, rationes indicentur.

The commentary on this law will be divided as follows: (1) The decision to allow or to disallow the publication of the work; (2) the grant of permission to publish; (3) the refusal of permission to publish; (4) the fee; (5) a summary.

Article I. The Decision to Allow or to Disallow the Publication of the Work

When the local ordinary receives the report of the precensor, he is furnished with an expert opinion on the merit of the work in question. On the basis of the precensor's verdict he is to render his own decision, which should not be given arbitrarily, but, in ordinary circumstances, should follow the verdict of the precensor.[1] Thus, if the precensor issued a "*Nihil Obstat*," the local ordinary is fundamentally obliged to allow the publication of the work. Similarly, if the precensor issued an "*Aliquid obstat*" the local ordinary is similarly obliged to disallow the publication of the work, either until the necessary corrections are made, or completely, as the case may warrant.[2] An arbitrary refusal to allow publication after the precensor

[1] Schneider, *Buechergesetze*, p. 138; Vermeersch, *De Prohibitione*, p. 140; Gagnon, *La Censure*, p. 169; Woywod-Smith, *Commentary*, II, 147.

[2] Gagnon, *La Censure*, pp. 169–170; Ojetti, *Synopsis*, I, 725; Schneider, *Buechergesetze*, p. 138; Wernz-Vidal, *Ius Canonicum*, IV, pars 2, 142; Jombart, *DDC*, III, 165.

has issued the "*Nihil Obstat*" would violate charity and justice, burdening the author with useless expense and waste of labor, as well as depriving him of the right to communicate the fruits of his labors to others, and perhaps depriving him of a chance to earn a decent livelihood.[3] Similarly, the arbitrary grant of a permit to publish after the precensor has issued an "*Aliquid obstat*" would violate the law of the Church.

However, it is not always mandatory for the local ordinary to follow the verdict of the precensor. For objective and weighty reasons he may set it aside. It may be evident to the local ordinary that the precensor (either the precensor appointed *ex officio*, or a deputed precensor) was incompetent to appraise the content of a particular book; or, that the precensor failed to allot mature deliberation to a work that demanded thorough scrutiny; or, that the precensor was influenced by purely personal reasons for or against an author. It might also happen that circumstances make it inopportune to publish a work, even after a precensor has issued a "*Nihil Obstat*," e.g., because of a change in policy by ecclesiastical authorities, or a decision of higher authorities which renders untenable some of the opinions cited in that work as probable, or tolerated, which they may have been at the time of writing.[4]

Hence, a local ordinary is to exercise great care in arriving at his decision, and particularly so if he overrules the decision of his precensor. It is good to remember that the Church does not demand peace at all costs. Sometimes it is useful, and even necessary, to allow the minds of the faithful to be disturbed by controversy, or to proclaim truth fearlessly, regardless of consequences. In ordinary circumstances free discussion is very useful, even though it raises the tempers of some. Too great a rigor in the name of peace limits freedom of discussion, hinders progress in clearing doctrinal and moral issues, etc. If the occasion demands, the local ordinary may consult with others.[5]

If a local ordinary has reason to doubt the verdict of a precensor, he may submit the work to another precensor. If he obtains two concordant verdicts, he should consider the matter settled. If the verdicts disagree, he may submit the work to a third precensor, with explicit instructions to weigh the matter which causes the disagreement. The designation of a second and third precensor should be executed in such a manner as to give

[3] Woywod, *HPR*, XXVIII (1928), 971.

[4] Vermeersch, *De Prohibitione*, pp. 139–140; Ojetti, *Synopsis*, I, 725; Bouscaren-Ellis, *Canon Law*, p. 711; Cappello, *Summa*, II, 425; Coronata, *Institutiones*, II, 328; Wernz-Vidal, *Ius Canonicum*, IV, pars 2, 142; Woywod, *HPR*, XXVIII (1928), 971–972; Gagnon, *La Censure*, pp. 169–170.

[5] Woywod, *HPR*, XXVIII (1928), 971–972; Ojetti, *Synopsis*, I, 725; Jombart, *DDC*, III, 166–167.

no indication of the identity of the first precensor.[6] If a board of precensors is available, or the council of vigilance, it might be prudent or advisable to secure a joint decision of the members.[7] If the case warrants it, the work may be submitted to the Holy Office.

At any time the local ordinary may act as precensor, if he so wishes. However, he may not allow publication until he is assured that there is a favorable verdict. It would be wrong to allow publication before the favorable verdict has been reached.[8] The local ordinary may also delegate any priest to act in his name in allowing or disallowing the publication of works, either in individual cases, or for all cases.[9]

Article II. The Grant of Permission to Publish

The act of allowing the publication of a work may be considered from two aspects. It is: (1) the official act whereby the ecclesiastical authority makes the judgment of the precensor his own—the official judgment that a work conforms to ecclesiastical standards, and contains nothing contrary to ecclesiastical standards;[10] (2) more precisely, it is the official administrative decree which allows the publication of a writing by the interested parties.[11] It is an act of voluntary jurisdiction.[12] At this moment the prohibition of the "*ne edantur sine censura*" ceases because the condition laid down by the Church has been fulfilled and verified.

Since the permission to publish is given by way of a rescript,[13] the following formalities are obligatory:

---

[6] Gagnon, *La Censure*, p. 170; Berutti, *Institutiones*, IV, 433, n. 3; Piat, *NRT*, XXXII (1900), 351; Cappello, *Summa*, II, 423; Wernz-Vidal, *Ius Canonicum*, IV, pars 2, 142; Woywod, *HPR*, XXVIII (1928), 971–972. The procedure outlined in the text is that presented by Benedictus XIV, const. "*Sollicita ac provida*," 9 iul. 1753, §§4,5,8 (*Fontes*, N. 426) for the Holy Office and the Sacred Congregation of the Index, in reference to books reported as worthy of condemnation.

[7] Pius X ordered the erection of a board of vigilance in every diocese in his litt. encycl. "*Pascendi*," 8 sept. 1907, §44, VI—*Fontes*, n. 680. This board still exists today, in virtue of a decree of the Holy Office, 22 mart. 1918—*AAS*, X (1918), 136.

[8] S.C.S.Off., decr., 29 mart. 1941—*AAS*, XXXIII (1941), 121.

[9] Cf. Gagnon, *La Censure*, p. 180.

[10] The verdict of the precensor is an expert, but private, opinion. Even the decision of the local ordinary is not an absolute guarantee that the work is free from all error. It is a legal assurance, which begets a presumption in favor of the work. At most, the decision is a negative approval of the work, and does not imply that the local ordinary subscribes to all or any of the opinions contained therein. Cf. *L'Ami*, XXXIX (1922), 197; Augustine, *Commentary*, VI, 452; Gagnon, *La Censure*, p. 171–172.

[11] *L'Ami*, XXXIX (1922), 197; Gagnon, *La Censure*, p. 172.

[12] Tummulo-Iorio, *De Censuris*, p. 812; Blat, *Commentarium*, III, partes 2–6, 347; Eichmann, *Lehrbuch*, p. 466.

[13] This formality is not to be identified with the formality of printing a notice of the granted permission in the book, which will be discussed in the following chapter. It is quite apparent that some fail to keep these two items apart.

(1) The document must contain the name of the author and the title of the work which the precensor's verdict concerns, and the verdict of the precensor. This is proof that the work was actually examined.[14] No particular formula is required for the verdict of the precensor, but the simplest and usual wording is "*Nihil Obstat.*" In some cases the "*Concordat cum originali,*" or any similar phrase, might be required.[15]

(2) The name of the precensor must be mentioned.[16] This identifies the person responsible for the favorable verdict. If the local ordinary performed the precensorship, that fact is to be mentioned.[17] The words "*inscripto eius nomine*" in canon 1393, §4, do not mean that the precensor must sign the document, but merely that his name must be mentioned.[18] A sufficient weight of reasons, however, may warrant that the name of the precensor be omitted on the document, and the mere fact of precensorship be noted. This is expressly allowed by canon 1393, §4, but only in extraordinary circumstances, and rarely.[19] It is not prescribed that the date of the issuing of the "*Nihil Obstat*" be recorded in this rescript, though its mention is evidence that the verdict was given before the grant of the permission to publish.[20]

(3) The formal grant of the permission to publish is the principal part of the rescript. No special form is required. The simple word "*Imprimatur*" (let it be printed) has been consecrated by long usage, and owes its origin to a time when the law prescribed that the *permission to print* be granted after precensorship. Today, however, the law demands that the *permission to publish* be granted after precensorship. Hence, the former term is archaic, and no longer fits the act which it is supposed to designate. It were better to

---

[14] *L'Ami*, XXXIX (1922), 197; Piscetta-Gennaro, *Elementa*, II, 91; Vermeersch-Creusen, *Epitome*, II, 508–509.

[15] The formula "*Nihil Obstat*" was prescribed by Pius X in his litt. encycl. "*Pascendi,*" 8 sept. 1907, §44, ad IV—*Fontes*, n. 680. This is not found in the present law. Cf. Woywod, *Commentary*, II, 127; De Meester, *Compendium*, III, pars 1, 268.

[16] Cappello (*Summa*, II, 422) stresses the point that the name and surname of the precensor should be clearly indicated. Perhaps he is thinking of the practice of some religious who sign themselves in the manner customary in their institute, which manner often abstracts from the use of the surname.

[17] Vermeersch, *Periodica*, IV (1909), 57; Gagnon, *La Censure*, p. 209.

[18] Some erroneously demand the signature of the precensor: Augustine, *Commentary*, VI, 452; Ayrinhac, *Admin. Legisl.*, p. 286; Woywod, *HPR*, XXVIII (1928), 972–973; Gagnon, *La Censure*, p. 208. This phrase dates back to the time when all documents were inscribed by hand, as is evident from the origin or the law. Even Pius X did not require the signature of the precensor.

[19] De Meester, *Compendium*, III, pars 1, 269; Gagnon, *La Censure*, p. 208; Boudinhon, *Nouv. Législ.*, p. 264.

[20] Beste, *Introductio*, p. 701.

use the word "*Publicetur,*" which is more precise according to the present law, and corresponds to the "*potestatem edendi*" of canon 1393, §4.[21]

Should a local ordinary desire to use any other formula, he should take care not to express the idea of positive approval unless he really means just that.[22] In itself, the permission to publish is nothing more than a negative approval, i.e., this work contains nothing contrary to ecclesiastical standards.

(4) The name of the person granting the permission must be mentioned in the rescript. Pope Leo X had required that the local ordinary sign this document, though this does not seem to be required by the present law.[23] The Code places this grant of permission on the same level as certain other official acts which are done in writing. Hence, a rubber stamp would suffice, provided the document be countersigned by the chancellor, for then the document would be regarded as authentic.[24] If the chancellor or another person has been delegated to grant the permission, he signs his own name, and subjoins a phrase indicating that he acts as delegate of the local ordinary.[25]

(5) The place and date of the concession must be mentioned in the document.[26]

(6) The rescript must be in writing. This does not appear to be a condition for the validity of the grant of the permission. It seems required, however, for lawfulness.[27] It need not be handwritten, but may be typewritten, or in a printed formula, in which the pertinent data are inserted. Two copies of the document should be made. One copy is kept in the diocesan archives,

---

[21] De Meester, *Compendium*, III, pars 1, 269; Gagnon, *La Censure*, p. 208; Boudinhon, *Nouv. Législ.*, p. 264; Berutti, *Institutiones*, IV, 434; Woywod-Smith, *Commentary*, II, 147. The term "*Imprimatur*" was formerly prescribed by Pius X.

[22] Bouix, *De Curia Romana*, p. 567; Schneider, *Buecbergesetze*, p. 140; De Meester, *Compendium*, III, pars 1, 269, n. 3. Goodwine mentions the peculiar modern American twist whereby publishers seek an *Imprimatur*, even for works on profane topics, but for commercial advantages.—*The Jurist*, X (1950), 182–183 (33–34).

[23] Leo X (in Conc. Lateranen. V) const. "*Inter Sollicitudines*," 4 maii 1515, §2—*Fontes*, n. 68. It is not found in the present legislation.

[24] Cf., Prince, *The Diocesan Chancellor*, The Catholic University of America Canon Law Studies, n. 167 (Washington, D. C.: The Catholic University of America Press, 1942), pp. 82–83.

[25] E.g., N.N., [Cancellarius], ab Episcopo die . . . mensis . . . anni . . . ad hoc delegatus.

[26] These items are required by canon 1394, §1, as in all official documents of this nature. Cf., Gagnon, *La Censure*, p. 209; Blat, *Commentarium*, III, partes 2–6, 348.

[27] Dilgskron, *Anal. Eccl.*, V (1897), 89; Pennacchi, *ASS*, XXX (1897–1898), 500; Vermeersch, *De Probibitione*, p. 140; Marc-Gesterman-Raus, *Institutiones*, I, 869; Wernz, *Ius Decretalium*, III, 130, n. (107); Gagnon, *La Censure*, p. 208; Piat, *NRT*, XXXII (1900), 352. Some older authors held that the written document was required for validity, e.g., Van Coillie, *Commentarius*, p. 86; Boudinhon, *Nouv. Législ.*, p. 265.

the other is sent to the author or the interested party which submitted the work, e.g., the publisher, the editor, etc.[28]

If a local ordinary is approached by an author who had obtained a permit to publish from another local ordinary who is not authorized to grant such a permit, he may, after securing an authentic copy of the original "*Nihil Obstat*," issue his own permission to publish on the strength of the former verdict of the precensor. He would also be within his rights in demanding a new precensorship.[29] This might happen when an author intended to publish his work in a certain diocese, obtained the "*Imprimatur*" there, and then made final arrangements to have the work published in a different diocese.

The local ordinary is to avoid unnecessary delay in granting the permit to publish. Older legislation was most explicit on this point, though the present law is silent in this regard.[30] A work may lose much of its current value, and an author and publisher suffer considerable financial loss, if a publication is unduly delayed. Justice and charity demand that culpable neglect be avoided.[31]

Article III. The Refusal of Permission to Publish

Permission to publish a work may be denied for any number of good reasons, all of them reducible to the fact that the intended publication fails to conform to ecclesiastical standards. In such cases the local ordinary is obliged to refuse the permission to publish. This refusal is not a canonical punishment, nor is it a prohibition imposed by the local ordinary. Rather, the local ordinary declares, in effect, that the original and general hypothetical prohibition—not to publish a work without permission—still remains.[32]

A work may be totally unfit for publication, or, as is usually the case, certain portions of the work are more or less objectionable.[33] In order to preclude any irregularity, or any attempts at arbitrariness, the Code prescribes that, if the permit to publish has been refused, the author may request the reasons for the refusal, and the local ordinary is obliged to tell them. A local ordinary may, if he wish, manifest the reasons for the refusal when reporting the unfavorable verdict. He need not discuss the reasons he adduces.[34]

---

[28] Woywod, *HPR*, XXVIII (1928), 972; Gagnon, *La Censure*, p. 209.

[29] This is in accordance with a decision of the S.C.Indicis, 9 maii, 1912—*AAS*, IV (1912), 370; *Fontes*, n. 5155.

[30] Leo X (in Conc. Lateranen. V), const. "*Inter Sollicitudines*," 4 maii 1515, §2—*Fontes*, n. 68.

[31] Périès, *L'Index*, pp. 188–189; Gagnon, *La Censure*, p. 212; Dilgskron, *Anal. Eccl.*, V (1897), 89; Boudinhon, *Nouv. Législ.*, p. 266.

[32] *L'Ami*, XXXIX (1922), 197–198.

[33] Boudinhon, *Nouv. Législ.*, p. 266.

[34] Cappello, *Summa*, II, 423; Vermeersch, *De Prohibitione*, p. 140; Boudinhon, *Nouv. Législ.*, p. 267; *L'Ami*, XXXIX (1922), 198; Gagnon, *La Censure*, p. 207.

If the phrase "*donec corrigatur*" is used in the local ordinary's refusal, it means that the work must be emended before the permission will be granted. It would not be proper to grant a conditional permission, i.e., so that the permit becomes automatically effective if the corrections are made, without the need of resubmitting the corrected portions.[35] It happens all too often that mistakes are made in the very corrections, and if these are not precensored, they are printed in the work, and the mistakes bear the *Imprimatur*. If the precensor make incidental corrections, that will obviate the necessity of a further precensorship.

Most authors, being in good faith, will readily submit to corrections. Some may not, and in this case the reason for the refusal to grant permission must be mentioned, if the author desires to know them. It may happen, however, that the local ordinary feels that it would be imprudent to reveal the reasons for the refusal. It could eventuate that the reasons would lead to the knowledge of the identity of the precensor and would be a source of hardship for him.[36]

When an author is refused permission to publish, various courses are open to him.[37] He may respectfully request a new precensorship, though this will appear useless in most instances. He may apply to another competent local ordinary for precensorship, though if he does this he must mention the fact of the previous refusal according to the norm of canon 1385, §2. There is no possibility of having recourse to a metropolitan, for an archbishop cannot overrule the decisions of his suffragans in this matter.[38] He may have recourse to the Holy Office, *in devolutivo*.[39] Rome has not made known what procedure then follows in such cases. Possibly it will require the local ordinary to submit his reasons; or it may perform its own precensorship.[40]

---

[35] This type of permission would be a "*permissio sub condicione suspensiva de futuro*," which is not allowed. Cf. Pennacchi, *ASS*, XXX (1897–1898), 499; Piat, *NRT*, XXXII (1900), 350; *L'Ami*, XXXIX (1922), 198; Woywod, *HPR*, XXVIII (1928), 973.

[36] The local ordinary is the judge of the sufficiency of the cause for withholding the reasons for the refusal to grant permission to publish. Cf. *L'Ami*, XXXIX (1922), 198; Ayrinhac, *Admin. Legisl.*, p. 287; Blat, *Commentarium*, III, partes 2–6, 348; Gagnon, *La Censure*, p. 208.

[37] The same would hold if the local ordinary refused to give his reasons, when asked; or if the local ordinary refused permission to publish after the corrections had been made. Cf. Woywod, *HPR*, XXVIII (1928), 973; Boudinhon, *Nouv. Legisl.*, p. 268.

[38] In the pre-Code law, the following held that the metropolitan had this power: Schneider, *Buechergesetze*, p. 138; Bouix, *De Curia Romana*, p. 566; Périès, *L'Index*, p. 204; Dilgskron, *Anal. Eccl.*, V (1897), 89; Piat, *NRT*, XXXII (1900), 349–350. Today, however, that view is not held. Cf. Boudinhon, *Nouv. Législ.*, p. 269; Gagnon, *La Censure*, p. 208.

[39] Boudinhon, *Nouv. Législ.*, p. 269; Ayrinhac, *Admin. Legisl.*, p. 287; De Meester, *Compendium*, III, pars 1, 269, n. 7; Gagnon, *La Censure*, p. 208; Berutti, *Institutiones*, IV, 433; Woywod, *HPR*, XXVIII (1928), 973.

[40] Boudinhon, *Nouv. Législ.*, p. 269.

The publication of a work for which the permission to publish was not received does not make that work a forbidden book, unless it happens to be one of those works for which such a penalty is enacted in law. However, such an action would be a violation of the law, and, if canon 2318, §2, were violated in that act, the penalty of excommunication could possibly be incurred.

Article IV. The Fee

The Code is silent about the possibility of a fee for the grant of the permit to publish.[41] In a somewhat parallel case, which also involves the use of voluntary jurisdiction, the quinquennial faculties of the bishops in the U. S. forbid the acceptance of a fee for the grant of permission to read forbidden books.[42] In any case, canon 1507, §1, would have to be observed.[43]

Article V. A Summary

The local ordinary, after receiving the report from the precensor, renders his own decision, and executes it by granting or refusing permission to publish the work in question. Fundamentally the local ordinary is bound by the verdict of the precensor, though, for weighty reasons, he may overrule it. If he has reason to doubt the verdict of the precensor, he may prescribe further examination of the work by other precensors, or he may even himself examine the work.

The grant of permission involves the official act whereby the local ordinary makes the verdict of the precensor his own, as well as the official allowance of the publication of the work. This is an act of voluntary jurisdiction, and the permission is given by way of a rescript.

The refusal of permission to publish is not a punishment or canonical penalty. It is a declaration that the general hypothetical prohibition, "works are not to be published without permission," still remains in force. If an author desire to know the reasons for the refusal, the local ordinary is obliged to manifest them, unless he judge that there is sufficient reason to keep them secret. The author who feels aggrieved may have recourse to Rome.

---

[41] Pre-Code law demanded that the permission had to be given gratis. Authors state that the mind of the Church seems to be the same, e.g., Coronata, *Institutiones*, II, 329; Blat, *Commentarium*, III, partes 2–6, 347. Wernz-Vidal state that "*ex natura rei*" it is demanded that the grant be made gratis.—*Ius Canonicum*, IV, pars 2, 143. Cf. also Gagnon, *La Censure*, pp. 212–213.

[42] Bouscaren, *Canon Law Digest*, II, 41.

[43] Eichmann, *Lehrbuch*, p. 467, n. 1.

The publication of a work that has not received permission is not, for that reason alone, a crime, unless it happen to fall under the tenor of canon 2318, §2, and then an excommunication reserved to no one is incurred. The work so published is not a forbidden book, unless it is expressly so mentioned in the law.

The Code is silent about the payment of a fee for the grant of permission to publish.

CHAPTER XI

REGULATIONS CONCERNING PRINTING (CANON 1394, §1)

Canon 1394, §1, requires that when a work is printed, notice of the grant of the permission be printed in that work. The text of the law reads:

> Licentia, qua Ordinarius potestatem edendi facit, in scriptis concedatur, in principio aut in fine libri, folii vel imaginis imprimenda, expresso nomine concedentis itemque loco et tempore concessionis.

The reason for this law is quite apparent. By this means the reader is furnished with an assurance that the work conforms to ecclesiastical standards. It is the simplest and most efficient way to acquaint the public with the fact that the permission was granted.[1]

The canon states that the permission to publish ("*potestatem edendi*") be printed. This means the permission granted by the local ordinary, and does not include the "*Nihil Obstat*" given by the precensor, nor even the name of the precensor.[2] The canon speaks of the permission to publish, but does not

[1] In a certain sense the printed notice of the granted permission in the work is equivalent to the divulgation of the promulgation of the decree. Cf. Boudinhon, *Nouv. Législ.*, p. 265; Piat, *NRT*, XXXII (1900), 135.

[2] Pre-Code law had demanded the printing of the name and of the verdict of the precensor, according to the tenor of the instruction of Clemens VIII, "*Catholicae fidei,*" 17 oct. 1595—*Fontes*, n. 426. The following hold that it is still obligatory to print the name and verdict of the precensor: Boudinhon, *Nouv. Législ.*, p. 263; *L'Ami*, XXXIX (1922), 197; Berutti, *Institutiones*, IV, 434; Beste, *Introductio*, p. 701; Claeys Bouuaert-Simenon, *Manuale*, III, 138; Blat, *Commentarium*, III, partes 2–6, 348; De Meester, *Compendium*, III, pars 1, 268–269; Marc-Gestermann-Raus, *Institutiones*, I, 870; Mothon, *Institutions*, I, 91; Pruemmer *Manuale*, p. 499; Raus, *Institutiones*, pp. 556–557; Seraphinus a Loiano, *Institutiones*, II, 635; Wernz-Vidal, *Ius Canonicum*, IV, pars 2, 142–143; Woywod, *HPR*, XXVIII (1928), 972–973. Many claim that this is demanded by canon 1393, §4, which is obviously a mistake, for that canon is not speaking of the printing, but of the document by which the local ordinary concedes the permission.

The following hold the opinion found in the text of this commentary: Bouscaren-Ellis, *Canon Law*, p. 711; Aertnys-Damen, *Theol. Moral.*, I, 754; Cance-Arquer, *El Código*, I, 843, n. 1; Coronata, *Institutiones*, II, 329; Gillet, *Jus Pontificium*, XI (1931), 61; Gagnon, *La Censure*, pp. 210–211; Nevin, *ACR*, II (1925), 56; Noldin-Schmitt, *Summa*, II, 642; Piscetta-Gennaro, *Elementa*, II, 91; Regatillo, *Institutiones*, II, 114; Tummulo-Iorio, *De Censuris*, pp. 812–813; Ubach, *Theol. Moral.*, I, 561; Van Hove, *De Legibus*, p. 263; Vermeersch-Creusen, *Epitome*, II, 509; Jombart, *DDC*, III, 166; Goodwine, *The Jurist*, X (1950), 176–178 (27–29). Sipos (*Enchiridion*, p. 714, n. 23) and Cocchi (*Commentarium*, VI, 155) and Woywod-Smith (*Commentary*, II, 148) mention both opinions and decline to take sides. In Rome it is the practice not to mention the name or verdict of the precensor. Cf. Vermeersch-Creusen, *Epi-*

specify whether it means the permission which follows precensorship and also the permission for which precensorship is not required, or whether it means the first alone. The common opinion of the authors, both before and after the appearance of the Code, applies the law only to the permission which attends precensorship.[3] It is not speaking of the perm'ssion obtained from a major superior, which need not be printed in the work.[4] Particular law, however, may demand that it be printed.

The common law does not demand the reproduction of the exact words of the concession or the granted permission.[5] The name of the grantor, notice of the date and the place of grant, and the fact that the permission was

---

tome, II, 509; Piscetta-Gennaro, *Elementa*, II, 91; Gagnon, *La Censure*, p. 211; Bouscaren-Ellis, *Canon Law*, p. 711. Boudinhon, who holds that the obligation still exists, is frankly baffled by the Roman practice.—*Nouv. Législ.*, p. 263.

Should it become necessary to ascertain the name of the precensor, that can easily be done by consulting the copy of the grant which is preserved in the diocesan archives. Jombart, *DDC*, III, 166; Gagnon, *La Censure*, p. 211.

[3] The following authors hold that the prescription of canon 1394, §1, applies only to writings subject to precensorship, to the exclusion of the permission of canon 1386, §1: Piscetta-Gennaro, *Elementa*, II, 91; Aertnys-Damen, *Theol. Moral.*, I, 754; Ubach, *Theol. Moral.*, I, 561; Coronata, *Institutiones*, II, 329; Vermeersch-Creusen, *Epitome*, II, 510; Tummulo-Iorio, *De Censuris*, p. 813; Ayrinhac, *Admin. Legisl.*, p. 286; Jombart, *DDC*, III, 168; Regatillo, *Institutiones*, II, 114; Bouscaren-Ellis, *Canon Law*, p. 711. Beste, (*Introductio*, p. 698) states that the permission of which canon 1386, §1, treats is ordinarily ("*ordinarie*") printed.

[4] The following hold that the permission given by the major religious superior must be printed: Ubach, *Theol. Moral.*, I, 561; Fanfani, *De Iure Religiosorum*, p. 316; Naz, ed., *Traité de Droit Canonique*, III, 166; De Meester, *Compendium*, III, pars 1, 260. In practice, this is not observed, particularly by members of lay institutes.

Popes Clement VIII (instr. "*Fidei Catholicae*," 17 oct. 1595, §II—*Fontes*, n. 426) and Leo XIII (const. "*Officiorum ac munerum*," 27 ian. 1897, n. 36—*Fontes*, n. 632) had obliged regulars to print the notice of this permission given by their major superiors. It is quite evident that the term "*Ordinarius*" of canon 1394, §1, means the same in canon 1393 and 1394, even though the word "*loci*" is not appended. It is clear from the context. The printing of the "*Imprimatur*" is an ecclesiastical assurance given to the faithful. There is no reason to be concerned about the special formalities to be observed by religious. Cf. Vermeersch-Creusen, *Epitome*, II, 510; Berutti, *Institutiones*, IV, 426; Piscetta-Gennaro, *Elementa*, II, 92; Keene, *Religious Ordinaries and Canon 198*, The Catholic University of America Canon Law Studies, n. 135 (Washington, D. C.: The Catholic University of America Press, 1942), p. 13; Regatillo, *Institutiones*, II, 111.

[5] The following allow liberty, provided the essentials are mentioned: Genicot-Salsmans, *Institutiones*, I, 386–387; Vermeersch, *De Prohibitione*, pp. 140–141; Goodwine, *The Jurist*, X (1950), 178–180 (29–31).

The following claim that the exact wording must be reproduced: e.g., Gennari, *ME*, X, parte 1 (1897–1898), 111–112; Cappello, *De Curia Romana*, I, 299; Hollweck, *Buecherverbot*, p. 58; Schneider, *Buechergesetze*, p. 139; Boudinhon, *Nouv. Législ.*, p. 264; Périès, *L'Index*, p. 185; Piscetta-Gennaro, *Elementa*, II, 91–92; Gagnon, *La Censure*, p. 210. The obligation is not mentioned in the present law.

actually given are the essentials. More is not required. The simple statement, "*cum permissu superiorum*," "*with ecclesiastical approval*," or any similar phrase, is not sufficient, for it does not specify which superior issued the permission, nor the place, nor the date of the concession. Without mention of these details, it cannot be known whether a new approbation was obtained for a translation or a new edition, whether the legitimate local ordinary was approached, which local ordinary is responsible for the permission, or whether the work was precensored and thereupon approved at all, as alleged.[6] Hence, such a simple statement does not meet the requirements of canon 1394, §1, and opens the way to deception of the readers.[7] The contrary opinion, that such simple statements suffice when printed on leaflets, holy pictures and books or booklets of minor importance, lacks foundation and cannot be sustained in view of the explicit wording of the canon.[8] No reasonable motive exists for omitting the prescribed details. If briefly expressed, they take up no more space than the formula "*cum permissu superiorum*" or the like.

The Code explicitly demands that the permission and the prescribed details be printed on all works, citing books, folios and images.[9] This list is not exhaustive, but exemplary. The permission should appear in each issue of periodicals subject to precensorship.[10] Translations and new editions must show the new approbation required by canon 1392, §1. If a work is printed and bound before permission is granted, or if printing the permit had been overlooked, the permission, with the required details, may and should be printed on a slip of paper and pasted in each copy of the printed work before distribution to the public.

---

[6] When printed in periodicals, especially in the U. S., it does not even signify precensorship.

[7] Claeys Bouuaert-Simenon, *Manuale*, III, 138; Mothon, *Institutions*, I, 92; Gagnon, *La Censure*, p. 210; Naz, ed., *Traité de Droit Canonique*, III, 166; Goodwine, *The Jurist*, X (1950), 179–180 (30–31).

[8] This opinion is still held by Vermeersch, *Periodica*, XIV (1926), (97); Vermeersch, *Theologia Moralis*, III, 542; Coronata. *Institutiones*, II, 329; Berutti, *Institutiones*, IV, 434; Seraphinus a Loiano, *Institutiones*, II, 634; Regatillo, *Institutiones*, II, 115; Bouscaren-Ellis, *Canon Law*, p. 711; Jombart, *DDC*, III, 166. It is based on the authority of some pre-Code authors. The phraseology of the "*Officiorum ac munerum*" (n. 36, 40) was less explicit and the law of precensorship was applied less rigorously to writings smaller than books in the strict sense. Cf. Piat, *NRT*, XXXII (1900), 136; Vermeersch, *De Prohibitione*, pp. 140–141. The above mentioned authors either fail to note that the Code is more exacting in this regard, or tailor the principle to fit the practice. Cf. Goodwine, *The Jurist*, X (1950), 179–180 (30–31).

[9] The following held that it was not necessary to indicate the permission on holy pictures and sacred images: Vermeersch, *De Prohibitione*, p. 93; Cappello, *De Curia Romana*, II, 282; Wernz, *Ius Decretalium*, III, 117, n. (69). This out-dated opinion still finds a following in practice. Cf. Jombart, *DDC*, III, 166.

[10] Goodwine, *The Jurist*, X (1950), 180 (31).

The canon allows the notice of the permission to be printed in the front or the back of the book. Similarly, it may be printed on the obverse or reverse sides of published holy pictures.

The canon does not make explicit mention of the case wherein it might be advisable to omit printing the record of the fact that the permission was granted. This might occur in publications intended for non-Catholics, the diffusion of which would be greatly hindered by the appearance of such a notice in the work.[11] Publishers are well aware of the difference such a notice makes in the diffusion of these works. Basically an indult from the Holy See is required in order to act contrary to this general law of the Church, but in urgent cases the local ordinary may dispense according to the tenor of canon 81.[12] The local ordinary possesses no general authority from the Code to dispense from this regulation; neither is it contained in the quinquennial faculties for the Bishops of the United States. However, in particular cases, a proportionately grave excusing cause may exist wherein the law does not oblige. In such instances the matter should be referred to the local ordinary for his judgment, lest abuses arise or the author or the publisher succumb to self-deception.[13]

Printing a work without the explicit mention of the grant of permission does not, for that reason alone, make that work a forbidden work, unless it happens to be one of those works which receive specific mention in canon 1399, 5°.[14] The intentional omission of the printed notice of the

---

[11] Bouscaren-Ellis, *Canon Law*, p. 711; *Theol. Mechlin.*, p. 226, n. 1; De Brabandere, *Compendium*, II, 518–519; Dilgskron, *Anal. Eccl.*, V (1897), 228–229; Vermeersch, *De Prohibitione*, p. 141; Coronata, *Institutiones*, II, 329; Haring, *Grundzuege*, II, 374, n. 3; Jombart, "De imprimenda licentia imprimendi," *Periodica*, XXI (1932), 189*–190*; Goodwine, *The Jurist*, X (1950), 180–181 (31–32).

[12] Coronata, *Institutiones*, II, 329; Haring *Grundzuege*, II, 374, n. 3; Berutti, *Institutiones*, IV, 434; Bouscaren-Ellis, *Canon Law*, p. 713; Eichmann, *Lehrbuch*, p. 467; Gagnon, *La Censure*, p. 210; Jombart, *DDC*, III, 166; Goodwine, *The Jurist*, X (1950), 181 (32).

[13] Jombart, *Periodica*, XXI (1932), 189*–190*; Jombart, *DDC*, III, 166; Goodwine, *The Jurist*, X (1950), 182 (33). Several authors assert a general power in the local ordinary to dispense or to allow the omission of the approbation, e.g., Dilgskron, *Anal. Eccl.*, V (1897), 228–229; De Brabandere, *Compendium*, II, 519; Boudinhon, *Nouv. Législ.*, p. 265; Vermeersch, *De Prohibitione*, p. 141; Coronata, *Institutiones*, II, 329; Piscetta-Gennaro, *Elementa*, II, 92; Regatillo, *Institutiones*, II, 115; Naz, ed., *Traité de Droit Canonique*, III, 166. Their "bestowing" such power upon the local ordinary seems only to mean that he may authoritatively declare the presence of an excusing cause. Jombart (*DDC*, III, 166) and Bouscaren-Ellis (*Canon Law*, p. 713) refer to it as a form of "*epikeia*."

Coronata (*Institutiones*, II, 329) and Regatillo (*Institutiones*, II, 115) state it as a general principle that, if anything subject to precensorship is published in magazines or papers ("*ephemerides*"), the permission for publication need not be printed. They assume that an excusing cause is always present.

[14] Berutti, *Institutiones*, IV, 434; De Meester, *Compendium*, III, pars 1, 269, n. 3; *Theol. Mechlin.*, p. 226, n. 1.

granted permission does not seem to constitute a grave sin, unless it were done in contempt, or implied a cause of grave scandal.[15]

In the pre-Code law it was obligatory to make a declaration, in the beginning of the lives of the servants of God, that the miraculous deeds and eminent sanctity narrated therein were based on the testimony of human credence alone, and that the grant of the *Imprimatur* gave no official sanction to the alleged miracles, etc. Pope Urban VIII had made this obligatory, but it was abrogated by Pope Leo XIII. At times, however, it may be advisable to make such a statement, when there is a probable danger that too great a credence will be placed in these works, but there is no obligation to do as arising from common law.[16] In the pre-Code law it was also obligatory to print the name of the author and publisher, together with a notice of the place and date of publication, etc. These requirements, though highly desirable and recommended by librarians, are no longer demanded by ecclesiastical law.[17] In the pre-Code law it was also required that, after a work was printed, and before it was published, it had to be resubmitted to the precensor, whose duty it was to compare the printed copy with the original manuscript that had received the "*Nihil Obstat*," in order to certify that the printed work was a faithful reproduction of the original. This is not required in the present law.[18]

Summary

Canon 1394, §1, requires that the notice of the grant of permission to publish be printed either in the beginning or at the end of the book. It is not required to reproduce the wording of the grant, as long as the essentials are mentioned, i.e., the fact of the grant, the name of the grantor, and mention of the place and date of the concession. It is not required that the verdict or the name of the precensor be mentioned.

This permission must be printed at least for that case in which precensorship preceded the permission. It is not required to print the notice of the granted permission which was given by the major religious superior.

---

[15] Vermeersch, *De Prohibitione*, p. 141.

[16] Coronata, *Institutiones*, II, 340; De Meester, *Compendium*, III, pars 1, 288, n. 6; Piscetta-Gennaro, *Elementa*, II, 92; Sonntag, *Censorship of Special Classes of Books*, pp. 27–28; Vermeersch, *De Prohibitione*, p. 15, n. 1, and p. 83; Lehmkuhl, *Theol. Moral.*, II, 761; Jombart, *DDC*, III, 166. Boudinhon (*Nouv. Législ.*, p. 131) and *L'Ami* (XLIV [1927], 567) still hold it to be obligatory.

[17] Piscetta-Gennaro, *Elementa*, II, 92; Coronata, *Institutiones*, II, 329; Ferreres, *Institutiones*, II, 152; Haring, *Grundzuege*, II, 373; Vermeersch-Creusen, *Epitome*, II, 510; Augustine, *Commentary*, VI, 453.

[18] Boudinhon, *Nouv. Législ.*, p. 263; Gagnon, *La Censure*, pp. 211–212; Woywod, *HPR*, XXVIII (1928), 972.

Mention of this granted permission must be printed in all published works, including holy pictures. In a case of necessity, the local ordinary may, according to the terms of canon 81, dispense from the obligation of printing the fact of the granted permission, though for a habitual procedure contrary to the demand inherent in the law, an indult from the Holy See would be required.

A work that is printed without mention of the fact of the grant of permission is not, for that reason alone, a forbidden work. Various pre-Code regulations no longer are in force.

CHAPTER XII

PENAL SANCTIONS (CANON 2318, §2)

Despite the fact that many penal sanctions existed in the pre-Code law, only one still exists today for violators of the law of precensorship. All penal sanctions, save the one enacted in canon 2318, §2, have been abrogated. The text of canon 2318, §2, reads:

> Auctores et editores qui sine debita licentia sacrarum Scripturarum libros vel earum adnotationes aut commentarios imprimi curant, incidunt ipso facto in excommunicationem nemini reservatam.

The commentary on this canon will consist in an explanation of the terms.

(1) The Scriptural Works Mentioned in the Canon

(a) *The Books of Sacred Scripture.* In scriptural language, the term "book" is used for any unit of the Bible. A canonical crime and penalty requires grave matter. However, the unauthorized printing of even one complete book of the Bible is held sufficient for the incurring of the penalty.[1] The penalty is incurred, regardless of the language in which the text of the Bible is edited, whether in the original language, in an ancient version, or in any modern vernacular translation.[2]

(b) *Annotations and commentaries.* The terms "annotations" and "commentaries" have been explained above in the discussion on canon 1385, §1,

---

[1] Regatillo, *Institutiones*, II, 399; Naz, ed., *Traité de Droit Canonique*, IV, 710; Pellé, *Le Droit Pénal de l'Eglise*, p. 370. The following consider even the smallest "book" of the Bible as constituting a grave matter: Cappello, *De Censuris*, p. 347; Cerato, *Censurae*, p. 71; Coronata, *Institutiones*, IV, 311; Cocchi, *Commentarium*, VIII, 232; Genicot-Salsmans, *Institutiones*, II, 560; Woywod, *Commentary*, II, 470; Sipos, *Enchiridion*, p. 715; Ciprotti, *De Consummatione Delictorum*, I, 28, who also cites Cipollini (*De Censuris*, [Taurini, 1925], p. 182); Gagnon, *La Censure*, p. 82.

[2] Ayrinhac, *Penal Legislation*, p. 205; Beste, *Introductio*, p. 961; Boudinhon, *Nouv. Législ.*, p. 310; Cappello, *De Censuris*, p. 346; Cerato, *Censurae*, p. 71; Claeys Bouuaert-Simenon, *Manuale*, III, 376; Cocchi, *Commentarium*, VIII, 232; Coronata, *Institutiones*, IV, 311; De Meester, *Compendium*, III, pars 1, 315; Vermeersch-Creusen, *Epitome*, III, 319; Pistocchi, *I Canoni Penali*, p. 40; Salucci, *Il Diritto Penale*, II, 36; Chelodi, *Ius Canonicum de Delictis*, p. 80; Ciprotti, *De Consummatione Delictorum*, I, 28; Regatillo, *Institutiones*, II, 399; Pellé, *Le Droit Pénal de l'Eglise*, p. 370; Naz, ed., *Trait. de Droit Canonique*, IV, 710. It does not matter that the edition be accurate, or that the translation be faithful, or that it be made by Catholics.—Sipos, *Enchiridion*, p. 715; Aertnys-Damen, *Theologia Moralis*, II, 760; Cappello, *loc. cit.;* Coronata, *loc. cit.* Anthologies of scriptural texts are not included.—Pellé, *Le Droit Pénal de l'Eglise*, p. 371; Ciprotti, *De Consummatione Delictorum*, I, 28.

1°.[3] Non-exegetical scriptural works, e.g., dissertations, homilies, biblical novels, etc., do not fall under the strict meaning of annotations and commentaries; but paraphrastic editions or versions of books of the Bible are included.[4] If the annotations or commentaries are printed without permission, they violate the law, even if they are written by Catholics, and even though they be in perfect harmony with Catholic doctrine.[5] It is quite immaterial if they be printed with or without the text of Sacred Scripture.[6] It suffices that the annotations or the commentary treat of a part of a book of the Bible.[7] It is disputed whether these works must reach the size of a book, in the strict sense, before grave matter is reached, or whether the size of a booklet suffices.[8]

(2) The Delinquents

The canon punishes only the authors and the publishers who have the books of Sacred Scripture or their annotations and commentaries printed without the requisite permission.

---

[3] Chapter VI, Article I.

[4] Regatillo, *Institutiones*, II, 399; Pellé, *Le Droit Pénal de l'Eglise*, pp. 370–371; Ciprotti, *De Consummatione Delictorum*, I, 28, who also cites Cavigioli (*De Censuris*, Torino, 1919, p. 138) and Cipollini (*De Censuris*, p. 182).

[5] Aertnys-Damen, *Theol. Moral.*, II, 760; Ayrinhac, *Penal Legisl.*, p. 205; Cappello, *De Censuris*, p. 346; Cerato, *Censurae*, p. 71; Cocchi, *Commentarium*, VIII, 232; Coronata, *Institutiones*, IV, 311; Sipos, *Enchiridion*, p. 715.

[6] De Meester, *Compendium*, III, pars 1, 315; Pistocchi, *Canoni*, p. 40; Salucci, *Diritto*, II, 367; Naz, ed., *Traité de Droit Canonique*, IV, 710; Coronata, *Institutiones*, IV, 311; Pellé, *Le Droit Pénal de l'Eglise*, p. 371. Boudinhon (*Nouv. Législ.*, p. 320), however, claimed that the text had to accompany the annotations.

[7] De Meester, *Compendium*, III, pars 1, 315; Vermeersch-Creusen, *Epitome*, III, 319; Cipollini, *De Censuris*, p. 182; Pernicone, *Prohibition*, p. 238. Cerato (*Censurae Vigentes*, p. 71), however, and Ciprotti (*De Consummatione Delictorum*, I, 28) postulate that the annotations treat of an entire book of the Bible; the latter author lays down the same requirement for the commentary.

[8] The following demand the size of a book in the strict sense: Beste, *Introductio*, p. 961; Cocchi, *Commentarium*, VIII, 232; Coronata, *Institutiones*, IV, 311; De Meester, *Compendium*, III, pars 1, 315; Naz, ed., *Traité de Droit Canonique*, IV, 710; Vermeersch-Creusen, *Epitome*, III, 319; Woywod, *Commentary*, II, 470; Gagnon, *La Censure*, p. 82.

The following state that it suffices for the annotations or the commentary to amount to a book or a booklet: Cappello, *De Censuris*, p. 347; Cerato, *Censurae*, p. 71; Heylen, *De Censuris*, p. 164; Pellé, *Le Droit Pénal de l'Eglise*, p. 371; Ciprotti, *De Consummatione Delictorum*, I, 28, who says that a booklet that can truly be called a commentary suffices. Genicot-Salsmans (*Institutiones*, II, 560) merely state that the matter must be notable.

Some authors hold that periodicals devoted, for the most part, to annotations or commentaries on the Sacred Scriptures and bound in fascicles, or bound in books, or destined to form a book, fall under the law of canon 2318, §2: Cappello, *De Censuris*, p. 341; Cerato, *Censurae*, p. 71; Cocchi, *Commentarium*, VIII, 232; Heylen, *De Censuris*, p. 164; Pellé, *Le Droit Pénal de l'Eglise*, p. 371; Vermeersch-Creusen, *Epitome*, III, 319; Woywod, *Commentary*, II, 470.

The term *author* ("*auctor*") as opposed to *publisher* ("*editor*") is sometimes used in a strict sense, to mean only the composer of a work, and sometimes in a broad sense, to mean the composer, editor, translator, etc. In canon 2318, §2, the term is understood in its broad sense. It would be absurd to demand the strict interpretation, for the real authors of the Bible have died long since. The Code is also legislating for editors, translators, etc., of the Bible.[9]

The term *publisher* must be understood as the person who makes copies of a work available to the general public, e.g., by selling them or by distributing them gratis, or by offering them for public sale or distribution.[10] This definition excludes the *printer*, unless he be the publisher at the same time.[11] However, the printer, because of the nature of his work, and others as well may be guilty of the crime of co-operation according to the terms of canons 2209 and 2231.

(3) The Delictual Act

The censure is inflicted upon the author and the publisher for having the books of Sacred Scripture or annotations and commentaries thereof printed without the proper permission.

The term "*imprimi curant*" means that the author or the publisher must be the principal and proximate moral cause of the printing of the work. This condition is verified if they print the work themselves or if they, personally or through another, engage a printer to print the work. If the author or the publisher is not the proximate moral cause of the printing, he is not guilty of the crime and does not incur the excommunication; e.g., an author may have donated his manuscript to another, without any stipulation about printing; or the manuscript may be printed against his wishes.[12] A publisher

---

[9] Cerato, *Censurae*, p. 70; Cocchi, *Commentarium*, VIII 233; Coronata, *Institutiones*, IV, 310; Pellé, *Le Droit Pénal de l'Eglise*, p. 368; Naz, ed., *Traité de Droit Canonique*, IV, 710; Blat, *Commentarium*, V, 206; Gagnon, *La Censure*, p. 82; Regatillo, *Institutiones*, II, 399; Ciprotti, *De Consummatione Delictorum*, I, 27. In regard to the annotations and commentaries, the foregoing authors limit the term to the writer who composed them; in like manner, e.g., Beste, *Introductio*, p. 961; Cappello, *De Censuris*, p. 345; Pistocchi, *Canoni*, p. 39; Salucci, *Diritto*, II, 34; Heylen, *De Censuris*, p. 164.

[10] The meaning of the term is more fully explained above in Chapter V, Article II, A, 7).

[11] Ayrinhac, *Penal Legisl.*, p. 205; Cappello, *De Censuris*, p. 345; Cerato, *Censurae*, p. 70; Cocchi, *Commentarium*, VIII, 233; Coronata, *Institutiones*, IV, 310; Genicot-Salsmans, *Institutiones*, II, 559–560; De Meester, *Compendium*, III, pars 1, 315; Vermeersch-Creusen, *Epitome*, III, 319; Boudinhon, *Nouv. Législ.*, p. 321; Heylen, *De Censuris*, p. 164.

[12] Cf. Lugo, *Disputationes*, XXI, n. 90; Arndt, *Commentarii*, p. 248; Genicot-Salsmans, *Institutiones*, II, 560; Konings, *Theologia Moralis*, II, 356; Ballerini-Palmieri, *Opus Theologicum Morale*, VII, 725; Hilarius a Sexten, *Tractatus*, p. 237; Pennacchi, *ASS*, XXX (1897–1898), 532; Vermeersch, *De Prohibitione*, p. 157; Coronata, *Institutiones*, IV, 310; De Meester, *Compendium*, III, pars 1, 315; Lehmkuhl, *Theologia Moralis*, II, 721.

who merely publishes such a work after it has been printed does not incur the excommunication, but he is an accessory to the delict after its commission, and is guilty of handling a forbidden book.[13] If one and the same man is the author and the publisher, only one penalty is incurred. If several persons are involved as moral principals of the delict, each one incurs the penalty.[14] When a publishing house is run, not by an individual, but by a board, then the principles of canon 2255, §2, and 2209, §1, may be invoked, i.e., only those individual members who decide on the printing incur the penalty; those who vote against the printing, and those who abstain from voting, are not guilty of the crime.[15]

The delictual act is consummated as soon as the entire work is printed, even before it is published. The canon uses the term "*imprimere*" rather than "*edere.*" The use of this term in connection with editions of Sacred Scripture is intentional, as can be learned from canon 1391, which treats of vernacular translations of the Bible. The term must, therefore, be understood in its proper sense.[16] However, only that printing which is done with a view to the publication of the work could constitute matter for the delictual act.[17] Private printings are not governed by the law on precensorship, and hence they are not meant here.[18]

---

[13] Cf. Cerato, *Censurae*, p. 70; Boudinhon, *Nouv. Législ.*, p. 321; Aertnys-Damen, *Theol. Moral.*, II, 760.

[14] Cerato, *Censurae*, pp. 71, 72, 147; Cappello, *De Censuris*, pp. 214, 215; Salucci, *Diritto*, II, 28.

[15] Cappello, *De Censuris*, p. 214; Cerato, *Censurae*, pp. 71–72; Chelodi, *Ius Canonicum de Delictis et Poenis*, p. 80; Coronata, *Institutiones*, IV, 304. Also cf. the authors' commentaries on canon 2334, 1°.

[16] Aertnys-Damen, *Theol. Moral.* II, 760; Beste, *Introductio*, p. 961; Cappello, *De Censuris*, p. 345; Cerato, *Censurae*, p. 70; Ciprotti, *De Consummatione Delictorum*, I, 28; Coronata, *Institutiones*, IV, 310; De Meester, *Compendium*, III, pars 1, 315–316; Heylen, *De Censuris*, p. 164; Salucci, *Diritto*, II, 37; Sipos, *Enchiridion*, p. 715; Vermeersch-Creusen, *Epitome*, III, 319; Wernz-Vidal, *Ius Canonicum*, VII, 449.

Some, however, hold that the censure is not incurred until the moment of publication, either because of the general tenor of the entire law of precensorship, or because of the phrase "*opere publici iuris facto*" of canon 2318, §1, e.g., Piscetta-Gennaro, *Elementa*, IV, 295; Cocchi, *Commentarium*, VIII, 233; Ayrinhac, *Penal Legisl.*, p. 205; Pistocchi, *Canoni*, pp. 40–41; Eichmann, *Das Strafrecht des Codex Iuris Canonici* (Paderborn, 1920), p. 132; Pellé, *Le Droit Pénal de l'Eglise*, p. 370.

[17] Aertnys-Damen, *Theol. Moral.*, II, 760; Beste, *Introductio*, p. 961; Cappello, *De Censuris*, p. 346; Coronata, *Institutiones*, IV, 311; Vermeersch-Creusen, *Epitome*, III, 319; Wernz-Vidal, *Ius Canonicum*, VII, 499.

[18] Augustine, *Commentary*, VIII, 296, n. 4; Tummolo-Iorio, *De Censuris*, p. 770; Coronata, *Institutiones*, IV, 311.

The crime is consummated when the printing is finished.[19] The printing of copies must be extensive enough to constitute an "edition," even if it be a small one; if only a few copies are printed, it is not an edition, and the censure is not incurred.[20]

The term *printing* must be understood not merely in the very restricted sense of reduplication by metal type and press, but also of those other modern forms of reduplication that have been mentioned under this term in the chapter on terminology, e.g., offset, plates, photolithography, multigraph, mimeograph, etc., provided the printing be done with a view to publication, and a sufficient number of copies are made to constitute an edition.[21]

The printing becomes a canonical crime through the fact that it is done without the proper permission ("*sine debita licentia*"). The due permission is that mentioned in canon 1385, §2, or that required in canon 1391. It is the permission which must be preceded by precensorship. The penalty is not incurred by a religious who fails to obtain the permission of a major religious superior, provided he obtains the called for permission from the ecclesiastical superior.[22] Nor is the penalty incurred as long as a valid, though illicit, permission has been obtained from a local ordinary.[23] If

---

[19] A book is not yet really printed when the type is set, or when galley or page proofs have been drawn. Some authors state that the delict is consummated when the work is put to press, e.g., Beste, *Introductio*, p. 961; Cappello, *De Censuris*, p. 346; De Meester, *Compendium*, III, pars 1, 315; Salucci, *Diritto*, II, 37; Vermeersch-Creusen, *Epitome*, III, 319. Most probably they merely wish to emphasize the fact that the delictual act consists in the printing of the work and not in the publishing of it. Sipos (*Enchiridion*, p. 715), however, holds that the excommunication is incurred "*statim post inchoatam impressionem.*"

[20] Cappello, *De Censuris*, p. 346; Cerato, *Censurae*, p. 70; De Meester, *Compendium*, III, pars 1, 316; Tummolo-Iorio, *De Censuris*, p. 770.

[21] Some authors require that the work be printed on a printing press, and exclude lithographic reproductions, e.g., Ciprotti, *De Consummatione Delictorum*, I, 27, n. 40; Heylen, *De Censuris*, p. 164. Perhaps they wish simply to imply that such reproductions are usually not intended for publication.

[22] The following pre-Code authors held this view: Suarez, *Opera Omnia*, XXIII, 658; Bassaeus, *Flores*, I, 460; Van der Velden, *Principia*, II, 861; Bucceroni, *Institutiones*, II, 399; Gabriel de Varceno, *Compendium*, II, 512; Pennacchi, *Commentaria*, II, 235–236; Arndt, *Commentarii*, p. 249; Piat, *NRT*, XXXIII (1901), 140; Vermeersch, *De Prohibitione*, p. 156.

This view was also held, after the appearance of the Code, by Blat, *Commentarium*, V, 206; Boudinhon, *Nouv. Législ.*, p. 320; De Meester, *Compendium*, III, pars 1, 316.

[23] For instance, if the author sought permission from a second local ordinary without mentioning a previous refusal; or, if the local ordinary issued the *Imprimatur* without having the work precensored. Cerato, *Censurae*, p. 71; Van der Velden, *Principia*, II, 861; De Meester, *Compendium*, III, pars 1, 316; *Constitutio* (Claromon-Ferrandi), p. 181.

Some authors maintain that the approbation of *any* local ordinary is valid, though it be illicit, if given contrary to canon 1385, §2, and suffices for the forestalling of the excommunication, e.g., Van der Velden, *Principia*, II, 861; Cappello, *De Censuris*, p. 346; De Meester,

permission is obtained before the printing of the work is completed, the penalty is not incurred.[24] The penalty is also incurred for the printing of new editions which lack the new approbation required by canon 1392.[25] If the permission should have been obtained for a first edition, but was not, it still must be obtained for subsequent editions.

If changes are made in an edition after the permission has been granted, the penalty is not incurred, unless these changes are so noteworthy that the greater part of the work consists of uncensored work.[26]

(4) The Penalty

The punishment is an excommunication incurred automatically when the printing is completed. The absolution is not reserved to anyone. When a penitent laboring under this penalty approaches for absolution, he must be disposed to recall or withdraw the edition and supply effective remedies, until the proper permission is obtained.

The work itself is a forbidden book.[27]

Compendium, III, pars 1, 316; Pellé, *Le Droit Pénal de l'Eglise*, p. 369; Heylen, *De Censuris*, p. 164. This seems to contradicit the canon which says "*sine DEBITA licentia*". Cf. Ciprotti, *De Consummatione Delictorum*, I, 28.

[24] Ballerini-Palmieri, *Opus Theologicum Morale*, VII, 275; Hilarius a Sexten, *Tractatus*, p. 237; Boudinhon, *Nouv. Législ.*, p. 320; De Meester, *Compendium*, III, pars 1, 316.

[25] Cerato, *Censurae*, p. 71; Ciprotti, *De Consummatione Delictorum*, I, 28. Coronata seems to agree with certain authors, whom he does not name, that the penalty is not incurred for one's printing without permission new editions of a work written by a Catholic and already approved by legitimate authority. Cf. *Institutiones*, IV, 311. He cites only Cavigioli, *De Cens. latae sent.*, n. 167. The same view is held by Jombart in *Traité de Droit Canonique*, ed. by R. Naz, IV, 710. Before the Code, Vermeersch (*De Prohibitione*, p. 148) did not consider the omission of permission in this case to be a grave matter.

[26] Van der Velden, *Principia*, II, 861; Gabriel de Varceno, *Compendium*, II, 512.

[27] Canon 1399, 5°.

CONCLUSIONS

1. The first record of pontifical legislation enacting precensorship for the entire Church is the Bull "*Inter multiplices*" of Innocent VIII (1482-149,2) issued Nov. 17, 1487.

2. The term *books* ("*libri*") in canon 1385, §1, 2°, must be understood in the extended juridic sense as defined by canon 1384, §2, since the use of the word in the strict sense is not evident.

3. Canon 1385, §1, 2°, subjects to precensorship: (*a*) all writings, large and small, which *ex professo* treat of a religious or moral topic, and (*b*) those writings on a profane topic which contain anything of particular interest to religion or morals.

4. The three groups of writings mentioned in canon 1385, §1, 2°, are not to be regarded as three entirely separate categories. The canon, in its text, progresses from the more frequent examples to an all-inclusive phrase at the end of the first and second groups; and, in turn, these groups are virtually contained in the final and all-embracing group: "ac generaliter scripta in quibus aliquid sit quod religionis ac morum honestatis peculiariter intersit." The more frequent kinds of writings on religious or moral topics are singled out for special mention, just as the books of Sacred Scripture and their annotations and commentaries are given special attention in canon 1385, §1, 1°.

5. The law on precensorship also applies to periodical publications whose principal scope it is to treat of a religious or a moral topic. The practical difficulty of exercising precensorship over periodicals issued frequently (e.g., weeklies) may necessitate a special arrangement or modification in the manner of performing precensorship. The appointment, however, of a censor who only reads each issue after publication and orders any necessary corrections to be inserted in the following issue, does not in and of itself fulfill the requirements of the law.

6. The permission of the major religious superior as required by canon 1385, §3, is a simple permission to publish. Though the particular law of the respective religious Institute may prescribe it, the canon does not demand precensorship by the major superior.

7. The permission mentioned in canon 1386, §1, is needed for the publication of works on merely profane matters. The word "*quoque*" does not cause the canon to include writings subject to precensorship.

8. The permission required by canon 1386, §1, is a simple permission without precensorship of the writings themselves. However, if a secular cleric or a religious writes for a periodical publication and the articles treat of matters mentioned in canon 1385, §1, all the rules governing precensorship must be observed.

9. Canon 1392 demands a new approbation not only for altered or enlarged new editions of an approved work, but also for mere reprint editions produced from new type or plates or by some other process, provided the work is truly being republished. Mere new impressions, i.e., new printings made from standing type or the original plates, are not new editions in the sense of the Code, at least if they are produced within a relatively short time after the earlier printing.

10. It is a false interpretation of canon 1393, §2, to restrict the precensor's competence to an examination of and judgment on the doctrinal content of the work. The precensor is appointed to give his expert opinion on the broader issue of whether the work can be published without harm to faith or morals or ecclesiastical discipline, whether in theory or in practice.

11. The identity of the precensor must not be revealed to the author unless and until a favorable verdict has been given. The observance of this prescription demands that ordinarily more than one precensor *ex officio* be appointed in each diocese; that the local ordinary do not instruct the author to send his manuscript directly to the precensor, but through the chancery; that, when necessary, the precensor do not communicate directly with the author, but indirectly and anonymously through the chancery office.

12. The name and verdict of the precensor need not be printed in the book or writing.

13. Canon 1394, §1, prescribes no other notice of the granted permission to be printed in the book or writing, or on the holy picture, than that of the local ordinary which follows precensorship. Neither the permission of the religious superior (canon 1385, §3) nor that which is mentioned in canon 1386, §1, need be printed, unless that be prescribed by particular law. The notice of the granted permission of the local ordinary must be printed in all works subject to precensorship, whether they be books, booklets, pamphlets, leaflets, single sheets, holy pictures, or periodical publications. The new approbation must receive printed mention in new editions.

14. To omit printing the notice of the granted permission of the local ordinary, an indult of the Holy See is necessary, or a dispensation granted according to the terms of canon 81, or the presence of a sufficiently grave excusing cause.

15. Printing the simple formula "*Cum licentia superiorum*" or the like does not satisfy the requirements of canon 1394, §1. According to the clear word-

ing of the canon, the name of the local ordinary, with mention of the date and the place of the grant must appear in all writings, including periodicals, pamphlets, leaflets and holy pictures. The observance of the law entails no extra expense and requires almost no additional space.

16. The term "author" is used in the broad sense to include not only the original composer of the work, but also the translator, reviser or editor.

17. Though it modified and abrogated several of the former regulations, the Code strengthened the law on precensorship: (1) by extending the meaning of the term "book" (canon 1384, §2) and subjecting all intended publications of whatever size or frequency to precensorship when they deal with matters mentioned in canon 1385, §1, or 1387-1391; (2) by explicitly demanding that the name of the local ordinary granting the *Imprimatur*, together with the date and the place of the grant, by printed in the writing, even if it be only a leaflet or a holy picture.

BIBLIOGRAPHY

SOURCES

Acta Apostolicae Sedis, Commentarium Officiale, Romae, 1909—

Acta et Decreta Concilii Plenarii Baltimorensis Tertii, A.D. MDCCCLXXXIV, Baltimorae, 1894 [Reimpressio].

Acta et Decreta Sacrorum Conciliorum Recentiorum Collectio Lacensis, 7 vols., Friburgi Brisgoviae, 1870–1892.

Acta Sanctae Sedis, 41 vols., Romae, 1865–1908.

Biblia Sacra Vulgatae Editionis, ed. H. Hetzenauer, Oeniponte, 1906.

Bouscaren, T. Lincoln, *The Canon Law Digest*, 2 vols. and Supplement through 1948, Milwaukee: The Bruce Publishing Co., [1934, 1943, 1949]

Bullarum, Diplomatum et Privilegiorum Romanorum Pontificum Taurinensis Editio, 24 vols. et Appendix, Augustae Taurinorum, 1857–1872.

Canones et Decreta Concilii Tridentini ex editione romana a. MDCCCXXXIV, repetiti, ed. Aem. Richter, Lipsiae, 1853.

Codex Iuris Canonici Pii X Pontificis Maximi iussu digestus, Benedicti Papae XV auctoritate promulgatus, praefatione, fontium annotatione et indice analytico-alphabetico ab Emo Petro Card. Gasparri auctus, Romae: Typis Polyglottis Vaticanis, 1929 [Reimpressio].

Codicis Iuris Canonici Fontes, cura Emi Petri Card. Gasparri editi, 9 vols., Romae [postea Civitate Vaticana]: Typis Polyglottis Vaticanis, 1923–1939 (Vols. VII–IX ed. cura et studio Emi Iustiniani Card. Serédi).

Collectanea S. Congregationis de Propaganda Fide, 2 vols., Romae, 1907.

Concilia Provincialia Baltimori habita ab anno 1829 usque ad annum 1849, ed. altera, Baltimori, 1851.

Concilii Plenarii Baltimorensis II, in Ecclesia Metropolitana Baltimorensi, a die VII ad diem XXI Octobris, A.D. MDCCCLXVI, habiti, et a Sede Apostolica Recogniti, Acta et Decreta, 2. ed., Baltimorae, 1868.

Concilium Plenarium Totius Americae Septentrionalis Foederatae Baltimori habitum anno 1852, Baltimori, 1853.

Corpus Iuris Canonici, ed. Lipsiensis secunda, post Aemilii Ludovici Richteri curas instruxit Aemilius Friedberg, 2 vols., Lipsiae, 1879–1881; ed. anastatice repetita, 1928.

Decreta Authentica Congregationis Sacrorum Rituum ex actis eiusdem collecta eiusque auctoritate promulgata sub auspiciis SS. Domini nostri Leonis Papae XIII, 5 vols. et Appendices, Romae, 1898–1927.

Enchiridion biblicum: Documenta ecclesiastica Sacram Scripturam spectantia auctoritate Pontificiae Commissionis de re Biblica edita, Romae, 1927.

Fontes Iuris Romani Anteiustiniani, Pars prima—Leges, ed. S. Riccobono, Florentiae: Apud S.A.G. Barbèra, 1941.

Index Librorum Prohibitorum Sanctissimi Domini Nostri Leonis XIII Pont. Max. iussu editus, ed novissima, Taurini, 1889.

Jaffé, Philippus, *Regesta Pontificum Romanorum ab condita Ecclesia ad annum post Christum natum MCXCVIII*, 2. ed. correctam et auctam auspiciis Gulielmi Wattenbach curaverunt F. Kaltenbrunner, P. Ewald, S. Lowenfeld, 2 vols. in 1, Lipsiae, 1885–1888.

Mansi, J.D., *Sacrorum Conciliorum Nova et Amplissima Collectio*, 53 vols. in 60, Parisiis, Arnhem, Lipsiae, 1901–1927.

Pii IX Pontificis Maximi Acta, 9 vols., Romae, 1854–[1878]

Schroeder, H.J., *Canons and Decrees of the Council of Trent*, St. Louis: B. Herder Book Co., 1941.

REFERENCE WORKS

Aertnys, J.—Damen, C., *Theologia Moralis secundum doctrinam S. Alfonsi de Ligorio Doctoris Ecclesiae*, 14. ed., 2 vols., Taurinorum Augustae: Marietti, 1944.

Aichner, Simon—Friedle, Theodorus, *Compendium Iuris Ecclesiastici*, 10. ed., Brixinae, 1905.

A. L. A. Glossary of Library Terms, prepared under the direction of the Committee on Library Terminology of the American Library Association by Elizabeth H. Thompson, Chicago: American Library Association, 1943.

Alphonsus de Ligorio, *Theologia Moralis*, ed. Michael Heilig, 10 vols. in 5, Mechliniae, 1852.

Alzog, John, *History of the Church*, translated from the German by Rev. Dr. F. J. Pabisch and Rt. Rev. Thomas S. Byrne, 3 vols., New York, 1912.

Arndt, Augustinus, *De Libris Prohibitis Commentarii*, Ratisbonae, Neo-Eboraci, & Cincinnati, 1895.

Arregui, Antonius, *Summarium Theologiae Moralis*, 13. ed., Westminster, Md.: The Newman Bookshop, 1944.

Augustine, Charles, *A Commentary on the New Code of Canon Law*, 8 vols., St. Louis, 1918–1922.

Ayrinhac, Henry A., *Administrative Legislation in the New Code of Canon Law*, New York: Longmans, Green & Co., 1930.

———, *General Legislation in the New Code of Canon Law*, New York, 1923.

———, *Penal Legislation in the New Code of Canon Law*, New York, 1920.

Ballerini, Antonius—Palmieri, Dominicus, *Opus theologicum morale*, 2. ed., 7 vols., Prati, 1892–1894.

Bargilliat, Michael, *Praelectiones Juris Canonici*, 37. ed., 2 vols., Parisiis, 1923–1924.

Baronius, C.—Raynaldi, O.—Laderchi, J.—Theiner, A., *Annales Ecclesiastici*, 37 vols., Bar-le-Duc, Parisiis, 1864–1883.

Bassaeus, Eligius, *Flores Totius Theologiae Practicae, tum Sacramentalis, tum Moralis*, 2. ed., 2 vols., Venetiis, 1690.

Benedictus XIV, *Opera Omnia*, 17 vols., Prati, 1839–1846.

Berutti, Christophorus, *Institutiones Iuris Canonici*, 6 vols. [Vol. II, Pars II, et Vol. V adhuc sub praelo], Taurini-Romae: Marietti, 1936–1943.

Beste, Udalricus, *Introductio in Codicem Iuris Canonici*, 3. ed., Collegeville, Minn.: St. John's Abbey Press, 1946.

Billot, Ludovicus, *De Virtutibus Infusis Commentarius in Secundam Partem S. Thomae*, 4. ed., Romae, 1928.

Bittle, Celestine, *Man and Morals: Ethics*, Milwaukee: The Bruce Publishing Co., [1950].

Blat, Albertus, *Commentarium Textus Codicis Iuris Canonici*, 5 vols. in 6, Romae, 1919–1927; Vol. III, Partes II–VI, 1923.

Bonal, Antoine, *Institutiones Theologiae ad usum Seminariorum*, 17. ed., 6 vols., Tolosae, 1891.

Boudinhon, A., *La Nouvelle Législation de l'Index*, 2. ed., Paris, 1925.

Bouix, Dominicus, *Tractatus de Curia Romana, seu de Cardinalibus, Romanis Congregationibus, Legatis, Nuntiis, Vicariis et Praefectis Apostolicis*, Parisiis, 1880 [Reimpressio]

Bouscaren, T. Lincoln—Ellis, Adam C., *Canon Law, A Text and Commentary*, Milwaukee: Bruce Publishing Co., [1946].

Brosnahan, Timothy, *Prolegomena to Ethics*, New York: Fordham University Press, 1941.

Brunsmann, John—Preuss, Arthur, *A Handbook of Fundamental Theology*, 4 vols., St. Louis: B. Herder Book Co., 1928–1932.

Bucceroni, Ianuarius, *Institutiones Theologiae Moralis*, 5. ed., 2 vols., Romae, 1908.

Cance, Adrien, *Le Code de Droit Canonique*, 2. ed., 3 vols., Paris, 1929.

Cance, Adriano—Arquer, Miguel de, *El Código de Derecho Canónico*, 2 vols., Barcelona: Editorial Liturgica Española, S.A., 1934.

Cappello, Felix M., *De Curia Romana*, 2 vols., Romae, 1911–1912.

———, *Summa Iuris Canonici in Usum Scholarum Concinnata*, 2. ed., 3 vols., Romae: Apud Aedes Universitatis Gregorianae, 1932–1940.

———, *Summa Iuris Publici Ecclesiastici*, 3. ed., Romae: Apud Aedes Universitatis Gregorianae, 1932.

———, *Tractatus Canonico-Moralis de Censuris iuxta Codicem Iuris Canonici*, 3. ed., Taurinorum Augustae: Marietti, 1933.

Castro-Palaus, Ferdinandus, *Opus Morale De Virtutibus et Vitiis Contrariis*, ed. nova, 3 vols., Lugduni, 1700.

Catholic Encyclopedia, The, 15 vols., Index and Supplement, New York, 1907–1922.

Cavagnis, Felix, *Institutiones Juris Publici Ecclesiastici*, 3. ed., 3 vols., Romae, [1896].

Cerato, Prosdocimus, *Censurae Vigentes Ipso Facto a Codice Iuris Canonici, Excerptae*, 2. ed., Patavii, 1921.

Chelodi, Ioannes, *Ius Canonicum de Personis*, 3. ed. curavit Pius Ciprotti, Vicenza: Società Anonima Tipografica, 1942.

———, *Ius Poenale de Delictis et Poenis et de Iudiciis Criminalibus*, 5. ed. a Pio Ciprotti, Vicenza: Società Anonima Tipografica, 1943.

Cicognani, Amleto Giovanni, *Canon Law*, tr. by Joseph M. O'Hara and Francis J. Brennan, 2. ed., Reprint, Westminster, Md.: The Newman Bookshop, 1948.

———, *Commentarium ad librum primum Codicis iuris canonici*, 2. ed. a Dino Staffa, 2 vols., Romae: Ex Officina Typographica Romana "Buona Stampa," 1939; Vol. II, Romae: Apud Custodiam Librariam Pontificii Instituti Utriusque Iuris, 1942.

Ciolli, A., *Commento breve della Costituzione leonina riguardo ai libri proibiti*, 2. ed., Roma, 1906.

Ciprotti, Pius, *De Consummatione Delictorum attento eorum elemento obiectivo in iure canonico*, Pars I, Romae: Apud Custodiam Librariam Pont. Instituti Utriusque Iuris, 1936.

Claeys Bouuaert, Ferdinandus—Simenon, G., *Manuale Juris Canonici ad usum Seminariorum*, 3 vols., Vols. I, III, 4. ed., 1934; Vol. II, 2. ed., 1935, Gandae et Leodii: Apud Seminaria.

Claeys Bouuaert, Ferdinandus, *Selecta Capita Codicis Iuris Canonici*, Gandae, 1919.

Cocchi, Guidus, *Commentarium in Codicem Iuris Canonici*, 8 vols. in 5, Taurinorum-Augustae, 1920–1930; Vol. VI (i.e. Lib. III, Partes IV–VI), 2. ed., 1927.

Constitutio APOSTOLICAE SEDIS Pii Papae IX qua Censurae Latae Sententiae, Limitantur annotationibus seu commentariis illustrata, Claromon Ferrandi, 1881.

Cornely, Rudolphus—Knabenbauer, I., *Historica et Critica Introductio in U. T. Libros Sacros*, Cursus Scripturae Sacrae Pars Prior, 2. ed., 3 vols. in 4, Parisiis, 1894–1897.

Coronata, Matthaeus Conte a, *Institutiones Iuris Canonici ad usum utriusque cleri et scholarum*, 5 vols., Taurini: Marietti, 1928–1936. [The 2. ed., published in 1936–1947, was also consulted]

———, *Ius Publicum Ecclesiasticum*, 2. ed., Taurini: Marietti, 1934.

Craisson, D., *Manuale Totius Iuris Canonici*, 7. ed., 4 vols., Paris, 1885.

Creusen, Joseph—Garesché, Edward, *Religious Men and Women in Church Law*, Milwaukee: The Bruce Publishing Co., [1931].

Crnica, Antonius, *Commentarium theoretico-practicum Codicis Iuris Canonici*, 2 vols., Sibenik: Typis Typographiae "Kàcic," 1940–1941.

Cronin, Michael, *The Science of Ethics*, 2. ed., 2 vols., New York: Benziger Bros., 1929–1930.

Cyclopedia of Law and Procedure, 40 vols., New York, 1901–1913.

Davis, Henry, *Moral and Pastoral Theology*, 3. ed., 4 vols., New York: Sheed & Ward, 1938.

De Brabandere, Petrus, *Iuris Canonici et Iuris Canonico-Civilis Compendium*, 3. ed., 2 vols., Brugis, 1882.

De Groot, Vincentius, *Summa Apologetica de Ecclesia Catholica ad mentem S. Thomae Aquinatis*, 3. ed., Ratisbonae, 1906.

De Meester, Alphonsus, *Juris Canonici et Juris Canonico-Civilis Compendium*, nova ed., 3 vols. in 4, Brugis, 1921–1928.

Denifle, Heinrich, *Die Entstehung der Universitaeten des Mittelalters*, Berlin, 1885.

Denifle, Henricus—Chatelain, E., *Chartularium Universitatis Parisiensis*, 4 vols., Parisiis, 1889–1897.

Dictionnaire de Droit Canonique, Paris: Letouzey et Ané, 1924—

Dictionnaire de la Bible, ed. F. Vigouroux, 3. ed., 5 vols. in 10, Paris: Letouzey et Ané, 1926–1928.

———, Supplément, ed. L. Pirot, Vol. I—, 1928—.

Dictionnaire de Théologie Catholique, 15 vols. in 30, Paris: Letouzey et Ané, 1903–1950.

Dobschuetz, Ernst von, *Das Decretum Gelasianum* DE LIBRIS RECIPIENDIS ET NON RECIPIENDIS *in kritischem Text herausgegeben und untersucht*, Texte und Untersuchungen, Dritte Reihe, Band 8, Heft 4, Leipzig, 1912.

Doctoris Seraphici S. Bonaventurae Opera Omnia, 10 vols. & Index, Ad Claras Aquas [prope Florentiam], 1883–1902.

Donat, Josephus, *Summa Philosophiae Christianae*, 3. ed., 8 vols., Oeniponte, 1923–1928; Vol. VII, 4. ed., 1928.

Eichmann, Eduard, *Lehrbuch des Kirchenrechts*, 2. ed., Paderborn, 1926.

———, *Das Strafrecht des Codex Iuris Canonici*, Paderborn, 1920.

Fanfani, Ludovicus, *De Iure Religiosorum*, 2. ed., Taurini, 1925.

Farges, Albert, *The Ordinary Ways of the Spiritual Life*, New York, 1927.

Ferreres, Joannes Baptista, *Compendium Theologiae Moralis*, 10. ed., Barcinone, 1919.

———, *Institutiones Canonicae iuxta Novissimum Codicem*, 2. ed., 2 vols., Barcinone, 1920.

Fessler, Joseph, *Sammlung vermischter Schriften*, Freiburg, 1869.

Frins, Victor, *De Actibus Humanis*, 3 vols., Friburgi Brisgoviae, 1897–1911.

Funk and Wagnalls, *The New College Standard Dictionary*, New York: The Funk and Wagnalls Co., 1947.

Gabriel de Varceno, *Compendium Theologiae Moralis*, 4. ed., 2 vols., Augustae Taurinorum, 1876.

Gagnon, Edouard, *La Censure des Livres*, Les Thèses Canoniques de Laval, n. 3, Québec, Université Laval, 1945.

Gatterer, Michael, *Katechetik oder Anleitung zur Kinderseelsorge*, 4. ed., Innsbruck: F. Rauch, 1931.

Genicot, Eduardus, *Addita et Mutata in editionibus secunda et tertia Institutionum Theologiae Moralis*, Lovanii, 1900.

———, *Institutiones Theologiae Moralis*, 4. ed., 2 vols., Lovanii, 1904.

Genicot, Eduardus—Salsmans, Iosephus, *Institutiones Theologiae Moralis*, 14. ed., 2 vols., Buenos Aires: Dedebec, Ediciones Desclee, De Brower, 1939. [The 16. ed., published in 1946 (Bruxellis: L'Edition Universelle) was also consulted].

Goepfert, Franz A., *Moraltheologie*, 5. ed., 3 vols., Paderborn, 1905–1906.

Gougnard, Armandus, *Collationes Theologicae*, 2 vols., Mechliniae: H. Dessain, 1932–1936.

Goyeneche, Servus, *Iuris Canonici Summa Principia*, 2 vols., Roma: Tip. Pol. "Cuore di Maria," 1938; Vol. I, Pro Manuscripto [no date].

Grannan, Charles P., *A General Introduction to the Bible*, 4 vols., St. Louis, 1921.

Gudenus, *Codex diplomaticus anecdotorum res Moguntinas illustrantium*, 5 vols., Francofurti et Lipsiae, 1757–1758.

Gury, Iohannes Petrus—Ballerini, Antonius, *Compendium Theologiae Moralis*, 12. ed., 2 vols., Prati, 1894.

Haring, Johann B., *Grundzuege des katholischen Kirchenrechtes*, 3. ed., 2 vols., Graz, 1924.

Hartzheim, Joseph, *Bibliotheca Coloniensis*, Coloniae, 1747.

Hefele, Carl Joseph von, *Conciliengeschichte*, 9 vols., Freiburg im Breisgau, 1869–1890; Vols. VII–IX, ed. J. Card. Hergenroether.

Heiner, Franz, *Katholisches Kirchenrecht*, 2. ed., 2 vols., Paderborn, 1897.

Heylen, V., *De Censuris*, Theologia ad usum Seminarii Mechliniensis, 4. ed., Mechliniae: H. Dessain, 1945.

Heymans, A., *De ecclesiastica librorum aliorumque scriptorum in Belgio prohibitione disquisitio*, Bruxellis, 1849.

Hilarius a Sexten, *Tractatus de censuris ecclesiasticis cum appendice de irregularitate*, Moguntiae, 1898.

Hilgers, Joseph, *Der Index der verbotenen Buecher*, Freiburg im Breisgau, 1904.

Hoepfl, Hildebrand, *Beitraege zur Geschichte der Sixto-Klementinischen Vulgata*, Biblische Studien, XVIII Band, 1–3 Heft, Freiburg im Breisgau, 1913.

———, *Introductionis in Sacros Utriusque Testamenti Libros Compendium*, 4. ed., 3 vols., 1935–1940, Vol. I, Romae: Editiones A. Arnodo, 1940; Vol. II–III, Romae: Anonima Libraria Cattolica Italiana, 1935–1938.

Hollweck, Joseph, *Das kirchliche Buecherverbot*, 2. ed., Mainz, 1897.

———, *Die kirchlichen Strafgesetze*, Mainz, 1899.

Howell, Herbert A., *The Copyright Law*, Washington: The Bureau of National Affairs Inc., 1942.

Hurley, Timothy, *A Commentary on the Present Index Legislation*, Dublin, 1907.

Jone, Heribert, *Commentarium in Codicem Iuris Canonici*, Vol. I, Paderborn: F. Schoeningh, 1950.

Jone, Heribert—Adelman, Urban, *Moral Theology*, 2. ed., Westminster, Md.: The Newman Bookshop, 1946.

Kapp, Friederich, *Geschichte des deutschen Buchhandels bis in das siebzehnte Jahrhundert*, 4 vols. & Index, Leipzig, 1886–1923.

Keene, Michael J., *Religious Ordinaries and Canon 198*, The Catholic University of America Canon Law Studies, n. 135, Washington, D. C.: The Catholic University of America Press, 1942.

Konings, Antonius, *Theologia Moralis*, 7. ed., 2 vols., Neo-Eboraci, 1892.

Kurtscheid, Bertrandus—Wilches, Felix, *Historia Iuris Canonici, Historia Fontium et Scientiae Iuris Canonici ad usum scholarum*, Romae: Officium Libri Catholici, 1943.

Lacroix, Claudius, *Theologia Moralis seu ejusdem in H. Busenbaum Medulam Commentaria a Zacharia, S.J., elucidata atque vindicata*, 2. ed., 4 vols., Parisiis, 1874.

Laemmer, Hugo, *Institutionen des katholischen Kirchenrechts*, Freiburg im Breisgau, 1886.

Laurentius, Iosephus, *Institutiones Iuris Ecclesiastici*, 3. ed., Friburgi Brisgoviae, 1914.

Lehmkuhl, Augustinus, *Theologia Moralis*, 12. ed., 2 vols., Friburgi, 1914.

Leitner, Martin, *Handbuch des katholischen Kirchenrechts*, 5 vols., Regensburg-Muenchen, 1918–1927.

Lercher, Ludovicus, *Institutiones Theologiae Dogmaticae in usum scholarum*, 4 vols., Oeniponte, 1924–1930.

Lexikon fuer Theologie und Kirche, herausgegeben von Dr. Michael Buchberger, 10 vols., Breiburg im Breisgau: Herder & Co., 1930–1938.

Lijdsman, Bernardus, *Introductio in Jus Canonicum cum uberiori fontium studio*, 2 vols., Hilversum in Hollandia, 1924–1929.

Lugo, Joannes de, *Disputationes Scholasticae et Moralis*, ed. nova accurante J. B. Fournials, 8 vols., Parisiis, 1890–1894.

Marc, Cl.—Gestermann, Fr. X.—Raus, J.B., *Institutiones Morales Alphonsianae seu Doctoris Ecclesiae S. Alphonsi Mariae de Ligorio Doctrina Moralis ad usum Scholarum accommodata*, 18. ed., 2 vols., Lugduni, 1927. [The 20. ed. (Lugdini: Typis Emmanuelis Vitte, [1940]–1946) was also consulted].

Maroto, Philippus, *Institutiones Iuris Canonici*, 3. ed., 2 vols., Romae-Madrid, 1919–1921; Vol. I, 3. ed., 1921; Vol. II, 1919.

McBride, James T., *Incardination and Excardination of Seculars*, The Catholic University of America Canon Law Studies, n. 145., Washington, D. C.: The Catholic University of America Press, 1941.

McCloskey, Joseph A., *The Subject of Ecclesiastical Law According to Canon 12*, The Catholic University of America Canon Law Studies, n. 165, Washington, D. C.: The Catholic University of America Press, 1943.

Merkelbach, Benedictus, *Summa Theologiae Moralis*, 3 vols., Parisiis: Desclée, De Brouwer, et Soc., 1931–1933; Vol. III, 2. ed., 1936.

Michiels, Gommarus, *Normae Generales Iuris Canonici*, 2. vols., Lublin, 1929.

———, *Principia Generalia de Personis in Ecclesia*, Lublin: Universitas Catholica, 1932.

Migne, Jacques P., *Patrologiae Cursus Completus*, Series Latina, 221 vols., Parisiis, 1844–1864; new ed., 1865–1896.

Moersdorf, Klaus, *Die Rechtssprache des Codex Juris Canonici*, Goerres-Gesellschaft zur Pflege der Wissenschaft im katholischen Deutschland, Veroeffentlichungen der Sektion fuer Rechts- und Staatswissenschaft, 74 Heft, Paderborn: F. Schoeningh, 1937.

Moriarity, Francis, *The Extraordinary Absolution from Censures*, The Catholic University of America Canon Law Studies, n. 113, Washington, D. C.: The Catholic University of America Press, 1938.

Moureau, H., *La Nouvelle Législation de l'Index*, Lille, 1898.

Mothon, Joseph P., *Institutions Canoniques*, 3 vols., Paris, 1922–1924.

Naz, Raoul, ed., *Traité de Droit Canonique*, 4 vols., Paris: Letouzey et Ané, 1948–1949; Vol. III, R. Naz, *Lieux et Temps Sacrés, Culte Divin, Magistère, Bénéfices Ecclésiastiques, Biens Temporels de l'Eglise*.

Noldin, Hieronymus—Schmitt, Albert, *Summa Theologiae Moralis*, 27. ed., 3 vols., Oeniponte-Lipsiae: F. Rauch, 1940–1941; Vol. III, 26. ed., 1940.

O'Brien, Joseph D., *The Exemption of Religious in Church Law*, Milwaukee: The Bruce Publishing Co., [1943].

Ojetti, Benedictus, *Synopsis Rerum Moralium et Iuris Pontificii*, 3. ed., 3 vols. & Index, Romae, 1909–1914.

Ottaviani, Alaphridus, *Institutiones Iuris Publici Ecclesiastici*, 2. ed., 2 vols., Romae: Typis Polyglottis Vaticanis, 1935–[1936].

Pellé, P., *Le Droit Pénal de l'Eglise*, Paris: P. Lethielleux, 1939.

Pennacchi, Iosephus, *Commentaria in Constitutionem APOSTOLICAE SEDIS qua censurae latae sententiae limitantur*, 2 vols., Romae, 1883.

Périès, G., *L'Index: commentaire de la constitution apostolique "Officiorum,"* Paris, 1898.

Pernicone, Joseph M., *The Ecclesiastical Prohibition of Books*, The Catholic University of America Canon Law Studies, n. 72, Washington, D. C.: The Catholic University of America, 1932.

Perrone, Ioannes, *Praelectiones Theologicae de Virtute Religionis deque Vitiis Oppositis*, Ratisbonae, 1866.

———, *Praelectiones Theologicae de Virtutibus Fidei, Spei et Caritatis*, Ratisbonae, 1865.

Pesch, Christianus, *Praelectiones Dogmaticae*, 9 vols., Friburgi Brisgoviae, 1895–1899; Vol. I, 2. ed., 1898.

Pejska, Iosephus, *Ius Canonicum Religiosorum*, 3. ed., Friburgi Brisgoviae, 1927.

Piscetta, A.—Gennaro, A., *Elementa Theologiae Moralis ad Codicem Iuris Canonici Exacta*, 5. ed., 7 vols., Torino: Societa Editrice Internazionale, 1938–1943; Vols. IV, VII, 4. ed., 1938, 1940.

Pistocchi, Mario, *I Canoni Penali del Codice Ecclesiastico Eposti e Commentati*, Torino-Roma, 1925.

Poulain, Augustin, *The Graces of Interior Prayer, A Treatise on Mystical Theology*, translated from the sixth edition by Leonora L. Yorke Smith, London, 1910.

Prince, John E., *The Diocesan Chancellor*, The Catholic University of America Canon Law Studies, n. 167, Washington, D. C.: The Catholic University of America Press, 1942.

Pruemmer, Dominicus, *Manuale Iuris Canonici in usum clericorum*, 3. ed., Friburgi Brisgoviae, 1922.

———, *Manuale Theologiae Moralis*, 2–3 ed., 3 vols., Friburgi Brisgoviae, 1923. [The 10th ed. by Engelbert Muench (Barcelona: Editorial Herder, 1946) was also consulted.]

Putnam, George Haven, *The Censorship of the Church of Rome*, 2 vols., New York, 1906–1907.

Ramstein, Matthew, *A Manual of Canon Law*, Hoboken, N. J.: Terminal Printing & Publishing Co., 1947.

Raus, J. B., *Institutiones Canonicae*, 2. ed., Lugduni, Parisiis: E. Vitte, 1931.

Regatillo, Eduardus, *Institutiones Iuris Canonici*, 2 vols., Santander-Madrid: Sal Terrae, Vol. I, 2. ed., 1946; Vol. II, 1942.

Reiffenstuel, Anacletus, *Ius Canonicum Universum*, 5 vols., in 7, Parisiis, 1864–1870.

Reusch, Franz Heinrich, *Der Index der verbotenen Buecher*, 2 vols., Bonn, 1883–1885.

Sabetti, Aloysius—Barrett, Timotheus, *Compendium Theologiae Moralis*, 34. ed. a Daniele F. Creeden recognita, Neo-Eboraci, Cincinnati: F. Pustet, 1939.

Saegmueller, Johannes Baptista, *Lehrbuch des katholischen Kirchenrechts*, 3. ed., 2 vols., Freiburg im B., 1914.

Salucci, Raffaele, *Il Diritto Penale Secondo il Codice di Diritto Canonico*, 2 vols., Subiaco: Typografia dei Monasteri, 1926–1930.

Santamaria Peña, F., *Comentarios al Código canónico*, 6 vols., Madrid, 1919–1922.

Santi, Franciscus—Leitner, M., *Praelectiones Juris Canonici*, 4. ed., 5 vols. in 3, Neo-Eboraci, 1904–1905.

Schaefer, Timotheus, *De Religiosis ad Normam Codicis Iuris Canonici*, 4. ed., Romae: Typis Polyglottis Vaticanis, 1947.

Scheeben, Mathias Joseph, *Handbuch der katholischen Dogmatik*, 4 vols., Freiburg im Breisgau, 1873–1897.

Schlecht, Joseph, *Andrea Zamometic und der Basler Konzilsversuch vom Jahre 1482*, Paderborn, 1903.

Schmalzgrueber, Franciscus, *Ius Ecclesiasticum Universum*, 5 vols. in 12, Romae, 1843–1845.

Schneider, Philipp, *Die neuen Buechergesetze der Kirche*, Mainz, 1900.

Schultes, Reginaldus, *De Ecclesia Catholica Praelectiones Apologeticae*, Parisiis, 1925.

Seraphinus a Loiano, *Institutiones Theologiae Moralis ad normam Iuris Canonici*, 5 vols., Taurini: Marietti, 1934–1942.

Sipos, Stephanus, *Enchiridion Iuris Canonici*, Pécs, 1926.

Sleutjes, Michael, *De prohibitione et censura librorum*, Galopiae, 1903.

Soglia, Ioannes, *Institutiones Juris Publici Ecclesiastici*, 5. ed., Paris, [1853].

Solieri, Franciscus, *Juris Publici Ecclesiastici Elementa*, Romae, 1900.

Sonntag, Nathaniel L., *Censorship of Special Classes of Books*, The Catholic University of America Canon Law Studies, n. 262, Washington, D. C.: The Catholic University of America Press, 1947.

Suarez, Franciscus, *Opera Omnia*, 2. ed., 28 vols., Parisiis, 1856–1878.

Tamburinus, Thomas, *Explicatio Decalogi*, 2 vols., Monachii, 1659.

Tanquerey, Adolphe, *The Spiritual Life, A Treatise on Ascetical and Mystical Theology*, 2. ed., Tournai: Society of St. John the Evangelist, Desclée & Co., 1932.

———, *Synopsis Theologiae Moralis et Pastoralis*, 3 vols., Neo-Eboraci, 1910–1912; Vol. I, 4. ed., 1912; Vol. II, 4. ed., 1910; Vol. III, 3. ed., 1912.

Theologia Mechliniensis, Tractatus de Censuris, Casibus Reservatis, Irregularitatibus et Libris Prohibitis ad usum Alumnorum Seminarii Archiepiscopalis Mechliniensis, 3. ed., Mechliniae, 1906.

Thomas Aquinas, St., *Summa Theologica*, Opera Omnia, ed. Leonina, 16 vols., 1882–1948.

Toso, Albertus, *Ad Codicem Juris Canonici Commentaria Minora*, 5 vols., Taurini-Romae, 1921–1927.

Tummulo, Raphael—Iorio, Thomas, *Compendium Theologiae Moralis*, 5. ed., 2 vols. & Suppl., Neapoli: M. D'Auria, 1934–1936; Supp., *De Censuris, Prohibitione Librorum, Irregularitatibus, Indulgentiis.*

Turner, Sidney Joseph, *The Vow of Poverty*, The Catholic University of America Canon Law Studies, n. 54, Washington, D. C.: The Catholic University of America, 1929.

Ubach, Josephus, *Theologia Moralis Codici Juris Canonici accomodatum*, 2. ed., 2 vols., Bonis Auris: Sociedad San Miguel, 1935.

Ubaldi, Ubaldus, *Introductio in Sacram Scripturam ad usum scholarum Pont. Seminarii Romani et Collegii Urbani de Propaganda Fide*, 5. ed., 3 vols., Roma, 1901.

Van Coillie, Constantinus, *Commentarius in constitutionem SSmi. Dni. Leonis XIII OFFICIORUM AC MUNERUM*, Brugis, 1899.

Van der Velden, Pius, *Principia Theologiae Moralis*, 2. ed., a Piato Montensi emendata, 2 vols., in 3, Parisiis, 1875–1884.

Van Hove, A., *De Legibus Ecclesiasticis*, Commentarium Lovaniense in Codicem Iuris Canonici, Vol. I, tom. II, Mechliniae-Romae: H. Dessain, 1930.

———, *De Rescriptis*, Commentarium Lovaniense in Codicem Iuris Canonici, Vol. I, tom. IV, Mechliniae: H. Dessain, 1936.

———, *Prolegomena ad Codicem Iuris Canonici*, Commentarium Lovaniense in Codicem Iuris Canonici editum a Magistris et Doctoribus Universitatis Lovaniensis, Vol. I, tom. I, 2. ed., Mechliniae-Romae: H. Dessain, 1945.

Van Noort, G., *Tractatus de Fontibus Revelationis necnon de Fide Divina*, Bussum, 1920.

———, *Tractatus de Vera Religione*, 4. ed., Hilversum, 1923.

Vecchiotti, Septimius, *Institutiones Canonicae*, 16. ed., 3 vols., Augustae Taurinorum, 1876.

Vermeersch, Arthurus, *De Prohibitione et Censura Librorum Dissertatio canonico-moralis*, 4. ed., Romae, 1906.

———, *Quaestiones de Iustitia*, 2. ed., Brugis, 1904.

———, *Theologiae Moralis Principia, Responsa, Consilia*, 4. ed., 4 vols., Romae: Apud Aedes Universitatis Gregorianae, 1944–1948.

Vermeersch, Arthurus—Creusen, Josephus, *Epitome Iuris Canonici cum commentariis ad scholas et ad usum privatum*, 6. ed., 3 vols., Mechliniae-Romae: H. Dessain, 1937–1946; Vol. I, 5. ed., 1933.

Voulliéme, Ernst, *Der Buchdruck Koelns bis 1500*, Bonn, 1903.

Vromant, G., *Ius Missionariorum, Introductio et Normae Generales*, Louvain, Museum Lessianum, 1934.

Webster's New Collegiate Dictionary, Springfield, Mass.: G. & C. Merriam Co., 1951.

Wernz, Franciscus, *Ius Decretalium*, 6 vols. in 10, Prati, 1908–1915; Vol. I, 3. ed., 1913; Vol. II, 3. ed., 1915; Vol. III, 2. ed., 1908; Vol. IV, 2. ed., Pars I, 1911, Pars II, 1912.

Wernz, Franciscus—Vidal, Petrus, *Ius Canonicum ad normam Codicis exactum*, 7 vols. in 8, Romae: Apud Aedes Universitatis Gregorianae, 1927–1938; Vols. II, V, 2. ed., 1928.

Wetzer und Welte, *Kirchenlexikon oder Encyclopedie der katholischen Theologie und ihrer Huelfswissenschaften*, 2. ed., 12 vols. & Index, Freiburg im Breisgau, 1883–1903.

Wittenberg, Philip, *The Protection and Marketing of Literary Property*, New York: J. Messner Inc., 1937.

Woywod, Stanislaus, *A Practical Commentary on the Code of Canon Law*, 3. ed., 2 vols., New York: Wagner, 1929.

Woywod, Stanislaus—Smith, Callistus, *A Practical Commentary on the Code of Canon Law*, rev. and enl. ed., 2 vols., New York: Wagner, 1948.

ARTICLES

Alpert, Leo M., "Judicial Censorship of Obscene Literature," *Harvard Law Review*, LII (1938–1939), 40–76.

Anonymous, *L'Ami du Clergé*, XXVI (1904), 186.

Anonymous, "Les nouveautés du Codex, Censure des Livres et Index," *L'Ami du Clergé*, XXXIX (1922), 113–118; 193–198.

Anonymous, *L'Ami du Clergé*, XLI (1924), 14; XLIII (1926), 400; XLIV (1927), 365; LII (1935), 88–89.

Anonymous, "De novarum Constitutionum editione et vi," *Periodica*, VII (1914), (8).

Anonymous [Vermeersch?], "Annotationes," *Periodica*, VII (1914), 165–168.

Bardy, G., "Gélase (Décret de)", *Dictionnaire de la Bible*, Supplément, III, 579–590.

Boudinhon, A., "Les Nouvelles Regles sur l'Interdiction et la Censure des Livres," *Le Canoniste Contemporain*, XX (1897), 129–137, 206–215, 297–310, 432–447, 665–677; XXI (1898), 16–35, 129–149, 241–254, 305–316, 382–390, 541–563, 656–668.

Brentford, Viscount, " 'Censorship' of Books," *Nineteenth Century and After*, CVI (1929), 207–211.

Brys, J., "De licentia scribendi in diariis et periodicis," *Collationes Brugenses*, XXXIII (1933), 408–413.

———, "De prohibitione librorum," *Collationes Brugenses*, XXVI (1926), 467–470; XXVII (1927), 44–49, 128–132, 200–207, 293–298, 372–376; XXVIII (1928), 35–40.

Cathrein, Viktor, "Die Andacht," *Zeitschrift fuer Aszese und Mystik*, VI (1931), 233–245.

Cram, Robert Vincent, "The Roman Censors," *Harvard Studies in Classical Philology*, LI (1940), 71–110.

Creyghton, Iosephus, "Vicariatus Generalis Diocesis Osnabrugensis Decretum 4 martii 1936," *Periodica*, XXVI (1937), 543–550.

Darling, Lord, "The 'Censorship' of Books," *Nineteenth Century and After*, CV (1929), 433–436.

Desjardins, [G.], "La Nouvelle Constitution apostolique sur l'Index," *Etudes religieuses de PP. Jesuites*, LXX (1897), 737–747; LXXI (1897), 208–219, 361–376.

Dilgskron, Carolus, "De revisione et approbatione librorum," *Analecta Ecclesiastica*, IV (1896), 422–428, 472–475; V (1897), 85–92, 129–137, 221–229.

Ellis, Havelock, "The 'Censorship' of Books," *Nineteenth Century and After*, CV (1929), 437–439.

Flahiff, G. B., "Ecclesiastical Censorship of Books in the Twelfth Century," *Mediaeval Studies*, IV (1942), 1–22.

———, "Ralph Niger, an introduction to his life and works," *Mediaeval Studies*, II (1940), 104–126.

Foot, Stephen, "The 'Censorship' of Books," *Nineteenth Century and After*, CV (1929), 440–443.

Forster, E. M., "The 'Censorship' of Books," *Nineteenth Century and After*, CV (1929), 444–445.

Gasquet, F. A., "Revising the Vulgate," *The Dublin Review*, CXLIII (1908,2), 264–273.
G[ennari], M[aria] C[asimiro], "Circa La Nuova Disciplina Sulla Proibizione e Sulla Censura de'Libri," *Il Monitore Ecclesiastico*, X (1897) parte I, 13–18, 33–40, 63–69, 80–86, 105–112, 132–136, 153–157.
Gfoellner, Johann, "Kirchliche Bildervorschriften," *Theologisch-praktische Quartalschrift*, LVIII (1905), 99–120.
Gillet, P., "De Censura Librorum," *Jus Pontificium*, XI (1931), 56–61.
Goodwine, John A., "Problems Respecting the Censorship of Books," *The Jurist*, X (1950), 152–183; reprint edition, [1950], pp. 1–34.
Goyeneche, S., "De censura librorum quando Ordinarius est editor, de Ordinario religioso editore, de superiore religioso concedente licentia," *Commentarium pro Religiosis*, VII (1926), 99–101.
Grumel, V., "Images (Culte des)", *Dictionnaire de Théologie Catholique*, VII, 766–844.
Gwynn, Denis, " 'Voltaire' and the Censors," *The Dublin Review*, CCIII (1938,2), 197–211.
Hansen, Joseph, "Der Malleus maleficarum, seine Druckausgaben und die gefaelschte Koelner Approbation vom J. 1487," *Westdeutsche Zeitschrift fuer Geschichte und Kunst*, XVII (1898), 119–168.
Harty, J. M., "Binding force of the Rules of the Index, Necessity of an Imprimatur, Prohibition of Books not having the necessary Imprimatur," *Irish Ecclesiastical Record*, 4th ser:, II (1906), 546–550.
[Heiner, Franz], "Welchem Bischofe steht die Approbation eines Buches rechtlich zu?" *Archiv fuer katholisches Kirchenrecht*, LXXVIII (1898), 186–188.
Hilgenreiner, Karl, "Buecherzensur," *Lexikon fuer Theologie und Kirche*, II, 605–606.
Hilgers, Joseph, "Buecherverbot und Buechercensur des 16. Jahrhunderts in Italien," *Zentralblatt fuer Bibliothekswesen*, XXVIII (1911), 108–122.
———, "Censorship of Books," *The Catholic Encyclopedia*, III, 519–527.
Hoepfl, Hildebrand, "Critique Biblique," *Dictionnaire de la Bible*, Supplément, II, 175–240
Huber, Max, "Die Pflege der Ascetik von Seiten des Clerus," *Theologisch-praktische Quartalschrift*, LIV (1901), 49–71, 332–351, 582–605; LV (1902), 43–60, 269–279; LVI (1903), 14–37, 304–313.
Jombart, Emile, "Censura praevia pro nova editione," *Periodica*, XXIV (1935), 36*–37*.
———, "Censure des Livres," *Dictionnaire de Droit Canonique*, III, 157–169.
———, "Quelques notions sur l'Index," *Revue des Communautés religieuses*, I (1925), 53–58.
———, "De imprimenda licentia imprimendi," *Periodica*, XXI (1932), 189*–190*.
Keating, Joseph, "Civil Censorship, Theory and Practice," *The Month*, CLIX (1932), 239–249.
Kober, Franz Quirin von, "Censuren, kirchliche," Wetzer und Welte, *Kirchenlexikon*, II, 2107–2110.
Lopez, Ulpianus, "Prelum catholicum et cinematographum," *Periodica*, XXIV (1935), 49*–66*.
M[ahoney], E[dward] J., "Imprimatur," *Clergy Review*, VII (1934,1), 251–253.
———, " 'Scribere' in Canon 1386, §1," *Clergy Review*, XIX (1940,2), 352–355.
Mangenot, E., "Septante, Version des," *Dictionnaire de la Bible*, V, 1623–1651.
Maréchal, P. [?], "Un décret récent du Saint-Office en matière d'inocographie religieuse," *Nouvelle Revue Théologique*, XLVIII (1921), 337.
Maroto, Philippus, "Animadversiones in s. congregationis Concilii decretum de gratiarum et oblationum in piis ephemeridibus evulgatione," *Apollinaris*, V (1932), 274–276.
Nevin, J.J., "Censorship of Books," *Australasian Catholic Record*, II (1925), 53–56.
Pallmann, Heinrich, "Des Erzbischofs Berthold von Mainz aeltestes Censuredikt," *Archiv fuer Geschichte des deutschen Buchhandels*, IX (1884), 238–241.

Pennacchi, Iosephus, "In Constitutionem Apostolicam OFFICIORUM AC MUNERUM Brevis Commentatio," *Acta Sanctae Sedis*, XXX (1897–1898), 33–96, 161–224, 289–352, 385–416, 481–534, 535–536; also published separately, Romae, 1898.

Piat, P., "Commentaire de la Constitution *Officiorum ac munerum* de Sa Sainteté le Pape Léon XIII sur la prohibition et la censure des livres et des décrets généraux qui l'accompagnent," *Nouvelle Revue Théologique*, XXXI (1899), 12–21, 131–142, 341–358, 565–584; XXXII (1900), 1–22, 131–139, 341–355, 466–479, 565–578; XXXIII (1901), 15–26, 132–145.

Planchard, J., "L'Index," *Revue théologique francaise*, II (1897), 21–35, 148—, 218—, 286—, 344—, 420—, 495—.

Quilliet, H., "Censures, Doctrinales," *Dictionnaire de Théologie Catholique*, II, 2101–2113.

Rest, J., "Die erste allgemeine paepstliche Zensurordnung," *Zentralblatt fuer Bibliothekswesen*, XXXI (1914), 68–69.

Romer, Carrol, "The 'Censorship' of Books," *Nineteenth Century and After*, CV (1929), 448–450.

Schubert, Franz, "Die Zukunft der Pastoraltheologie," *Theologie und Glaube*, XVI (1924), 119–129.

———, "Neubau der Liturgik," *Theologie und Glaube*, XIX (1927), 238–254.

Thaler, "Die Bitte des kirchlichen Zensors," *Archiv fuer katholisches Kirchenrecht*, XCII (1912), 361.

Thouvenin, A., "Index," *Dictionnaire de Théologie Catholique*, VII, 1570–1580.

V., J., *Nouvelle Revue Théologique*, XXX (1898), 108–113; XXXI (1899), 436–438.

Van Ruymbeke, L., "De la prohibition des livres," *Nouvelle Revue Théologique*, XXXV (1903), 657–671; XXXVI (1904), 98–109, 134–142.

Vermeersch, Arthurus, "Notae Canonicae," *Periodica*, IV (1909), 56–57.

———, "Annotationes ad Responsum S.C.Relig. diei 15 jun. 1911," *Periodica*, VI (1912, 66–68.

———, *Periodica*, VIII (1919), 26.

———, "De librorum conscriptione," *Periodica*, XI (1923), (15)–(17).

———, "De prohibitione imaginum," *Periodica*, XIV (1926), (93)–(98).

Vigouroux, Fulcrain, "Commentaires de l'Ecriture," *Dictionnaire de la Bible*, II, 877–878.

Villada, P., "Están sujetos los diarios a la censura eclesiástica previa?" *Razón y Fe*, XXIV (1909), 213–217.

———, "Una objeción sobre la censura previa de los periódicos," *Razón y Fe*, XXIV (1909), 352–354.

Vindex, "Domicilium et Quasi-Domicilium," *Jus Pontificium*, VI (1926), 34–55, 112–126, 154–158.

Wetmore, Edmund, "Copyright," *Cyclopedia of Law and Procedure*, IX, 889–976.

Whitman, Edmund A., "Literary Property," *Cyclopedia of Law and Procedure*, XXV, 1488–1501.

Wintersig, Athanasius, "Pastoralliturgik," *Jahrbuch fuer Liturgiewissenschaft*, IV (1924), 153–167.

Woolf, Virginia, "The 'Censorship' of Books," *Nineteenth Century and After*, CV (1929), 446–447.

Woywod, Stanislaus, "Law of the Code, Ecclesiastical Censorship," *Homiletic and Pastoral Review*, XXVIII (1927–1928), 628–631, 861–869, 966–973.

———, "Printing of Books and Pamphlets as Manuscript without Ecclesiastical Approbation," *Homiletic and Pastoral Review*, XXXVI (1935–1936), 970–971.

PERIODICALS

Analecta Ecclesiastica, Romae, 1893–1911.
Apollinaris, Romae, 1928—.
Archiv fuer Geschichte des deutschen Buchhandels, Leipzig, 1878—.
Archiv fuer katholisches Kirchenrecht, Innsbruck, 1857–1861; Mainz, 1862—.
Australasian Catholic Record, Sidney, 1924—.
Canoniste, Le, Paris, 1924–1926 (originally *Le Canoniste Contemporain*, Paris, 45 vols., 1878–1922)
Clergy Review, London, 1931—.
Collationes Brugenses, Brugis, 1896—.
Commentarium pro Religiosis (1935—: *Commentarium pro Religiosis et Missionariis*), Romae, 1920—.
Dublin Review, The, London, 1836—.
Etudes religieuses des PP. Jesuites, Paris, 1856— (1856–1861: *Etudes de théologie, de philosophie, et d'histoire;* 1862–1896: *Etudes religieuses, philosophiques et historiques*).
Harvard Law Review, Cambridge, 1887—.
Harvard Studies in Classical Philology, Cambridge, 1890—.
Homiletic and Pastoral Review, The, New York, 1900— (1900–1917: *Homiletic Monthly and Catechist;* 1917–1918: *Homiletic Monthly;* 1918–1920: *Homiletic Monthly and Pastoral Review*).
Irish Ecclesiastical Record, The, Dublin, 1864—.
Jahrbuch fuer Liturgiewissenschaft, Muenster in Westf., 1921—.
Jurist, The, Washington, D. C., 1941—.
Jus Pontificium, Romae, 1921–1940.
L'Ami du Clergé, Langres, 1879–1939, 1947—.
Mediaeval Studies, Toronto, 1939—.
Monitore Ecclesiastico, Il, Roma, 1876–1948 (1949—: *Monitor Ecclesiasticus*).
Month, The, London, 1864—.
Nineteenth Century and After, London, 1877—.
Nouvelle Revue Théologique, Paris, 1869—.
Periodica de Religiosis et Missionariis, 8 vols., Brugis, 1905–1919; *Periodica de Re Canonica et Morali utilia praesertim Religiosis et Missionariis*, 7 vols., Brugis, 1920–1927; *Periodica de Re Morali, Canonica, Liturgica*, Brugis, 1927–1936, et Romae, 1937—.
Razon y Fe, Madrid, 1901—.
Revue des Communautés religieuses, Louvain, 1925—.
Theologie und Glaube, Paderborn, 1909—.
Theologisch-praktische Quartalschrift, Linz, 1848—.
Westdeutsche Zeitschrift fuer Geschichte und Kunst, Trier, 1882–1913.
Zeitschrift fuer Aszese und Mystik, Innsbruck, 1926–1944; 1947—: *Geist und Leben*, Wuerzburg.
Zentralblatt fuer Bibliothekswesen, Leipzig, 1884—.

ABBREVIATIONS

AAS—Acta Apostolicae Sedis.
ACR—Australasian Catholic Record.
AGDB—Archiv fuer Geschichte des deutschen Buchhandels.
AKKR—Archiv fuer katholisches Kirchenrecht.
Anal. Eccl.—Analecta Ecclesiastica.
ASS—Acta Sanctae Sedis.
BRT—Bullarum Diplomatum et Privilegiorum Romanorum Pontificum Taurinensis Editio.
CB—Collationes Brugenses.

CC—Le Canoniste Contemporain.
CE—The Catholic Encyclopedia.
CLP—Cyclopedia of Law and Procedure.
Coll. Lac.—Acta et Decreta Sacrorum Conciliorum Recentiorum Collectio Lacensis.
Collectanea—Collectanea Sacrae Congregationis de Propaganda Fide.
CpR—Commentarium pro Religiosis.
CR—Clergy Review.
DB—Dictionnaire de la Bible.
DBS—Dictionnaire de la Bible, Supplément.
DDC—Dictionnaire de Droit Canonique.
Decr. Auth.—Decreta Authentica Sacrae Congregationis Sacrorum Rituum.
DTC—Dictionnaire de Théologie Catholique.
Etudes—Etudes religieuses des PP. Jesuites.
Fontes—Codicis Iuris Canonici Fontes.
FW—Funk & Wangnalls, *The New College Standard Dictionary.*
HPR—The Homiletic and Pastoral Review.
JE—Jaffe, Regesta Pontificum Romanorum (ed. by Ewald: from 590–882).
JLW—Jahrbuch fuer Liturgiewissenschaft.
L'Ami—L'Ami du Clergé.
Lexikon—Lexikon fuer Theologie und Kirche.
Mansi—*Sacrorum Conciliorum Nova et Amplissima Collectio.*
ME—Il Monitore Ecclesiastico.
MPL—Migne, Patrologiae Cursus Completus, Series Latina.
NRT—Nouvelle Revue Théologique.
Periodica—Periodica de Re Morali, Canonica, Liturgica.
RCR—Revue des Communautés religieuses.
RTF—Revue théologique francaise.
TuG—Theologie und Glaube.
ThPrQs—Theologisch-Praktische Quartalschrift.
WZGK—Westdeutche Zeitschrift fuer Geschichte und Kunst.
ZB—Zentralblatt fuer Bibliothekswesen.

BIOGRAPHICAL NOTE

Donald Herman Wiest was born on April 12, 1908, at Plain, Wisconsin. After completing his elementary education at St. Luke's Parochial School in the same town, he began in 1922 his studies for the Priesthood at St. Lawrence College, Mt. Calvary, Wisconsin. He entered the Capuchin novitiate at Detroit, Michigan, in 1927, where he made his religious profession on August 5, 1928. He pursued his philosophical and theological studies at St. Anthony Friary, Marathon, Wisconsin. At the end of the theological course he received the degree of Bachelor of Theology from the School of Sacred Theology of the Catholic University of America. He was ordained to the priesthood on June 17, 1934, at Marathon, Wisconsin, and was thereafter appointed professor at St. Lawrence College, Mt. Calvary, Wisconsin. In November, 1934, he was enrolled in the School of Canon Law of the Gregorian University, Rome, where he received the degrees J.C.B. and J.C.L. in the years 1935 and 1936 respectively. In October, 1936, he entered the School of Canon Law of the Catholic University of America as a candidate for the degree of Doctor of Canon Law.

ALPHABETICAL INDEX

8177—Gal. 4 Univ Litho Marsh

8177—Gal. 5 ALL Univ Litho Marsh

CANON LAW STUDIES*

327. KOESLER, REV. LEO J., O.S.B., J.C.L., Entrance into the Novitiate by Clerics in Major Orders (Canon 542, 2°).
328. MCFARLAND, REV. NORMAN E., A.B., J.C.L., Religious Vocation—Its Juridic Concept.
329. WIEST, REV. DONALD HERMAN, O.F.M.CAP., S.T.B., J.C.L., The Precensorship of Books.
330. DEWITT, REV. MAX GEORGE, A.B., J.C.L., The Cessation of Delegated Power.
331. MATHIS, REV. MARCIAN JOHN, O.F.M., J.C.L., The Constitution and Supreme Administration of Regional Seminaries Subject to the Sacred Congregation for the Propagation of the Faith in China.
332. SCHORR, REV. GEORGE F., A.B., J.C.L., The Law of the Celebret.
333. SHEEHY, REV. ROBERT FRANCIS, A.B., J.C.L., The Sacred Congregation of the Sacraments: Its Competence in the Roman Curia.
334. SHIELDS, REV. JOSEPH A., A.B., J.C.L., Deprivation of the Clerical Garb.
335. URICHECK, REV. GEORGE EDWARD, A.B., J.C.L., De forma celebrationis matrimonii in Ecclesiis Orientalibus ante Motu Proprio *Crebrae Allatae* et post.
336. DEPAUW, REV. GOMMAR ALBERT LEO JULIAN MARIA, J.C.L., The Legal Status of Catholic Elementary Schools in Belgium, 1830–1950.

* For a complete list of the available numbers of this series apply to the Catholic University of America Press, 620 Michigan Avenue, N.E., Washington 17, D. C.

www.ingramcontent.com/pod-product-compliance
Lightning Source LLC
LaVergne TN
LVHW050239080826
844660LV00012B/559